Winning Ways of Women Coaches

Cecile Reynaud, PhD

Editor

HUMAN KINETICS

Library of Congress Cataloging-in-Publication Data

Names: Reynaud, Cecile, 1953- editor.
Title: Winning ways of women coaches / Cecile Reynaud, editor.
Description: Champaign, IL : Human Kinetics, 2023. | Includes
  bibliographical references and index.
Identifiers: LCCN 2021054929 (print) | LCCN 2021054930 (ebook) | ISBN
  9781718203228 (paperback) | ISBN 9781718203235 (epub) | ISBN
  9781718203242 (pdf)
Subjects: LCSH: Women coaches (Athletics) | Coaching (Athletics) |
  Coach-athlete relationships. | BISAC: SPORTS & RECREATION / Coaching /
  Baseball | SOCIAL SCIENCE / Women's Studies
Classification: LCC GV711 .W57 2023 (print) | LCC GV711 (ebook) | DDC
  796.07/7--dc23/eng/20211222
LC record available at https://lccn.loc.gov/2021054929
LC ebook record available at https://lccn.loc.gov/2021054930

ISBN: 978-1-7182-0322-8 (print)

Copyright © 2023 by Human Kinetics, Inc.

The web addresses cited in this text were current as of October 2021, unless otherwise noted.

Managing Editor: Hannah Werner; **Copyeditor:** Chernow Editorial Services, Inc.; **Indexer:** Laurel Plotzke Callahan; **Permissions Manager:** Martha Gullo; **Graphic Designer:** Denise Lowry; **Cover Designer:** Keri Evans; **Cover Design Specialist:** Susan Rothermel Allen; **Photographs (cover):** Katharine Lotze/ Getty Images; Otto Greule /Allsport/Getty Images; Tim Casey / © 2015 University Athletic Association. All Rights Reserved.; **Photo Asset Manager:** Laura Fitch; **Photo Production Manager:** Jason Allen; **Senior Art Manager:** Kelly Hendren; **Illustrations:** © Human Kinetics; **Printer:** Versa Press

Human Kinetics books are available at special discounts for bulk purchase. Special editions or book excerpts can also be created to specification. For details, contact the Special Sales Manager at Human Kinetics.

Printed in the United States of America   10 9 8 7 6 5 4 3 2 1

The paper in this book is certified under a sustainable forestry program.

Human Kinetics
1607 N. Market Street
Champaign, IL 61820
USA

United States and International
Website: **US.HumanKinetics.com**
Email: info@hkusa.com
Phone: 1-800-747-4457

Canada
Website: **Canada.HumanKinetics.com**
Email: info@hkcanada.com

E8286

Tell us what you think!
Human Kinetics would love to hear what we can do to improve the customer experience. Use this QR code to take our brief survey.

CONTENTS

PREFACE

Some of you may have already read a 2004 book of a somewhat similar nature titled *She Can Coach!* That book, by weight of the works contributed by many of the finest female coaches at that time, made a case for why women with equal or greater knowledge, ability, experience, and concern for athletes are every bit as good as their male counterparts.

Fortunately, because that case has been substantiated time and again by women coaches everywhere since then, we have entered a new era of women in coaching. So, a fresh take is in order—one that effectively shares the unique expertise and experiences of women who have not only broken coaching barriers but have also established new standards of excellence in their coaching roles.

Winning Ways of Women Coaches presents the stories, insights, and advice of 20 highly successful women coaches. They come from 15 different sports and from multiple countries. Each coach has led teams or individuals to national or world championships or Olympic competition, or been a pioneer in earning a coaching position in Major League Baseball or the National Football League. In short, they have all proved themselves big-time in the coaching profession—because the way they do things works.

Moreover, as you will read, these coaches highlight the fact that far more important than coaching their sport is how they communicate with, care for, and develop the athletes under their guidance. Please keep that in mind as their stories inform you how successful coaches handle the many important areas of coaching covered in this book and encountered every day as you coach your own team.

The content is organized into three categories that reflect the emphasis of the material in each section:

Part I: Coaching Career Path and Considerations

Part II: Program Development and Management

Part III: Athlete Engagement and Growth

Within each of those parts are chapters that more specifically address how to deal with each of these aspects of coaching as successfully as possible. And because culture is now properly recognized as one of the most important factors in coaching success, each chapter's author-coach explains how she ensures the culture of her team and program is the best it can be. Here's a brief preview of what you'll find in the following pages.

We start out with a chapter on checking your coaching competencies. What abilities do you need to be a great coach? We learn that you can become an elite conference's Gymnastics Coach of the Century and the third winningest NCAA gymnastics coach of all time without ever having competed as a gymnast. You need to discover your why, and then it is all about the ability to work with people.

Chapter 2 focuses on getting a coaching position and growing as a coach. Keep educating yourself to be the best in your field, even if it means putting yourself out of your comfort zone.

You may already be in a coaching position but want to think about changing coaching roles and advancing your career. Chapter 3 takes a look at knowing your role and excelling in that position. You should always be prepared to be the head coach; however, it may be that you want to have a different experience and serve as an assistant coach for a while. It is OK to move between various positions and back again. We have seen some longtime head coaches change to become assistant coaches. They provide an extra valuable insight from having served as a head coach. Be ready to adapt to what the head coach needs and wants, but venture out and see if that is what you want.

A critical part of being a successful coach is having a strong assistant coach. Chapter 4 covers thriving as an assistant coach. Not everyone strives to be a head coach. Some people are completely satisfied serving as an assistant or associate head coach. The roles are completely different, but in order to achieve success in this position, a person must be loyal to the head coach while bringing their best suggestions into meetings. It is most rewarding when you enjoy where you work and who you work with.

Many coaches want to know if it is possible to be in coaching and raise a family at the same time. Chapter 5 gives coaches some constructive advice on ways of making it all work. We are seeing more and more women with their children in the gym or on the field. While it takes a good support system, coaches with children find they become stronger in both areas.

Coaches spend most of their time managing their athletes on and off the court or field. It is important to be reminded that coaches need to take good care of themselves before they can attend to others' needs. Chapter 6 is about managing yourself. We forget that it is not all about the athletes. Make sure to study yourself as a coach and understand how you communicate, share information, and conduct yourself with the team, staff, and the public.

Chapter 7 provides good insight into working with administrators. Take the time to build and maintain a positive relationship with the administration around you. Coaching can be rocky at times, and you need to make sure you have built up the support you need for yourself and your program.

Coaches work hard to have winning seasons, but what does it take to do that year after year? Chapter 8 gives us ideas on building and sustaining a winning program. One way might be to reach back to past teams to build strong future teams and keep the program legacy alive.

Team culture will make or break your program. Chapter 9 takes the reader through establishing a high-performance culture and how it sets the stage for years to come. Work hard to get the daily process set up and keep checking on it.

We are familiar with how important it is to have the proper technical skills and well-thought-out tactical game strategies. Chapter 10 is about developing and implementing a strategy for your overall program that will keep you on track. Set it up for the future and refer to it every day.

Chapter 11 shows us the importance of recruiting, organizing, and mentoring a staff. Surround yourself with the people who best complement your coaching style and can fill in where you need the help. No matter the level of the program, find people to assist in managing a team. They may be volunteers at a high school or club level or at a top NCAA Division I program. It is imperative to keep them organized and growing as coaches.

As you know, the speed of the leader determines the rate of the pack. Being an organized coach is critical to your success and everyone around you. Chapter 12 provides constructive ways for planning, scheduling, and delegating.

Chapter 13 has tips on selling your program. The media should be an important part of your program and how it is perceived by the public. Take the time to establish personal relationships with those covering your program.

Recruiting is the name of the game in college athletics. Chapter 14 is about recruiting athletes to your program. Make sure there is a good strategy in place to keep the program stocked with the players who fit into the culture that has been established.

Chapter 15 is about defining and adjusting athletes' roles. This can be a huge issue in many programs with athletes as well as their parents. Being able to define each athlete's role will go a long way in being transparent with a team. Knowing when adjustments need to be made and how to make them to keep the program strong is key.

Leading effectively and coaching people up is covered in chapter 16. Know the athletes and be able to communicate clearly with them about expectations and how they can continue to improve with quality feedback.

Chapter 17 is on taking an athlete-centered approach. Student-athletes deserve to have a strong voice in their athletics program. This chapter explains how to give them the opportunities to be involved in decisions about the team.

Strengthening the coach–athlete relationship is discussed in chapter 18. The team is a large family. Taking time to develop and maintain strong coach–athlete relationships will carry a coach through the years.

The people on teams being coached are so much more than athletes. Chapter 19 provides insight into growing athletes holistically. Coaches need to be prepared to have real-world discussions with their athletes. Being creative in coaching will keep your athletes engaged in ways that reach them where they are.

The final chapter is about keeping it fun while instilling the values. Fun is probably the thing coaches forget to plan for because it might not provide an obvious path to winning. Take time to enjoy the daily process of seeing the team live out the values you teach in practices, games, and in the community.

These chapters provide a wealth of coaching wisdom from women who have been there, done that. And, after reading what they've written, you'll appreciate even more that success and the payoff in coaching are not defined by wins and awards but rather by the positive impact made on the people you had an opportunity to influence and develop. We wish you success in doing just that as we continue to demonstrate the merit and value of women coaches.

ACKNOWLEDGMENTS

This book was made possible by the Human Kinetics staff, who believe it is important to learn from our best women in coaching. Thank you to Ted Miller for the support and guidance throughout this process. His experience in publishing educational resources was vital for this project. Hannah Werner, the project manager, was a pleasure to work with.

Thanks to the coaches who agreed to volunteer their time and expertise in putting this book together. Each one is tremendously successful in her sport, and they all have extremely busy lives. I thank them for taking the time to share their expertise and experience.

Special thanks go to Dr. M. Dianne Murphy for her assistance in reviewing material and to Megan Kahn, former CEO of WeCOACH, for sharing her connections to many of the coaches included in this coaching resource.

I offer my deepest appreciation for the women coaches I had as role models when I was a student-athlete and a young coach: Dr. Mary Jo Wynn, Linda Dollar, Dr. Rhonda Ridinger, Reba Sims, Dr. Billie Jones, and a close friend and mentor, Pat Summitt.

I appreciate the support of my family, friends, and colleagues who have understood my passion for coaching education as I worked on this project in order to give back to the coaching community.

Cecile Reynaud, PhD
Editor

PART I
COACHING CAREER PATH AND CONSIDERATIONS

CHAPTER 1

CHECKING YOUR COACHING COMPETENCIES

Valorie Kondos Field

The most interesting fact about me as a coach is that I was never a gymnast. I never had one gymnastics lesson. I was a professional ballet dancer, and I went to UCLA in 1982 strictly as the dance coach for the gymnastics team. This was a great opportunity for me because I was enthralled with the sport and I wanted to go to college. I found out who the head coach was, gave him a call, told him about my credentials, and they offered me a full scholarship to go to school. That is how I got to UCLA.

So, when people ask how a dancer got involved in athletics, it's very simple: I made the *ask*. My entire career would have never ever happened if I had not made the ask. In 1990, I was called into the athletics director's office and asked to take over as the head gymnastics coach. Not only did I not know anything about gymnastics, but I quickly realized I did not know what a healthy team culture looked like. I didn't grow up in the world of athletics, so I had no models or memories of good and bad athletic experiences. I did not know what competencies I needed as a coach. I did not know what core skills I needed to be a successful coach. I was the classic case of someone who didn't know what I didn't know. Most importantly, I did not know to ask the question, "Does all winning equal success?" I was now a college gymnastics coach, and all I knew was that I was hired to win.

So, when I took over as head coach, I did what I thought was prudent and just mimicked other head coaches of various other sports who had won. The paradigm that I had in my mind was that coaches were tough, relentless dictators with a "my way or the highway" mentality. I thought to be a strong leader you couldn't show any cracks in your foundation. You couldn't show vulnerability. You had to have all the answers, and if you didn't have the answers, then don't leave yourself open to scrutiny—say something and act like it is the right answer.

I took over a program that had been extremely successful, consistently ranked in the top three nationally. However, in my first year as the head coach, we finished dead last in the conference and did not make it to the NCAA National Championship. For my career and the long-term success of the program, I was forced to rethink my approach. I was either going to resign or I was going to figure it out.

LEARN FROM OTHERS

I decided to resign. I honestly didn't think of myself as a failure. I remember thinking that I obviously didn't know how to be successful as a coach so I'll go find another job that is more suited to me.

On my way to the athletics director's office to hand in my resignation, I was walking through the campus bookstore and saw a book on leadership by former UCLA men's basketball coach John Wooden. When I picked it up, it magically opened to his definition of success: "Success is peace of mind which is a direct result of self-satisfaction in knowing you made the effort to become the best you are capable of becoming."

It was shocking to me that here was a quote from Coach Wooden, touted as the greatest coach that ever lived, and he doesn't mention winning in his definition of success or even in the entire book. Coaches are hired to win, so I thought it was such a fluff description of success. I read it over and over, mulling over its meaning, until I finally had the biggest "aha moment" of my professional career. Success is peace of mind in knowing that *you* have done *your* best. By mimicking other coaches, I had been trying to be them, and I quickly realized that whenever you try to be someone else, you will always be a second-rate them. Worst of all, it prevents you from becoming a first-rate you.

With this bit of enlightenment, I didn't resign and instead went back to my office and thought about what *my* best would look like if I brought my best self to this job as the head coach of a premier athletic team. The first thing I asked myself was, "Why was athletics important?"

KNOW YOUR WHY

As Simon Sinek, author and inspirational speaker, would say, I had to figure out my *why*. All coaches should take time to silence all the outside noise and listen internally to their why. Why do they feel athletics is important, and why do they love to coach? If some coaches are being honest, they will say it's "because I get to stand up on a pedestal and be revered." It is a prestigious title. When someone says, "What do you do?" and you say, "I'm the head coach of this team," you can see their positive reaction. When I started thinking about my *why*, I thought, "Athletics is about figuring out how to win." Winning is about bragging rights. That's where I got hung up. There has to be more to this amazing world of athletics than bragging rights. I remember walking into our beautiful athletics facility at UCLA one day and looking around at all the trophies for all the sports, and I thought this is all about being able to say, "Ha-ha, we beat you." From youth sports to the NCAA to World Cup Soccer, the NFL, the NBA, and the Olympic Games, how many trillions of dollars are spent on bragging rights? There has to be more to athletics than just "ha-ha, we beat you."

I very quickly connected my mental dots and realized that *sport is a master class in teaching life lessons that you don't learn in the classroom.* All sports, especially team sports, teach the importance of preparation, proper progressions, resiliency, how to win with humility and lose with grace—which is often very hard to do, especially when the loss comes down to a contested call by an official. Team sport teaches us how being a part of something greater than ourselves is so much more rewarding than anything we could earn on our own. And among many other things, sport teaches us there is no shortcut to success. Sport teaches us the importance of taking control of our mind and our thoughts. And sport teaches us to be courageous. Courage is taking a step toward a goal without any guarantee of a result. My *why* all of a sudden became clear to me. I was excited to develop champions in life through the sport of gymnastics. Later on in my career, whenever I was asked what I did for a job, I answered, "I develop superheroes."

KNOW YOUR HOW

Once coaches figure out their *why*, coaches need to figure out their *how*—meaning how are they going to implement their coaching philosophy on a daily basis. How are they going to stick to their culture's foundation when the times get tough and it is so much easier to switch back to coaching from a *win-at-all-costs* mentality? It is far too easy to become dictatorial when focusing on the win, which is why we all need to constantly hit our internal refresh button as to the importance of our *why*.

When I refocused my purpose on developing superheroes in life through sport, I no longer focused on the win but on asking, "How can I motivate this athlete to want to do this because I know it will empower her to be her best self?"

Time after time I found that when I coached an athlete from the inside out—fortifying the whole human that was the athlete—the result was far greater than had I just coached their gymnastics.

One reason I have always felt it is important for gymnasts to compete in college is because it is truly the first time they experience what it's like to be a part of a team sport. I've asked a few of the national team gymnasts and Olympic gymnasts who came to our program if competing for our country felt like a real team effort. They all said, "Almost, but not entirely," because even though they competed with national pride, they still wanted to beat their teammates for the medal.

In college, that team trophy and team success are celebrated many times more than any individual title. To foster that feeling every day in the gym, I felt it was imperative that the athletes realize we are all part of the greater good. I often use the metaphor that we are like a jigsaw puzzle. We each are our own unique piece of the puzzle. All different yet all essential to the whole. Without that one piece, our puzzle will not be complete. That's why everyone is important. Everyone, all of us coaches included, need to strive every day to bring our best selves to our team puzzle so that we are powerfully connected, and through that connection we build trust.

Often, after a big win, some of our athletes wouldn't feel that they had earned the right to feel proud because they hadn't competed or contributed to the team's success. I would remind them about the puzzle, and how each of them was recruited for different strengths. Yes, some were recruited to compete all the time and score really high. Others were recruited as "utility players," athletes who could compete in any event at any time and give us a solid, decent score. And others were recruited for their character, work ethic, and enthusiasm, having been told by me that they probably wouldn't compete much. I know it sounds harsh, but I wanted them to realize what they were signing up for, and if competing in college was really important to them, then they should consider another school.

One of my favorite memories was when Katelyn Ohashi, UCLA superstar, was asked in an interview who she felt was the most inspiring person on the team. She answered, "Sara Taubman." The reporter

Katharine Lotze/Getty Images

said, "Who?" Katelyn replied, "Exactly. I know you thought I'd say one of our Olympic gold medalists, but actually it's Sara Taubman. Sara is a walk-on who will probably never compete, but Sara's contribution to our team is priceless. Sara shows up every day so appreciative, grateful, and enthusiastic to be a part of this program that she reminds me how important it is to show up every day appreciative, grateful, and enthusiastic. Sara definitely makes our team better, and I know she makes me better."

COACHING IN TODAY'S ENVIRONMENT

Coaches have got to be more careful than ever to make sure that they are giving instruction without crossing over and making it personal. Thankfully, student-athletes are having louder voices and are being heard, and the wise coaches are taking notice.

More than ever, coaches need to understand that the "old school" way of coaching may have produced medals and trophies, but there often was emotional, mental, and even physical damage that came with that philosophy. It is possible to produce excellence in a program while giving the athletes the space to feel heard and appreciated.

If I could offer one bit of advice for new coaches it would be that your best way to be a successful coach is to model the behavior that you want to see from your staff and student-athletes. We want our student-athletes to come to us respectfully, with an open mind, and be able to listen to something different. We want them to own up when they screw up, because we all screw up at some point. We want them to be able to have a safe space to apologize and be heard. We can't expect them to act like that unless we model that behavior.

Young adults enjoy listening to and are seeking out books and podcasts by research professor Brené Brown, and her research shows that leaders that come from a place of humility and vulnerability are far more successful than those that come from a place of having to know all the answers. Vulnerability is the first step to courage, so we need to redefine what courage looks like.

Courage isn't bullish. Courage is literally having the confirmation within yourself to confidently take that next step toward your goal without any guarantee of a certain result.

I taught a graduate course on transformative coaching and leadership at UCLA. We studied a different coach each week for 10 weeks, such as Phil Jackson, Pat Summitt, John Wooden, Bobby Knight, Sue Enquist, and others. The commonality with all these coaches was really interesting. There were definitely differences, but there were a lot of common behaviors, such as a maniacal attention to preparation, understood nonnegotiables, and a passion for their work. Along with the books

Don Liebig/ UCLA Photography

on each of the coaches, the students also were assigned to read Brené Brown's *Dare to Lead: Brave Work. Tough Conversations. Whole Hearts.* (2018). At the end of the course, when we discussed what they learned, every single student said they never thought of vulnerability as being a strong skill to have and not a weakness.

We are at an age now that we have the research that shows that coming from a place of empathy and compassion is actually going to get you a better result as a leader in any type of career. We are also in an era where emotions are heightened. While the "win at all costs" culture may have produced winners, the damage that can be done along the way can have an irreparable cost.

After reading up on the different generations, particularly our current youth Generation Z, it has become glaringly apparent that we as coaches and parents need to understand how the influences on our youth are far different from how we were raised. The first step in the equation of providing a healthy athletic environment for an athlete is to make sure that the parent and the young athlete are on the same page about what success means, and then the parent and the coach need to be on the same page. It's futile to work with an athlete on developing a characteristic that you, as a coach, feel is imperative to becoming a champion if once the athlete gets home, the parent tells them something different. The most successful coaching experiences I had were when the stakes were the highest. When an athlete disregarded the team rules and I either suspended them or didn't renew their position on the team, if the parent and I were on the same page giving the athlete the same message, 100 percent of the time the athlete took some time off, took responsibility for what was their part in the issue, chose how they wanted to live their life, and came back to the team and had a powerfully positive impact for the rest of their UCLA career. A hundred percent of the time.

COACHING ESSENTIALS

In my long career in coaching and reading about and observing successful coaches, several basic factors stand out. So, if I were advising anyone hiring a coach, I would strongly recommend that they ask these questions:

What is the moral foundation you want to establish with your team?

What is the moral foundation going to look like when you start to see cracks developing?

How do you go about fixing the cracks in the foundation?

I truly believe that the moral fiber and character of the person being considered are the most fundamental and important factors in determining any coaching hire. In other words, would that individual be a person you would entrust with one of your children?

During my last season at UCLA, we were competing at Oklahoma and we were horrible. We not only lost the meet, but some of our team acted in ways not in alignment with our team's moral foundation. My coaching philosophy is about respect, self-respect, respect for others, honesty, decency, and civility. We talk about all those things constantly. The reason we lost that meet wasn't because of gymnastics or lack of preparation. It was because of the cracks in our foundation. When we got back to UCLA, I brought up specific incidents that I saw on the road that didn't jibe with our team mettle. Those were the clear cracks in the foundation. We then discussed how to go about filling in and fortifying the cracks. To this day, those same team members will use the metaphor "cracks in the foundation" when they describe a situation that's gone wrong.

COMMUNICATING WITH YOUR ATHLETES

If you are not being honest with your athletes, you are not being respectful. If you are not being honest with a student-athlete and you are telling them only what they want to hear, then you are telling them they are not strong enough to handle the truth. The key is to say what you have to say as a coach, respectfully.

Respect is honesty and communication and grace. Grace is giving us all the benefit of the doubt. It's knowing we are going to make mistakes and we are going to hurt each other's feelings, but the first thought we have is that I'm going to give you the benefit of the doubt that your intention was not to hurt me.

In coaching, our intentions are often to make a point that is going to hit home. Then, as we all know, on any given day, somebody takes something that you say out of context, and you have to do damage control—or not. If you're interested in understanding why the athlete took what you did or said in that way, then the only way to see that clearly and come to a resolution is through communication. Have a respectful private conversation and let them know you are showing up wanting to give them a safe space to speak honestly. Then turn off your phone, shut off any other distractions, and listen. In serious situations with your athletes or staff, it is never a good idea to be flippant or sarcastic. Simply *listen*, and then formulate a response that is in alignment with your goal, which is usually, "How do we move forward?"

TAKEAWAYS

- To be an effective coach, you must know *who* you are, know your *why*, and know your *how*. Trying to be like another coach isn't a good idea.

- Coaching styles can range from very strict and demanding to more flexible and permissive. The keys to making any style work is to be authentic and athlete-centered, which means being true to yourself and also having the athletes' best interests and development foremost in your mind and the actions you take.

- In terms of rules, be clear with your athletes and staff on the negotiables and the nonnegotiables. Hold them accountable. But never resort to shaming, belittling, or bullying.

- The old-school way of winning, in any professional or athletic environment, is to figure out how to win regardless of the costs. Thankfully, we are living at a time where we have hard research data that reveals that the "costs"—the damage—of a win-at-all-costs environment is the mental, emotional, and even physical well-being of those we lead. It is incumbent on anyone who has the privilege of leading another human being to realize that there is always a path to success that does not compromise the human spirit.

CHAPTER 2

GETTING A COACHING POSITION, GROWING AS A COACH

Rachel Balkovec

When I was an undergraduate, a mentor said to me, "When you're young and you're growing as a coach, find the best in the world and go work for them. Be willing to work for free. Don't worry about the money. Don't worry about the title."

So, that's what I did. Before I was hired full-time in 2014 by the St. Louis Cardinals, I worked six unpaid internships with various top-level baseball organizations while supplementing my income with waitressing jobs along the way. Even after working full-time for five seasons with Major League Baseball organizations, I kept the same mentality.

One of the most difficult career decisions I made was to leave the Houston Astros after winning the World Series and go back to school for a second master's degree. The choice of which college to attend for that purpose was also a challenging one. Going to the University of Southern California and living in sunny and warm Los Angeles was a very tempting option. The other opportunity was to go to Amsterdam and work with the best researcher in the world in motor learning and eye tracking for baseball and cricket batters. The decision was a difficult one, but I remembered what my mentor had said at the beginning of my career. So, I picked up and moved literally halfway across the world to a rainy, cold city, depleting my entire life savings in the process. It was a long way from the big leagues.

CHARTING A PATH TO A COACHING CAREER

Throughout my career, I have worked hard to gain a variety of experiences in different philosophies of coaching. I believe that the ideal head coach is a generalist who can oversee and have an understanding of many different areas of performance. Armed with that knowledge, a leader can more accurately evaluate players and coaches, determine how they can improve, and then help them do so. If a head coach is a specialist in one area and doesn't have any knowledge of the other coaching specialties, it makes her or him very fragile and unable to evaluate player development strategies being employed by their coaches. This is a very common issue and leads to subpar coaching and someone remaining at a post for long periods of time. It's likely because the person above them doesn't even know that their work is subpar. Being at the helm of a program or organization requires that you know the ins and outs of as many disciplines as possible relevant to your sport or industry.

Success in coaching collegiate sports is often gauged by the team's number of wins versus losses. In Minor League Baseball, the priority of coaches is player development, not the team's record. The organization is constantly moving players up and down the minor league system. Therefore, winning is not the best way to evaluate the coaches. The administrators must have a grasp of all areas of player development in order to evaluate their coaches. The same can be said for assistant coaches in college. Head coaches should know many facets of the game to be able to accurately evaluate their coaching staff. Being an *expert coach* means you are a generalist in many different areas while having one or two main areas of expertise.

If I were building a *super coach*, I would recommend various topics to study instead of just one. For example, I would recommend that coaches get a kinesiology and anatomy background so they can understand the human body and the way that it works. This ties into the last point of being a generalist.

One thing that has become mainstream at almost every level of sport is incorporating strength and conditioning into team sport athletes' training regimen. Coaches need to be able to understand and evaluate their strength and conditioning staff members. Ideally, they should be able to work closely with strength and conditioning staff due to their knowledge of the details of movement in their sport, and they should integrate this knowledge into their sport coaching.

Another area I would strongly recommend coaches understand is behavioral psychology. Many things may have changed in sports over the years, but behavioral psychology has not. People largely think and act in the same way, especially in a group setting. I will cover this more in depth later with examples. Motor learning is another area. Understanding how an athlete is able to perceive things, process the information, and react is critical and extremely useful for a coach. I have gotten less enchanted with the body and more fascinated with skill acquisition, psychology, the eyes, the brain, and how the body acts out the requests of the brain.

One other thing related to both the physical and the mental aspect of coaching is practice design and periodization. This is a foundational concept learned in strength and conditioning curricula. We are taught early on how to manage load throughout a year. However, in sport coaching, many athletes just want to do more all the time. Hitting is no exception. Pitchers have adhered to "pitch counts" for the last decade; they cannot throw over a certain number of pitches in a game to protect their arm. This varies dependent on the time of year and the athletes. However, in hitting, swing counts do not exist in practice. There is very little thought given to periodization of volume in hitting for the maximization of power output. Players will hit hundreds of balls without giving consideration to their intensity or the quality of the swings. In part, this has happened because of the traditionally used methods to measure a pitcher's intensity. For decades, pitch velocity has been tracked using radar guns. It's easy to tell when a pitcher is getting tired because his velocity may drop off. However, in hitting, we are just now starting to have the ability to easily measure how hard they are swinging and how far they are hitting the ball, which is vital in understanding the level of intensity of their practice.

Cliff Welch/Icon Sportswire via Getty Images

One other skill that a coach could consider is being well versed in analytics. This is vitally important in this evolving and changing world of technology. Being able to interpret data and statistics will increase a coach's ability to analyze situations objectively. Furthermore, it allows coaches to be able to communicate areas of improvement to the athletes objectively. When a coach is armed with this tool in their arsenal, it removes some of the emotion out of tough conversations. If the coach can effectively communicate data to the players, then the players are less likely to think it is simply the coach's opinion. Increased accessibility to technology comes with big datasets, and using the tech is a separate skill set from collecting the data and turning it into usable information for player development. A coach who can do this will have an extra tool to use in player communication and evaluation.

GAINING COACHING EXPERTISE

The head coach or manager is crucial to charting and correcting the course for a program and team. However, the more specific input and work of each member of the coaching staff is critical to the success of that journey. It's also where a coach can develop an area of "expertise." That is why I thought it was important to cross over into the world of hitting. My ultimate goal was to be in a managerial or high-level leadership position. While I had learned quite a bit in many areas, I wanted to zero in on one specific area before moving steadily toward management.

Though I worked hard to become a top strength and conditioning coach, I began to outgrow that role 10 years into my career and sought to have a bigger impact in the overall culture of the organization I was working for. My journey transitioning to a hitting coach really began in 2016, while serving as a strength and conditioning coach with the Houston Astros. I had heard the hitting coaches talking about eye tracking for hitters. As I often did, I dropped into some of the pitch recognition and vision meetings with the players during some spare time I had in my schedule. My interest was immediately piqued. I played college softball but had never heard about this concept, let alone how to coach it or train it. It had always been important to me as a strength coach to attend hitting and pitching meetings. Not just to stay on top of things regarding the strength training area, but also to understand the game from a more holistic approach. In this case, I could have never predicted where the information regarding pitch recognition would take me in my career.

When I decided to leave strength and conditioning and make the move to hitting, I knew I would need a skill set that separated me far and away from the male competition. Not only would I be switching careers in professional baseball, but I was doing it as a woman. I believed that eye tracking was valuable, but from a career perspective, I knew that not too many people were into eye tracking, and no one really knew a lot about it. I thought, "Rare is valuable." I had a desire to learn more about it, but an added benefit would be that having that skill would make me a rarity. If you want to set yourself apart, get to know a new area of focus and delve deeply into it before anyone else has a chance to do it. That creates a competitive edge in your career.

Eye tracking is not only a passion of mine and a unique lens through which to look at ball sport coaching. It was also a vehicle for me to be hired as the first full-time female hitting coach in Major League Baseball by the New York Yankees alongside Rachel Folden, who was hired at around the same time by the Chicago Cubs. When the news broke that I was hired as a hitting coach for the Yankees in the fall of 2019, there was speculation that it was a publicity stunt or a minority hire. However, there is no doubt in my mind that by being a generalist in multiple facets of the sport *and* acquiring a highly unique skill in an uncharted area of baseball, I was able to distinguish myself and earn the job. Furthermore, my boss with the Yankees was none other than the person that introduced me to eye tracking in the first place, my old colleague from the Houston Astros, Dillon Lawson. After working together for three seasons with the Astros, he had seen my curiosity, professionalism, and drive firsthand as a strength coach and knew that I would thrive as a hitting coach as well under his guidance.

Being a Coachable Coach

One of the best things you can do as a coach is to continue to be coached yourself for as long as possible. When you are struggling and someone is trying to help you get better, you realize what you sound like to your own players. It is a delicate balance of letting someone figure it out and giving them direct and honest feedback. Part of being an expert coach is being able to be coached.

I personally seek being coached as much as possible and as formally as possible. This takes on many forms. For example, in 2015, I was trying to be competitive in the sport of beach volleyball. I sought out a 16-and-under program full of high school freshmen and sophomores and asked to be a part of their training. Humbling yourself in that way is not something that people often do. I immersed myself in a sport that I knew nothing about and was publicly embarrassed every single practice in front of 16-year-olds who were kicking my ass. Learning a *truly* new skill is humbling—not sitting at a conference, privately learning in your own head and jotting down a few notes of new things you may have picked up. That's not hard enough. If you want to get inside the mind of your athlete, find something you are truly bad at and make a genuine attempt at learning it. Hire a coach. Feel the frustration and embarrassment that your athletes feel and then take note of how you feel when your coach says: "Just relax." *Right, thanks.*

Continuing education is not simply reading a book or attending a webinar. Continuing to learn new skills (physical or mental) that are difficult for you is just as much continuing education as anything else. Learning about the learning process in real time by learning a new skill is more valuable than reading about motor learning in a book. Sometimes the former isn't possible, but seek it out as often as you can.

ESTABLISHING YOURSELF ON A STAFF

As a new coach, you very rarely walk into a perfect scenario. Typically, you are brought in to improve a situation and correct problems. Winning coaches don't get fired, so a new coach is likely taking over a losing culture. Sometimes you can start with a clean slate and build it from ground zero, but often you are entering what has been a negative culture and need to clean it up.

While it is essential to develop a working rapport with your athletes as a new coach, you also need to make clear to them that you are not their equal. It's a fine line, and one that is especially hard to walk as a woman working with male athletes.

When I was younger and less experienced, I would overdo it and be standoffish. As the only woman coach around, I was a novelty and felt that it was even more important to draw the line. Reflecting back, I could have opened up a bit more, but I just thought "better safe than sorry" in that regard. That's not a very good position from which to form positive coach–player relationships, and I have adapted over time. However, growing older as the players stay the same age has created an age gap that makes it easier for me to be more of an "older sister" figure or even a "mom" at times.

The players I have typically worked with in the minor leagues are ages 16 to 20. At the lowest levels of the developmental system in Minor League Baseball, they are often from the Caribbean or South America and may or may not have a high school degree. They are gifted athletically but have very raw skills and usually don't speak English. I am a Caucasian woman from Omaha, Nebraska. So, there was quite a cultural gap between us when I first got into professional baseball. Seeing this, I quickly adapted and resolved to learn Spanish in order to close that gap. Many coaches in professional baseball forgo this step, but I saw it as absolutely necessary because of my gender and over time viewed it as one of the easiest ways to show them that I cared. By learning their language I was going to them and not expecting them to do all the work to communicate. I gained their respect and trust through a shared vulnerable point. While they were struggling to learn English, I was very publicly struggling to learn their language as well. They became my teachers just as much as I was their teacher, and it created a closer bond between us.

One other key way to enlist players' support is to give them leadership opportunities. It's easy to assume that players lack the initiative and experience to be leaders and handle the many responsibilities that role entails. Sometimes this is the case, but many times the lack of leadership and maturity comes from coaches underestimating their athletes' ability to move into a role like that. As coaches interested in

Mary DeCicco/MLB Photos via Getty Images

the holistic development of our athletes, it is important that we at least try to promote their leadership capabilities.

I took the idea of creating a "peer council" from the book *Legacy* (2013) by James Kerr. We assigned certain players to a peer council that we perceived as having leadership qualities. Then we put them in charge of seemingly remedial tasks, such as ensuring that their "unit" showed up on time. If someone was late, we told them, it was their fault. The task itself was irrelevant. The fact that the coach showed that level of trust in them made them feel appreciated, and they flourished in the role because of it. In coaching, we must be willing to turn some control over to captains and other leaders on the team to show we trust them, and they will, in turn, gain trust in us.

USING A CONSTRAINTS-LED APPROACH

I have developed a presentation called the "Constraints-Led Culture" in which I detail how to change the environment in order to require the desired behavior. The concept is rooted in a strength and conditioning and motor learning theory called the constraints-led approach. In this theory, the less you say as a coach the better because the body doesn't process words for action. It processes barriers, hurdles, and tasks to complete. Therefore, in a cultural sense, words and slogans like "We need to focus" are not much help.

Athletes need, and secretly want, more specific guidance—something they can turn into tangible action then demonstrate repeatedly with success until they own it. Instead of saying "We need more focus in practice," the solution is to change the practice to something that requires more focus. Every coach at some time has benefited from adding in a competition to practice because the athletes raise their level of intensity. You don't have to say, "Hey, go hard!" Just create a competition and watch the effort and focus go up a notch or two. That's positive behavior change produced by change in the environment.

Some coaches use this approach intuitively. Constraints-led coaching is a style of coaching where the coach takes a particular technique, skill, or tactic from the whole game and isolates the skill and lets the players find the answers themselves within the environment that the coach creates.

Say, in volleyball, you have an outside hitter who has trouble hitting the ball to a certain area of the court. Using the constraints-led approach, you might put up barriers that won't allow the player to hit anywhere else. Instead of coaching the player to "turn your hips this way" or "turn your body that way," the player now has a clear external goal. There is a wealth of research to indicate that external cues or the constraints-led approach is more effective in making change in someone's physical behavior.

However, the same concept applies to mental behavior, and yet we continue to say "Hustle!" "Work hard!" and "Focus!" without the external cues to really require the behavior.

CREATING A WINNING CULTURE

I have always had a deep curiosity about organizational culture, but coaches who have enjoyed tenured success over a long period of time regardless of the talent of the players, such as Bill Walsh, Bill Belichick, and Sue Enquist, are of particular interest to me. Talent comes and goes, and those coaches have achieved a long-term success based on their systems. Both from my reading and my experiences in nine different top-level institutions, I believe there are four core concepts involved in coaches developing a consistently winning culture.

The first is *detailed standards*. Just as I mentioned previously about the need for more specific language and expected tangible actions tied to those words in gaining understanding and support for a direction you want to take a team or individual athlete, the same is true in establishing a culture. "Hustle!" doesn't cut it. "You have 30 seconds or less to get to the next station" defines what hustle means in a clear manner that both the coach and the player can understand, and it's a clear metric that can be measured. Did you hustle or didn't you? There is no gray area. The clock tells us.

While generations have changed, behavioral psychology and team dynamics have not. Love has been introduced into the coaching language much more in recent years. But how do we let the athletes know that we love them? This doesn't mean that we take it easy on them and treat them all as individuals to make sure that they know they are special. It means that we give them clear boundaries to work within and make sure they have all of the tools to meet the standards that we have set. Setting clear boundaries is the first step for setting a foundation of clear and objective feedback mechanisms. You can't get mad if you didn't tell them. No matter *how* intuitive the task might seem.

So, not surprisingly, the second element is to provide *detailed steps to meet the standards*. Many coaches miss this step. Coaches lay out high standards, but the players are only able to achieve so much because the coach has not given them a detailed road map to achieve the standards. For example, "Our goal is to go to the Women's College World Series!" Great goal. But we have to work backward from that and say exactly what that would take. How many runs per game do we need to score based on previous teams and their paths to the WCWS? How many home runs? What strike percentage? Quantifying clear steps that can be laid out is crucial to provide mini wins along the way. The goal itself doesn't have to be realistic. In fact, I support unrealistic goals. However, the steps to reach that standard or goal should be clearly laid out and very reachable in incremental steps.

The third concept is *group competition*. As previously mentioned, it's the secret sauce, and every coach knows it. It's a surefire way to get teammates foaming at the mouth, 100 percent locked in and ready to compete, even in a seemingly routine practice drill. However, if you study the University of North Carolina soccer team and coach Anson Dorrance, you would discover that it is a daily practice that is intentionally cultivated in what he calls the "competitive cauldron." Every single day there is intentionally scheduled competition. There are individual competitions versus one another, and there are also small societies within the team that are competing against each other every day. The individuals and teams are awarded points, and each day the players can see exactly where they stand on the board based on the points that they've earned. I'll talk more about this later.

The last core concept of a dynasty is *exclusivity*. While it is a coach's job to mentor young athletes, if you want to win championships and you want the athletes to buy in and work hard, then you must let players go if they are not holding the standard over a long period of time. If the standards have been laid out clearly and the majority of the players understand how to meet them (meaning, you've done your job), then a player who is continually failing to meet the standards must go. This is much less about punishing a noncompliant athlete than it is about letting all of the other players on the team know that they are being rewarded for holding the standards and have earned the right to continue to be a part of the team. As everyone reading this book knows, just one wrong person in the clubhouse can be toxic to the environment and cause a downshift in energy. More importantly, allowing a player to hang around who has not held the standards causes the contributing members to lose trust in you as a coach because it shows a lack of integrity.

FORMING SMALL SOCIETIES FOR TEAM SUCCESS

In Maslow's hierarchy of needs, the top of the pyramid is self-actualization. If you think about that from a sports standpoint, that would mean: "I care about my team. I care about the athletics department. I care about this school. I care about this sport or my country." They would be playing for the greater good in some capacity related to their team and their sport.

However, at the beginning levels of baseball, some of the guys in the Dominican Republic and Venezuela literally don't get three meals a day. That means they're not even fulfilled in physiological need, the bottom of the pyramid, and we're trying to get them to care about their teammates. It's almost impossible! We have to take them through the process and give them the next step up after physiological needs, which is personal safety needs. This means boundaries and instruction. They need to understand what they will be rewarded for and what actions will elicit a negative consequence. We walk through the steps of the process physically and also emotionally to get them where we want them to be at the top of the pyramid. We can't get upset about them not caring about their teammates when they are just trying to survive. . . . In a collegiate setting, maybe their boyfriend just broke up with them, or they aren't playing, or it is that time of the month for young girls, and then we jump on them for not caring about the team.

During one off-season, I put the competitive cauldron to work full tilt in a strength camp of 50 players. My idea was to create set teams in which they would compete for points through the entirety of the camp. The coaches and I set out to form teams. Instead of deciding on the number of teams based on the number of players we had and then assigning captains, we asked, "Who out of this group can lead?" We came up with five players we thought could lead a team and built the teams around them. We chose to go this route because we wanted to make the teams even by leadership. We knew the camp was going to be very challenging, both physically and mentally, and we needed someone that would hold the line and be someone we as coaches could count on in each group. We separated them into these small societies, assigned the captains to the peer council, and began the strength camp.

Each team led by a peer council member earned points for everything from the dynamic warm-up to the weight room to cleaning up the cafeteria after lunch. If someone hit one of their goals in the weight room, he got points for his team. On the other end of the spectrum, if someone was late by even a minute, it was minus 10 points for his team. This created peer accountability. We never had to get mad at anyone because the team did that job for us. Being late is much worse if they know it directly affects their teammates. And the teammates would let them know that behavior was unacceptable! That's what we created with the competitive cauldron. In a sport like baseball, in which individualism is pervasive in every aspect, we created accountability to their teammates. No one wanted to let each other down. Therefore, individual effort levels rose and team effort levels rose to beat their competition. They checked the point board that we placed in a public area incessantly each morning to see which team was in the lead. This was also a crucial piece because the winning team was to get a day at the local beach resort paid for by the organization. A high prize for young men!

The way the coaches chose the teams was very deliberate. We considered letting the peer council choose, but we wanted to make sure that the teams were even by character. First, we identified the individuals with the strongest leadership qualities. Then we identified who were most likely to be "energy suckers" (as Sue Enquist calls them). We spread those people out among the five teams so that the leadership on each team would not be overtaken. We then listed a co-captain or junior leader for each team, and then the remaining 35 athletes were distributed as evenly as possible to make the groups roughly equal in character so their mental approach to the challenge would be the same. Typically, teams are separated by age or physical ability, but we thought this to be much less important in this competitive cauldron. We wanted to construct super teams with an ideal leadership structure, as we believed this would make them even.

The point system went way beyond physical tasks to ensure that we were rewarding all the behaviors we valued. This camp was held at our Dominican Academy, where the players were housed, fed in the cafeteria, and took English classes nightly. Therefore, as coaches, we saw opportunities for players to get points for attending English class and also for something we called "pride duties." Each week every team would be assigned a pride duty, which included cleaning the cafeteria after a meal, serving food to their teammates during lunch (hair nets, gloves, and all), and tidying the weight room. The concept was rooted in having them "take pride" in their facilities and appreciate the support staff that was helping them each day. They were awarded points based on how well they kept up with their weekly duties. Points were deducted if they failed to meet our standards set ahead of time.

The peer council was vital. We met with the captains each Sunday and gave them their pride duties and schedule for the week. After our meeting, they knew it was their responsibility to get their team to where they needed to be on time. Furthermore, they were to assign individual players to the pride duties daily. We didn't tell them how to do those things. That was on them. We worked hard to communicate with the peer council as much as possible and empower them as leaders wherever we could. We tried not to address the teams unless we had to, so the peer council had the ultimate authority over their teams. It's my opinion that the best teams are run by the players. But oftentimes, the players don't get that opportunity because the coach wants to be in charge. Of course, there are times when this is necessary, but as much responsibility as possible should be given to the players. That camp was one of the highlights of my career with that group of athletes because I saw that if I set up the right environment and got out of their way, they would outperform my expectations. Don't be the limiting factor for your athletes. Let them surprise you.

One reason we don't grow as coaches or move up in the profession is that we are concerned about doing something different and failing because of it. That's what we did in the example of establishing small societies within the team—an approach often used in military training but often frowned upon in team sports for fear of creating disharmony among the athletes. We took a "risk" in some ways as this had never been implemented in our organization. I was told that this would be too hard for those kids and that they needed more guidance. Of course, the opposite couldn't have been more true. The leaders we appointed excelled, and overall the players enjoyed hard work more than I had ever seen because they were working for their team. This seems like a given in collegiate athletics, but it is a rarity in professional sports.

We should have the confidence to take a chance and be a leader in the field or discipline. It is easier to stay home and be comfortable as opposed to moving halfway around the world to learn from the best. When we consider doing something different to get better the naysayers may attempt to pull you back. However, if you're attempting to be a coach of a dynasty, that will require you to do something that's different from everyone else. That means everyone else around you will have an opinion about what you're doing. That's what you sign up for if you want to be at the top of any endeavor, and it is certainly true in the coaching profession as well.

TAKEAWAYS

- Determining a desired coaching position and gaining the experience and expertise to capably fulfill it are key initial steps in a coaching career.

- Collaborating effectively with staff and demonstrating leadership abilities with players are essential functions of coaches.

- Using a constraints-led approach in coaching can help to focus and motivate athletes in their learning and performance.

- Establishing a winning culture includes providing standards and detailed steps to meet them, creating a competitive environment in which positions and playing time are earned, and excluding athletes who fail to adhere to the standards.

- Creating a peer council of leaders within a team, and groups of athletes assigned to each of them, can improve cohesion, competition, and accountability in a program.

CHAPTER 3

CHANGING COACHING ROLES, ADVANCING YOUR CAREER

Carol Owens

I was a restricted earnings women's basketball coach at the University of Michigan when I learned of an opening for a full-time assistant coach at Notre Dame. I called Head Coach Muffet McGraw, who said she wanted to interview me. When I asked when she wanted to schedule the interview, she said, "Tomorrow." I stammered, "I don't know if I can do that." She said, "Don't worry about it being formal. Just wear some nice dress pants and come on."

I made the trip there, and we spent the whole day talking about her philosophy and my thoughts on various parts of coaching. The process was more a conversation than a formal interview. We went to dinner with her husband, Matt, at a Chinese restaurant. Fortunately, I had learned how to use chopsticks proficiently while playing professional ball in Japan.

At the end of the visit, Coach McGraw said, "I have basketball camp all next week." I said, "That's fine; I am also working at a camp all next week." We agreed that she would call me after camp. I wanted to write her a letter and let her know how much I enjoyed the interview process, seeing the campus and meeting with her, but at the camp where I was working, the only quick form of written communication available was a fax machine. So I drafted a long letter and even improvised my own fax cover sheet. Since the camp was in Arizona, I drew pictures of mountains and stick figures on the top of my homemade cover sheet and faxed it with my thank-you letter.

When camp was over on Friday, I was expecting Coach McGraw to call me. I waited and waited and waited. Finally, I called her office. Her secretary answered and said, "Coach McGraw is in camp, but she will call you right back." She called me 20 minutes later. While she was talking, in my mind I was thinking she was going to tell me that she offered the job to someone with more experience. Then she said, "I just want to know if you want the job?" I said, "Uh, *yes!*"

Fast-forward 15 years later, and she still has that cover letter with the mountains and stick figures I had drawn. One day not too long ago she pulled it out of a file. The paper was so old it was yellow. I was shocked that she had kept it for so many years.

Coach McGraw took a chance on me. I think she liked my passion and energy. I was young and two years removed from playing basketball professionally overseas. I was eager to hit the ground running.

DIFFERENCES IN COACHING ROLES

Every staff is different in terms of the assignment of responsibilities according to a staff member's job designation. But here is how it has worked at the places I've coached and how the roles are generally designated in most coaching settings.

The head coach is the CEO who oversees the entire program—the staff, athletes, budget, recruiting, scheduling, and so on. A head coach sets the plan, guides its implementation, and makes the final decisions about the most important matters that arise involving the program.

Someone with the title of associate head coach is typically the head coach's closest confidant, someone she can consult with on broader issues and who can assist her in overseeing aspects of the program that need extra attention. An associate coach might also be delegated a certain facet of the program, such as scheduling.

A person with the title of assistant coach has more specific, assigned responsibilities. One assistant might focus on offense; another assistant might focus on defense. Or the responsibilities of the assistant coaches might be organized by player positions, meaning one might work with perimeter players and the other works with post players.

In any case, the coaching role designations and duties are determined by the head coach's management style, assessment of the experiences and skill sets of staff members, and the perceived best allocation of those assets to maximize their effectiveness within the program.

The head coach must make clear to the associate head coach and assistant coaches how they are expected to handle a whole array of things—from their comportment in public as a representative of the program to their recruiting pitches and their communication with and assessments of players. If those things are understood and embraced by the staff, it can take a lot of pressure off the head coach and reduce the number of things she needs to concern herself with on a daily basis. Of course, assistants should consult the head coach and suggest solutions and new approaches, but the ultimate decisions on matters of significance are made by the head coach.

MY EXPERIENCE IN COACHING ROLES

When I became associate head coach at Notre Dame, my responsibilities started to change in many different ways. I began taking some things off the head coach's plate in terms of running our leadership group and monitoring team disciplinary actions. The role meant not just having my own responsibilities but also being an advisor to the head coach. If Muffet was out of town, I would conduct practices and go to the head coach's meetings. Muffet would trust me in making day-to-day decisions within the program if she was not there. It takes a lot of experience to know what the head coach wants. As the associate head coach, you are in the position where the other younger or inexperienced assistants will come to you for advice. You'll be mentoring the other staff members as well. The role includes not just holding people accountable but making sure everyone is on the same page.

My role changed a bit after I left Notre Dame for a head coaching job elsewhere and then came back to Notre Dame as associate head coach; same title, but an expanded role. Coach McGraw's trust in me grew, knowing that I had experience as a head coach. She really relied on me and was able to be vulnerable around me because I could say, "We need to be thinking about this or reviewing a certain game film." That is how my role evolved at Notre Dame the second time around with the same head coach, Muffet McGraw. She would bounce information off me before she would address it with the staff, so I was virtually in her shadow.

We now have a new head coach at Notre Dame, Niele Ivey, and in my associate head coach role, I am even more of an advisor to her because I served as her mentor for many years. She has stepped into a role without having any head coaching experience. We have biweekly meetings—we call them "advisory meetings"—and talk about everything with the rest of our staff. We talk about goals with the team and how we want to see that discussion go in a team meeting. We give her ideas on what she needs to emphasize with the team.

With everyone on staff having different skill sets, we contribute in different ways. The assistant coach and I take as many things as we can off the head coach's plate. For example, we started working on staff guidelines we thought we needed to have in place, such as what time all the women's basketball coaches needed to be in the office and how the staff should communicate with one another. We drafted the staff guidelines along with a code of conduct.

We also drafted the standards and expectations for the players and reviewed it with Coach Ivey to get her feedback, and she was able to communicate these expectations to the team. Those are things that she did not have to worry about. As a new head coach, she needed to be involved in speaking engagements with alumni, fans, and other

Andy Mead/YCJ/Icon Sportswire via Getty Images

stakeholders. Coach Ivey has relied on me for guidance as we tackle some obstacles that she's been facing early on as a new head coach.

For me, it has been a big change from working with Coach McGraw, who had so much experience, to working with a new head coach with no previous head coaching experience. Before, in a game situation, I was just reaffirming what the head coach thought. Now I am giving more suggestions on what the head coach needs to be thinking about. We now have two coaches with head coaching experience assisting our new head coach in adjusting to her role. If you have not had any head coaching experience and you are offered a job as a head coach, I strongly recommend that you have one assistant on the staff with head coaching experience.

The policies and procedures for a new head coach's staff are extremely important to lay out early because each head coach is going to run things differently. If you are working for an experienced head coach, more than likely things have been in place for a long time and everyone knows how the program is going to be run. With a new head coach, it is important to learn the coach's expectations, how she works and what she wants out of everybody individually, and to adapt to her overall coaching philosophy and style.

Sometimes, head coaches make a change and go to another college or university as an assistant coach. That is such a plus for the program acquiring that kind of experience on the staff, and it can help young head coaches learn to navigate their way through the wide range of coaching and leadership roles and responsibilities.

Everyone thinks they want to be a head coach, but people don't realize the enormous responsibilities that job entails. Coaching is probably only 10 percent of the job. It is all the other responsibilities that can be overwhelming. Every situation is different, and every program has its challenges or runs a totally different way. It is hard to put certain things into place or into a particular order such as A-B-C-D. How many coaches have made a plan for their first 100 days, and how often do they get through that first-100-days list? You may be stuck on the first 25 days because of all the things that come up. If you have other staff members around you who have that experience, they can take some of those things off your plate.

A lot of former head coaches are not coaching anymore and are not looking to take anyone's job—they just want to help out other coaches. Everyone has their own personal "advisory council" of people they rely on for advice and counsel. Why should it stop when you are in the role of a head coach? As a head coach, you feel like you are on an island by yourself. There were so many times as a head coach that I was alone in having to make tough decisions that were not popular decisions but needed to be made for the benefit of the program, and so you feel alone in that sense.

When I was an assistant coach, the players were always coming to me, hanging out in my office, and then when you step into the role of head coach, all of a sudden they are tiptoeing around your office so they don't have to come in to see you. You need to have people who understand that and can bridge the gap between the players and the head coach. Athletes are different now in the way they think and communicate. It is important for an assistant coach to be able to put players in an environment that can relieve some of the anxiety involved in talking with the head coach.

Once you move to the head coach chair, you realize your decisions affect everything and everybody. The buck stops with you. As an assistant coach, when you are recruiting and you see a great athlete, you tell the head coach, "We have got to have this player." As a head coach you have to make the final decision: "Am I going to offer a scholarship to this particular player?" It is not as easy as you think, because you have to consider this player's impact on your program. Are there challenges with this prospect, and do I want to coach this particular type of player? Each one of those recruiting decisions affects every area of your program, so it takes a while to make those important decisions that shape the future of the team. The assistant coaches are saying "Go for it," but they don't have everything at stake. It is also a matter of trust and having people around you that you can trust to make the right decisions in other areas.

You don't have to bring everything to the head coach. For assistants to be more effective, we need to be solution-oriented. You can tell the head coach about the issue, but you should also bring the head coach some well-thought-out solutions to consider, not just problems. Head coaches have got to surround themselves with people they trust so they feel comfortable with others handling a lot of things that go on, such as a player missing a class.

Staff Chemistry

Rapport, respect, and trust are essential for a coaching staff to get along and perform effectively. But relationships and chemistry must be nurtured all the time. A coaching staff needs to do things together, besides just having a retreat once a year.

Make a conscious effort to keep the staff engaged with one another personally. Spend time around each other off the court and out of the office to learn more about each other. At Notre Dame, we do some activities such as a wine and painting event and go off campus to another facility and talk about different things that we each value. You have to invest time in your staff's growth and connection. If it is during a slower time, we will start our staff meetings by asking about everyone's weekend and what they did, and everyone looks forward to it. It is such a simple thing, but it shows you care about each other as people.

It is just as important that we build relationships with each other as we do with our players. We get to know everyone's personality. We have a good mix of different types of people. One of us is fiery, one is more Zen and calm, and of course the younger assistants are watching all of this and learning how we need to connect with one another.

Some coaches tend to hire their friends, and that is not necessarily the best idea. If you are going to hire someone who you consider a friend, then there has to be mutual respect for each other's position on the staff. I have seen those types of hires go wrong if they don't have honest conversations about what they value and how the program is going to be run.

Staff Makeup and Movement

I believe it is best to have a variety of personalities and backgrounds on a staff. That is good insurance against groupthink and also provides a breadth of perspectives and experiences from which to create and problem-solve.

Coach McGraw used to always have a male on staff because she thought it might be too much to have all women together and that you needed to have balance and diversity of thought. Then one year we had all women on the staff, and I was a little nervous. In the back of my mind, I thought that if we weren't successful, then everyone will question whether it was because we didn't have a male coach in the program. Fortunately, we were successful, so that blunted the second-guessing and criticism over our staff makeup. Coach McGraw would also talk about how wonderful it was to have such a great group of women on staff. Then a reporter asked her one day if she would ever hire a male and she said no. Of course, that discussion went viral. There seemed to be a stigma that maybe women weren't as good as men at the Xs and Os, but we are just as good at that part of the game.

There are so many great game coaches who are women. I don't mind having a diverse staff, but we want to make sure women are recognized as having the same qualities as men. It is great having a coaching staff of all women because our players look at us and think, "OK, I can do this," and they see the pride that we have in being a unified staff. We allow the players to have voices and see other women in all different positions—not just basketball, but other positions where they are managing people. They need to see that.

Changes in a coaching staff are common. The responsibility is on the head coach, but it is also on her assistant coaches, because they need to make sure they are prepared to move on to another coaching position. That can be accomplished by head coaches allowing assistants or associates to get an opportunity to take the seat of the head coach during practice games so they can see how it feels. If you have started gaining more responsibilities in the program and are interested in moving up, this will be important.

I knew I wanted to be a head coach. I don't know that I ever thought I was ready, and I had been an assistant for 10 years. You are not ever going to feel 100 percent ready, but you are going to be anxious to take that next step if you have been in a program long enough and that program has been successful. You have more and more responsibilities, and you feel comfortable with helping to make decisions. I think that's when you start thinking, "Hey, I think I can do this," or "I don't want any part of being a head coach."

When things don't work out as a head coach, it's not the end of the world, as my own experience would attest. More and more programs are recognizing the value of hiring former head coaches as assistants and consultants and acquiring all the experience and wisdom that such individuals can offer. Of course, those former head coaches have to be comfortable with their new role and defer to their head coach once they accept an assistant or associate head coaching position. Otherwise, there will be friction and tension, and the chemistry among staff won't be what it should be.

Staff and Team Culture

The foundation for the culture in a program is set by the coaching staff. Yes, the athletes must be engaged, committed to, and involved in sustaining the culture, but the coaching staff will establish its parameters and principles.

Of course, a good team culture is much easier to develop and maintain if you have the right kind of coaches and players in the program. That's why the head coach's decisions on the assistant staff and who to recruit or seek as athletes are so important. I know at the high school level you can't recruit like we do in college, but the same principle applies. Good people equal good culture.

That has been a big focus for us—getting the right people to join our team. We have passed on a few players that other basketball programs have recruited. Chemistry and culture have always been positive in our program. We look for an unselfish player who values academics along with basketball.

At Notre Dame, we put our heads together, and our staff identified the general boundaries of what we wanted and needed to be successful. First, we want our players to be responsible in how they communicate and in the decisions they make. We have three team rules:

1. Be respectful.
2. Be on time.
3. Communicate.

Being respectful encompasses a lot of things, and disrespectful behavior falls along the lines of being late and not communicating with the professors or staff or anyone that touches our program. Disrespectful behaviors could include not responding to texts, emails, and phone calls. Showing respect is a big umbrella, but players have control over

Adam Lacy/Icon Sportswire via Getty Images

Culture Paying Off at Crunch Time

At the beginning of 2018, we set goals and determined what our core values were for the team. We lost four players to ACL injuries. So, when we got to the point in the season where we had lost horribly to Louisville, the goals seemed in jeopardy.

We had lost our point guard and needed someone to step into that role right away. What we had to do as a team was lean on our core values and make sure everyone knew the core values didn't change in terms of everybody needing to be accountable, everyone having to be responsible to each other. We went back to talk about those core values and to show the team that the goals don't have to change if we don't want them to change, but everybody has to do a little bit more.

I think back on that year and what we had in place when we felt like we weren't going to achieve our goals because of all the injuries and the adversity that came along with it, and it really made our team closer because we realized we needed each other. The team began to believe that we could do this. A true testament is when we played Tennessee; we were down in the first half and were playing like we did against Louisville earlier in the season. At halftime, Coach McGraw came into the locker room and said, "You know what? We have talked about this." She reminded each player on the team what they were going to need to do to be successful. She gave specific instructions on what we needed to do, but reminded us we all needed to do it tougher and together and rely on our core values. As coaches, we had to believe that our goals hadn't changed, and we were a united front. When the team witnessed the staff still having the same confidence and the same expectations for the team, they followed us and trusted the process.

it. What does that look like? If someone texts you about something, text them back. If someone calls you, call them back. If someone emails you, email them back. Players need to have examples of what types of behavior are important.

We also have a three-strike rule that allows some leeway. Let's say an athlete was 15 minutes late for class. That would be one strike, and the athlete would undergo awareness training. She will do an extra workout and carry that strike forward for the season. When athletes get three strikes, they run the risk of being suspended a game, but they always have an opportunity to erase a strike by getting a plus. Yes, there are rewards built in also. Players can show exceptional behavior by being helpful to teammates, encouraging first-year students who are struggling, making great progress academically, and so on. They can reduce any strikes they have back down to zero with positive behaviors that we are seeking to promote in our program. The key thing is that the athletes are in control of all those situations, and it helps them be more responsible and encourages them to communicate.

We work on development in all areas, including life skills. We bring alumnae back to talk about their journeys and what they did in college, the mistakes they made, what they learned. We give current players opportunities to ask questions. We also show respect for their opinions. We work hard to establish that trust factor that is so important in a team.

GETTING INTO COACHING

Anyone wanting to get a job in coaching needs to be a member of their national coaching association, like the Women's Basketball Coaches Association (WBCA). They can also attend an educational event such as A Step Up—Next Level, run by Felicia Hall Allen & Associates for coaches wanting to move up. Many head coaches and assistant coaches attend those types of programs, so that is a way to get noticed. There are numerous camps and clinics that coaches can work and get to know many others. Let everyone in your network know you are looking for a coaching position.

Girls who want to get into coaching are so needed because these young women today need a lot of mentoring. We need coaches who are in it for the right reasons. Our coaching jobs are fantastic, and we get paid fairly well in the sport of basketball, but the real reward is seeing young ladies graduate or seeing Brianna Turner in the WNBA with the leading field-goal percentage. It is great to see her so happy and doing so well. You just hope you had a small part in her ability to be successful.

You have to enter coaching for the right reasons. I think a lot of times people don't know what they want to do, so they think, "Maybe I'll just be a coach." I'll say, OK, let's talk about this. Is this what you really want to do? I have had at least three conversations with young women who have been graduate assistants (GAs) trying to figure out their path. When I ask them why they wanted to be a GA, they say, "I wanted to get my master's degree and I played basketball, so I thought about coaching." Then I ask some more questions, such as *why* do you want to coach?

Coach Val, in chapter 1, emphasized the importance of each coach determining their why, and I advise every aspiring coach to give this a great deal of thought. Sometimes their answer leads them to shift into more of a sport administration career path. Other times they just seem to be checking out different options and haven't matured to the point that they know their direction, much less why they want to take it.

A career in coaching is a commitment like no other. So, decide if you want to be committed to mentoring and being an example to young women to show them that they can do it too.

The biggest challenges vary from year to year. Sometimes it is the recruiting; sometimes it is your game schedule. Other times it is making sure that the team gets what they need from an administrative standpoint. I always tell people who are looking to be head coaches to just make sure their vision aligns with the vision of your athletics administration. Are their expectations of you and your expectations the same? That can be a challenge if you take a new job and it is not what you thought it was going to be.

But as a veteran coach, I can, without reservation, encourage young women who are properly motivated and have sufficient skills and experience to enter coaching. It is an extremely challenging but rewarding profession. Being in a position to help members of the next generation improve their athletic, academic, and life skills is a big responsibility and is very rewarding.

Communication is key, whether you are seeking a job or counseling players. How do you get the best out of your players without them feeling you are threatening them or pushing them too hard, mentally? Even though she was a very successful coach early in her career, Coach McGraw recognized her "my way or the highway" approach wasn't going to cut it anymore. She had to learn how to be more collaborative. She might have accomplished what she wanted to accomplish, but she knew it was better to make the athletes feel like they are a part of the process and have a voice on the team. Sometimes we have to do that as coaches and how we approach things. I am a lot different—and hopefully much better—now in how I approach players than I was 20 years ago. It can be hard when athletes aren't great communicators, but you have got to find a way to build those relationships so that whatever you are saying, they know it is coming from a good place.

If I am not enjoying the job and continuing to learn about the game and what it involves, then this may not be the profession for me. But it was. I just had to determine my *why*. When it comes down to it, I find the role of mentoring young, motivated people fulfilling, and I enjoy doing so in a sport setting. That is why I coach.

TAKEAWAYS

- The keys to success for a coaching staff include the head coach's self-awareness of her management style, the clear designation of duties to assistants that optimizes their abilities, ownership and a solutions-finding approach taken by the assistants in those roles, trust and communication among all members, and a shared vision of where the program wants to go and how to get there.

- The entire coaching staff must be devoted to modeling, nurturing, reinforcing, and monitoring the program's culture and be willing to intervene with corrective measures quickly whenever there are lapses.

- Coaching is a career path that we should encourage in all young women who aspire to stay involved in sports and who have a passion to develop their athletes to their full potential, on and off the court or field.

CHAPTER 4

THRIVING AS AN ASSISTANT COACH

Denise Corlett

We had an assistant coach one year who stood up during the match and was ready to throw his clipboard. I looked up at him and told him, "Sit down." He said, "Why?" I said, "It is not your job as the second assistant to throw your clipboard." He said, "Well, the head coach isn't going to throw his." I said, "That's not your business. It is the head coach's job to disagree with the referees if he wants to and it's your job to sit down." He sat down, but that's when I knew he was ready to move on.

UNDERSTANDING THE ASSISTANT COACH'S ROLE

My mom was my physical education teacher and volleyball coach through 10th grade. I grew up on the volleyball courts and I helped coach the seventh- and eighth-grade team when I was a junior and senior in high school. I was so fortunate that I had played sports and had that taste of coaching in my background.

Of course, I could never have anticipated then the good fortune I would have during my athletic and coaching career, being part of 15 national championship teams. We won nine NCAA Volleyball National Championships while I was coaching at Stanford, and my team won a national title from the Association for Intercollegiate Athletics for Women (AIAW) when I played basketball at UCLA and another championship in badminton. I also played on teams winning two USA Volleyball Nationals and two Amateur Athletic Union (AAU) Basketball Championships.

My coaching career at Stanford began as an assistant for Don Shaw, who loved the volleyball aspects of coaching and studying the rotation tapes of teams. That forced me to learn the administrative duties of coaching, which I found I enjoyed, but that most coaches don't like to do. I also got heavily involved with recruiting and basically did everything Don did not have time for. However, he was probably one of the best game coaches or tacticians I have ever worked with. Serving as his assistant was a great start to my volleyball coaching career.

John Dunning was the next head volleyball coach at Stanford. I told him to tell me what he wanted me to do, and I felt confident I could address whatever role he needed me to fill. He let me continue doing many of the same things I had been doing previously with the administrative work and organizing our recruitment.

Kevin Hambly came in as the new Stanford head volleyball coach at the beginning of 2017. I basically worked where Kevin needed me. With all these coaches, I tried to be flexible and take on any assignments as needed. One year I worked with the setters, another year with our defense, and another year I called blocking signals for the team. I benefited and grew as a coach from not being tied to just one aspect of the game.

Each program is different depending on the strength of the staff members, but many times an assistant coach will serve as the primary recruiting coordinator. Or you might be the practice planner. Some assistants are assigned defense or offense, so you can have those separation of duties, depending on the sport and the number of assistants on staff.

It is important as an assistant or associate head coach that you branch out and learn all areas of coaching. Don't just have one strength. If you don't know something, find out about it. If you are not the main recruiter, ask to sit in the recruiting meetings so you can learn about recruiting strategies. Request to be in the budget and fundraising meetings so you understand those important facets of a program. Be ready to assist in planning team trips, learn how to put together the player notebook, plan a practice, run a team meeting, set up summer camps, and do anything else the head coach will let you do. You will need a good knowledge of every aspect of running a program so that if and when you want to go to the next level, you have broad experiences. Young assistants now usually just want to go in the gym or on the field and coach the players. It is important that assistants are excellent teachers and understand the technical and tactical parts of their sport. Assistants will be evaluated and earn respect from others based on the progress of the players they work with and how much they improve as athletes in the program. When assistants first begin, they do not have a complete understanding that it is not just about being in the gym and conducting a practice. It should go without saying that whatever your responsibilities are, be the best at whatever task is given to you.

Some programs have two associate head coaches. Football and basketball started adding a variety of titles to their coaching staffs, so they could promote their coaches and get them a salary increase. It is just a title with probably no real change in responsibilities.

GETTING AN ASSISTANT COACHING POSITION

When someone once asked me, "How do I get a job like yours?" I said, "Get a job working with someone who wants to do everything you don't want to do." The goal is to make the head coach successful because if the head coach is successful, then the team is going to be successful and you will be able to stay in that job. If that head coach is not successful, you probably won't get to stay there if they let the head coach go. Don't go into a job interview and say, "I want to do this." Instead, convey that you are willing to do what the head coach and program need you to do.

Be prepared to answer a variety of questions when you are interviewed:

- Why do you want to work here?
- What do you bring to this program?
- What are the characteristics of an ideal assistant coach?
- What are your strengths and the areas you may need to improve?
- Tell me about a critical situation you were involved in and how you handled it.
- What does loyalty mean to you?
- What brings you joy in coaching—in other words, why do you like to coach?

Understand your own coaching philosophy and the philosophy of the person you want to work with. Once you work for them, don't be afraid to disagree with or provide a different perspective on things to the head coach in a respectful way. They don't need someone to agree with them on everything, but challenge them with different points of view. Then, when a decision is made on a topic, you will need to support it 100 percent, whether it aligns with your philosophy or not.

You should also be prepared with your own list of questions during the interview:

- What is the coaching philosophy of the head coach?
- What roles and responsibilities would you see for me if I get this job?
- What would I be doing during practices and games?
- What is the philosophy of the head coach on winning and losing?
- What are your expectations of your assistants?

Stanford Athletics

STAYING AT ONE INSTITUTION

There are good reasons I stayed at one institution. First, I loved that academics are emphasized so strongly at Stanford, where the university admissions process is very unique and highly selective. Students and student-athletes truly care about academics. You must honor that academic component, or you won't be successful at Stanford. I liked helping student-athletes and getting to know them and their families as we worked through recruiting and admissions.

I did not want to leave Stanford because we had student-athletes that were driven, and we were always competing for an NCAA National Championship. Even when we were having a down year, I thought we had a shot at winning another championship. I probably could have gone anywhere to coach, but getting a bigger salary and having a big house was not important to me. My two-bedroom condo and 1,200 square feet is fine for me.

People need to choose what makes them happy, and being a head coach wasn't going to drive me. I didn't have a dream of being a head coach. I know how big the differences are in being an assistant and being the head coach. I don't like being in the limelight and in the front row, so the role as an associate head coach was more suitable for me.

The only other place I might have wanted to be a coach was at UCLA, because that is where my family lives. I've been fortunate to be involved with two great institutions in my career, and so that makes me kind of picky. There are several assistant coaches in other sports who have stayed at the same place for years, maybe because they went to school there or their families are there and they grew up there. I talk periodically with some of those coaches and we jokingly say, "When are we ever going to make a move?" When you have family around you and your spouse or partner has a great job, there are reasons you don't want to move to another place.

There are lots of factors to consider if you are thinking of making a move. Assistant coaches who are in good situations, working in successful programs and maintaining a positive working relationship with their head coach, really have no reason to leave, unless they are seeking to move up the coaching ladder.

MOVING FROM ASSISTANT TO HEAD COACH

You can tell when an assistant coach or associate head coach is ready to move on. With all the assistants we have had in our volleyball program, there is a point where I tell them, "You need to start looking," because they start wanting more and maybe getting out of their roles. Sometimes they ask me why I am telling them that. I say to them, "You are starting to challenge the head coach in a different way and probably in an inappropriate way in front of the team." You have to check your ego when you are an assistant. Most head coaches will listen to you, but I have always believed there is one voice, and that is the head coach. But when an assistant coach needs to start having the last word, then you know it is time for them to try being a head coach.

Some individuals are just not cut out to be assistant coaches. A telltale sign is when an assistant wants things to be the way they see it and wants to do things their way. You can tell they don't like it when their idea isn't accepted. Most head coaches ask for opinions and suggestions, but then it is their right to take and use that input or not. Assistants that show dissatisfaction or respond to a head coach in a negative way can be very disruptive, not only to the coaching staff but also to the team and the entire program. Assistants need to do their job and do it in an appropriate and right way. Don't ever talk over the head coach, and be prepared to apologize if or when it happens unintentionally. Understand the head coach is the one who makes all the final decisions and move on. Egos can't get involved.

Some assistants wanting to get to the next level might not be getting there because either the head coach doesn't recognize it or is not giving

Assistant Coach Checklist

☐ Always be loyal to your head coach, staff, and school. At some point you might find you aren't happy working there. Ask the head coach to help you find another position instead of becoming a burden in the program. Remember, the head coach will be the person giving you your next job recommendation. You need to realize which team you are on, and that is always the staff team. The head coach writes a recommendation or makes a call for you, not the athletes on the team or the other assistant coaches. Think of your role as an assistant as an internship observing the head coach.

☐ Know your sport inside and out. Continue to be a student of the game, studying all aspects of it, and take time to learn the areas you don't have responsibilities for currently but may in the future.

☐ Be able to teach the game to the athletes. Master coaches are master teachers. Study other great coaches and how they teach their athletes.

☐ Effective communication with coaching staff, athletes, administrators, recruits, parents, and the fans will be key to your success, professionally and personally. Make sure you are listening intently when someone is speaking to you. Maintaining eye contact with the person speaking is a great way to let them know you are engaged in the conversation.

☐ Demonstrate professionalism at all times. This means the way you dress in the office, in the gym, and while traveling, recruiting, and scouting. Dress appropriately, even when you are on your own time and out in public. Eyes will be on you everywhere, and you should cherish that. When you meet people for the first time, you want to make a good impression. Be aware of your posture, your body language, and your facial expressions. All of those things say everything about you.

☐ Develop positive relationships with the parents of your athletes and the department support staff that works with your program, as well as officials, other head and assistant coaches, support staff at other schools, and the media. It will serve you well to have strong relationships and a positive reputation with high school and club coaches you meet in recruiting. They should continue to want to work with you, even if you change schools or positions.

☐ Get involved coaching in USA summer programs—a high-performance program or one with youth and junior national teams. Attend coaching clinics and conventions to continue to grow your knowledge as well as your network and contacts in the field.

the assistants the responsibilities they want. That is when you must continue to learn. If you are starting to think you want to be in charge, then that's when it is time for you to start looking for a new job.

In preparing for the possible next step as a head coach, take good notes on every aspect of the program you may want to incorporate into your own program when you become a head coach. Also, write down things you want to make sure you don't do in your program, so keep track of the good and the bad. Keep that folder updated like a résumé or portfolio on how you will run a program as a head coach. When the opportunity comes along, you'll be ready to go. Have a conversation with your head coach on whether they feel you are ready or not to move up. If they agree you are ready to move up, they can help be on the lookout for the right place for you. If they don't feel you are quite ready yet, take advantage of every opportunity to get better in those areas that need strengthening.

GOING FROM ASSISTANT TO HEAD COACH, THEN BACK TO ASSISTANT

Sometimes when you are an assistant at a successful program, suddenly you are the name that everyone is trying to hire, and it is enticing. Then you take that position, and you realize it is not all you thought it would be, because the grass isn't always greener on the other side. If you have a pretty good gig, then maybe there isn't a reason to move on. You have no idea what is going to happen. Maybe you aren't going to be a great head coach, and maybe you are just really good at what you are doing at your school.

Obviously, some people move on and are very successful as a head coach, and other coaches may decide to coach at a different level. If they are in a NCAA Division I program, they might go to a Division II or a Division III school where the volleyball is still great, but it is a different level of commitment. They end up loving it because the recruiting is different and not as intense.

Recruiting at a Division I school is hard because of all the travel to get out to see prospective student-athletes in tournaments, in practices, in high school matches, and meeting with high school counselors and coaches. The demands of college recruiting are nonstop. We have a recruiting calendar, but it is still nonstop. Some young coaches want to be the first ones in the gym in the morning and the last ones to leave the tournaments at night, and that wears on you after a while, especially if you are trying to have a family life. The quality of life can be a challenge if you don't do a good job of managing it all.

I want to be a mentor to people. My path was different, and it is hard to give advice to people about moving on because I didn't do it or want to do it. The main thing is to be prepared and know what you are getting into. Find out what your passion is and go with that.

If you become a head coach, you can't just hire your friends. Hire people who are good and can help you be successful. Look for people you can not only trust, but who will make you the best coach you can be. People feel like they should hire people they know, but they don't really know their strengths, and then it doesn't work. I find that new coaches that come into the profession never seem to understand the amount of paperwork and planning that must been done in the office; it is not just about practice and games. If the head coaching position doesn't work out, we are seeing that they can go back to being assistants at top programs.

Those head coaches returning to be assistants are so valuable because they bring a completely different perspective to the program. They don't want to be in charge, so they are extremely loyal to the head coach. They can see everything much more clearly after having been responsible for an entire program. They are less stressed and enjoy the process of coaching more because the pressure is not on their shoulders anymore. They will give their honest feedback to the head coach and then do whatever is asked of them. Remember, assistant coaches give suggestions and the head coach makes decisions.

FACILITATING COMMUNICATION IN THE PROGRAM

As an assistant or associate coach, you must have a good rapport with the student-athletes and have their trust. Lots of athletes feel more comfortable talking with an assistant coach. Whenever there was an issue I thought the head coach needed to hear about, I told the student-

Stanford Athletics

athlete, "You need to go talk to the head coach. If you need help, I'll go with you." I would never throw a player under the bus to the head coach, but I'll listen to them, think about it, and then maybe make suggestions about something that could change.

Oftentimes, it comes down to recommending that they take a different approach when talking to the head coach. One time, an athlete told our head coach, "I've got a plane ticket to go home and I'm going to miss practice." Obviously, the coach did not take that well. When the disappointed athlete came to me, I told her if she had just presented her case better, telling the head coach, "I've been on campus without a break for a long time, so I'd like to go home for the weekend and see my family," the coach probably would have said, "OK, just be sure to keep up your workouts while you're gone."

Helping athletes communicate more effectively with each other and with the coaching staff is a big part of an assistant's job. Cultivating relationships with the athletes and the head coach will be a vital link that you fulfill. It is easy for me to talk to the players because I did most of the recruiting and know them a little bit better, as well as being close to their families through the years of recruiting. In fact, I stayed close to some of the families when the athletes went to another school.

I am usually very engaged with the parents of our student-athletes. I am always honest with them. A lot of that honest relationship is about being transparent with the admissions process. As the recruiting process went on and commitments got earlier and earlier, you had to make the right decision. Having to ask a prospective student-athlete as a sophomore, and their parents, to wait for a year to get their admissions application approved was stressful. So, I needed to be talking with them throughout that process and advocating for them.

I probably talked to more moms stressed out during that year because parents are parents. They want to help their child, but they were having to wait for the admissions process and time line, and there was nothing they could do about it. It was out of our hands. I talked to the parents every week and said, "This is the right fit, so let's move on and let the process play out." They understood that.

Once they were at the university, I kept in touch with the parents when they would come into town or visit us when we played on the road. The conversations were never about volleyball; it was more like a friendship and talking about family and everything that was going on. I would talk to them about anything positive or negative and tell them I understood. If they said, "You don't understand because you don't have any kids," I'd remind them that "while I don't have my own children, I have quite a few young people I'm involved with." I would tell them, "I know you are her parents, and you want your daughter to have everything be perfect, but sometimes you have to let her make mistakes and fail. You have to let her do that because that is part of life. We're here to help shape them, but I'm not going to tell them what to do and follow them around at school. They are college students, and everyone has to let them grow up." At first, the parents might have thought I was going to be their gatekeeper, but I said, "I am not their mom or dad here. I might be more like their aunt, but I'm not going to tell them they can't do certain things." I think the parents respected me and trusted me for having that conversation with them.

Many coaches don't want to talk to parents and say, "I'm not going to be coaching the parents." But the parents are still the decision makers, and if the parents are comfortable with the coaching staff at a school, they are probably going to be comfortable with their daughter going there. If the coaches are not communicating with the parents when they are recruiting the student-athlete, they are going to be hesitant through the whole process, and when their daughter is not starting, they probably are less likely to trust that decision. When their daughter wasn't seeing much playing time at Stanford, the parents believed in us and knew us personally, so they weren't as unhappy. Indeed, we only had one player transfer out in the 31 years I was there.

KNOWING YOUR BOSS

Learn how to manage up, and be aware of the preferred communication style of the head coach. How do they want to get information from you? Is it in a meeting, in an email, in a text, in a phone call, and what is the timing of what you share with them? Do you keep in touch with them all hours of the day or night, or do they want boundaries? Know what is important to your boss. Is it the quality of work that you do? Is it the quantity of work you do? Is it done on time? If your head coach doesn't tell you something you need to do to get a job done, ask them for more direction. It is better to know what and how they want something done than to guess at what will make them happy and successful. Show initiative, and take care of small issues without being told to do so. If the floor needs to be swept, do it.

Understand what the head coach's hot buttons or nonnegotiables are. There should be no surprises for the head coach. You must inform them of everything, even if it doesn't need their attention yet, and never lie to the head coach. When you are presenting them with a problem or issue with the team or program, bring a solution as well. Not being transparent or truthful could cost you your job, and it probably should. One of the most important things you can do to keep your job is to help your boss be successful and to be loyal to them. It doesn't matter if you agree or not with what your head coach is doing unless it is something that is illegal or immoral.

ASSISTING IN CULTIVATING TEAM CULTURE

Communicating individually with athletes and with their parents is important, but just as vital in communication for assistants is the interaction with the team as a whole and groups within the team. We have had some very fine collections of individuals with whom to work over the years, but the key with all of them is to get them to a point where they truly believe in each other.

Some teams act like they are best friends, but they really aren't. When we have had concerns with certain teams, it is when the leaders were not on the same page. It is hard when one person thinks it should be this way and another one thinks it should be another way. We talk about everyone being different and being able to understand people's differences and being OK with it. We have to all be vulnerable and not be fake with each other. We all have to be there for the same reason. If you are only there for yourself, it is not going to be a good situation. It is important for everyone to get to know one another on a personal basis. You don't have to be their best friend, but you do have to care about them and make sure you are helping them. They might do things you don't like. There are players who might like to go to parties and some who don't. The players who don't like to go to parties can be offended when some of the others go out. They can't let those differences have an effect on the team. We have athletes who like to study a lot, and some players were offended when they were studying in the locker room. They didn't think they were focused enough before the game. We had to honor their behavior because that it just how they are. They still came out and performed well after studying right before the match.

We were at the NCAA Championship as one of the top-four teams left, and it was our head coach John Dunning's first year. Our starting setter had a final exam during the last film review meeting before we played. John asked me what to do, and I said, "We're fine. The players are used to this," but he wasn't used to it, and thankfully knew enough to ask about our past team culture. Someone might be in the locker room reading their chemistry book before practice, but they are able to step on the court and concentrate and perform just fine.

We have had some other differences among athletes, like some wanting to dance before practice or a match and others preferring to be quiet at those moments. We had to convince them to trust that everyone knew what they, individually, needed to do to be ready to play their best. Having trust and understanding that we are all different yet all in this together is a big key to having a good team culture.

While athletes are more likely to come to you to talk, remember you are not their good friend but an assistant coach. You will need to listen and care for them, but be mindful that you are one of the coaches, and you need to uphold the standards and behavior expected as a member of the coaching staff.

A strong culture is important among the coaches as well. We work closely together as a staff and try to make sure we are always on the same page. We take time to get to know one another as individuals outside the office. It is important that we show the team we are committed to each other and the athletes.

TAKEAWAYS

- Assistant coaches are most successful when they have a broad skill set, a range of experiences, and an understanding of their role in serving the head coach while effectively complementing the other assistants on staff.
- When seeking an assistant coaching job, make sure your values and philosophy are consistent with the head coach's and the institution's.
- Staying with one institution or team for an entire career is very rare in coaching these days. While there is much to be said in "growing where you're planted," the option of staying with one program isn't always an assistant coach's choice or what is best, for a variety of reasons.
- The desire to move from an assistant coaching position to a head coaching job is a natural one that is often reflected in wanting more decision-making power in the program. When that urge strikes, it is essential that the assistant talk to the head coach, who may be able to give the assistant experiences to prepare for the role and help the assistant find a head coaching job elsewhere.
- Returning to an assistant coaching job after having been a head coach can be a relief for coaches who discover the administrative and other duties associated with the head coaching job are unappealing.
- One of the most important functions of an assistant coach within a sports program is to facilitate communication. You must be an excellent communicator with athletes, other members of the coaching staff, and other staff involved in the program.

CHAPTER 5

COACHING AND RAISING A FAMILY

Ellen Randell

Rowing was the one sport I excelled at. The dream of being the best rower in the world drove me from my early teens. Although I did make two national teams and won several events, at 166 centimeters (5'5") and 73-75 kilograms (161-165 pounds), it became clear as I competed on the elite level that I did not have the physiology or anthropometrics to be the best rower in the world. After being told by our national team selectors that the only option for me to possibly gain a spot on the team was to row lightweight, I tried that for a season but found the 57-kilogram (126 pounds) weight limit unsustainable and, quite frankly, joy-sapping. So, from there, I began my coaching journey.

Initially, I helped out at my local rowing club as a volunteer coach while I studied for a bachelor's degree in sport science and worked part-time as a cardiac technician. I then applied for a coaching apprenticeship at the Australian Institute of Sport. With success in my first few years (a gold medal in my first Junior World Championship), I discovered coaching as a pathway to realize that dream of being the best. After coaching and achieving gold medals at World Championship regattas and coaching at two Olympic Games, I was preparing for the Sydney Olympics when the start of a new adventure began. I was about to become a mother.

MOTHERHOOD

Having children completely changed my worldview. No longer was it about me anymore. I now had two kids to help navigate through life with a husband who supported my career choice. I found that having children broadened my perspective, honed my time management skills, prepared me for being able to function under sleep deprivation, and most of all, I found deep satisfaction in becoming an enabler, teacher, motivator, and life coach for other people. I discovered that facilitating others to achieve their best physically and to help them on their way to becoming better human beings was more rewarding than what I had hoped to achieve just for myself.

I was about to turn 37 when I had decisions to make for my own family after the Sydney 2000 Olympic Games. I remember discussing with my husband, Adam, whether we should wait another Olympic cycle or try for our first child post-Sydney. We decided that we would try after the Games, so off to my GP I went to make sure I would be physically ready to conceive. I knew quite a few friends who had had trouble conceiving, and I was about to spend three months traveling with the team, so I took advice to stop taking contraception to give my body a chance to get back to normal. One month later, I found myself pregnant with still seven months to go before the Sydney Olympic Games. My first thought was, "Oh no, they are not going to let me coach," as the team hadn't been named yet.

Our sport was male-dominated, and at that stage I was the only woman who had coached Australian rowing crews at Olympic Games and one of two who had coached at the Senior World Championship level. I was acutely aware of being "the other" in this environment and was very conscious of not sticking my head up too high. I had spent most of my career trying to fly under the radar and let my results speak for themselves. I was also aware of the support of those mentor coaches close to me who supported me politically in our sport. So, I kept the knowledge of my pregnancy quiet and, for the first 12 weeks, told no one in rowing.

My first pregnancy was a challenge. I struggled with morning sickness from six weeks and was due to board an airplane to Europe at 12 weeks. I was pretty much vomiting every couple of hours through the day and at times through the night as well. I would be sick on the way to training and then knew I had a good 90 minutes before I would start feeling nauseous again, but that would get me through a training session. Then after 45 minutes or so of the nausea building, I would be sick again, and so the cycle continued.

Coming toward the flight to Europe, I worried about how I would cope away from my home environment and the familiar food I was using to control the nausea and whether I would be able to hide being ill. Miraculously, the morning I was due to fly out of Sydney I felt well, and this lasted for the month or so that we were overseas until the flight back. Then the nausea returned, and I was sick throughout that flight and for the month after. Luckily, the third trimester of my pregnancy was good. I told my mentor and club head coach (Tim McLaren) just before I left for overseas. He was surprised but very supportive. Then, at around 20 weeks pregnant, I thought it was safe enough to tell our national team head coach, Reinhold Batschi. I was pleasantly surprised by the support he showed. At 26 weeks, I started to show, and during the Sydney Games I was seven months pregnant. Most of the team did not know until a few weeks before the Olympic Games, but they were thrilled for me.

My first child, Jessicca, was born in late December following a successful Games and coinciding with the end of my contract at the club I was working with (in our sport, coaching contracts are often renewed every four years to coincide with an Olympic cycle). It was clearly messaged to me that I should take some time as a new mother to work out whether and when I would want to go back to coaching work again and even what that would look like. Maternity leave was not an option. I did not argue the decision not to renew my contract, but I was hurt by the assumption that being a mother would mean that I somehow could not continue to do the job I had been doing up to that point. What I knew was that I wanted to coach and that I would find a way to show I could be a mother and coach full-time.

COACHING CAREER AND MOTHERHOOD

I was soon approached by Jenny Clarke, an ex-rower I had coached internationally in the 1990s, who was running one of Sydney's school rowing programs. I took up the head coach position at Presbyterian Ladies' College (PLC) Sydney in term 2 of 2001 and coached there for three years. PLC supported me with maternity leave for my second child, Alicia. I very much enjoyed the opportunity to be doing what I loved, and I found that although challenging, it was possible and rewarding to be both a mother and a coach. In time, I missed the challenge of international racing and the opportunities to travel across the world to compete at the highest level in sport. So, after three years, I went back to my club and resumed my international coaching career.

In Australia and around the world, rowing was first of all a men's sport, and coaches were men. Even when women began to take up rowing, it was mostly men who coached them. Gradually, women began to take up coaching positions. Coaching is a career pathway where being a teacher, mentor, and life skills coach is extremely rewarding. Enabling young people to achieve what they are either driven toward or may not have yet realized possible, while encouraging them to be better human beings, is a valuable contribution to society. Diversity within a coaching staff is important, and as with any organization, a lack of diversity can be limiting for decision making, innovation, problem solving, and perspective. Rowing like most other sports has struggled to achieve gender diversity in coaching.

Women make up just under 50 percent of the world's population. Traditionally, in families with children, it has been the women who have been responsible for the major parenting roles. This has limited their opportunities to take up demanding working positions outside the home. It is important, however, for female role models to exist in all workplaces, including the sporting arena, and that women as well as men see a clear pathway progression to top-level sport. Raising children is also a reality of life, and with good support networks in place, especially now that men are more commonly taking up the opportunity to assist with parenting responsibilities, a coaching career and motherhood can be compatible and very rewarding.

One of the pressures I felt particularly during my early coaching years was the perceived "token female" coach position, where I have felt the "pressure" of needing to be successful so that other women would be able to have an opportunity in the future and managers could not say, "We gave a woman a go, but it didn't work out." My experience has been that male coaches who fail initially are given an opportunity to learn from that experience, but female coaches are often not given the same opportunity.

It is important for both men and women to see women (and mothers) in leadership positions (such as coaching), as this normalizes their

Rowing Australia/Delly Carr

presence in this space. The saying "You can't be what you can't see" is particularly relevant for younger women considering career opportunities. There are, however, steps to be considered along the way.

SUPPORT OF PARTNER, INVESTMENT OF SELF

Choosing a partner in life wisely is an important consideration for everyone. I was already fully immersed as a national coach when I met Adam, and he was aware of what he was getting into. I was nervous about committing to a life partnership, but I was sure he would be a good father. We married after the 2004 Athens Olympic Games and a three-month engagement.

I have been extremely fortunate to be married to Adam, who runs his own IT business and continues to support my career choice. He has been closely involved in raising our two children, looking after our girls at home while I have spent weeks and often months in Europe. As a result, we have raised two very independent women.

Having children engenders good time management and efficiency. I have found myself excelling at multitasking, but also being able to compartmentalize when needed. I have also been fortunate to have a partner who does not let me second-guess issues that might be going on at home. With all couples, direct, open, and honest communication is important in a relationship. It is also important to look after yourself both mentally and physically. At times of extreme exhaustion, I have found it better to get a good night's sleep and start again in the morning anew. Each morning starts with a clean slate.

I have found it important to give my partner and children quality time and to be present when I am at home. This can be hard to do when sleep-deprived and exhausted from dealing with other people all day. As with all relationships, building trust is important, as is looking for a broader perspective if things are getting off the rails—either forgiving or being forgiven and moving on. Mistakes are great learning opportunities both at work and at home.

Coaching is demanding because of the hours required and the constant emotional investment with people. But making time for family is important, as well as making time for your own self-care. For me, that is going for walks as I listen to podcasts or music, or walking the dogs with Adam, or getting the occasional massage. I also practice mindfulness.

Role modeling a coaching career pathway is important for my own children, as is lifelong learning, and I try to keep some degree of study going while I coach. I have been enrolled in part-time degree courses throughout my rowing career because I believe it is valuable to keep a broader perspective and an active brain—to be aware of what is going on in the world other than just in sport. I am interested in issues of justice, development, and climate change and how they affect our world.

I did need to make some adjustments to my career when the girls were young. This involved limiting my availability for national team coaching to non-Olympic crews until they were both well into secondary high school. My times away from home were limited to three- to five-week stints rather than the 10 to 14 weeks at a time that were necessary with the Olympic teams. Doing this put a pause on my Olympic coaching career, but it was necessary to find a way to keep pushing toward what I was aiming for. Today, many sporting organizations are much more aware of the need to support mothers when they travel with teams, often allowing for support people to travel with them.

SEPARATION OF FAMILY FROM JOB

I personally have kept my family a little separate from my job. That is just a personal choice that has worked for us, although I am aware that for many others it works successfully to blend more. This comes back to your partner and the support people around you and what is possible.

I found it difficult to have my children around when I was coaching and organizational support was not available or offered. Keep in mind, my coaching was out on the water and not the safest place to have young children. It would be quite different in a more controlled environment, such as a gym or outside on a field, where others could help keep an eye on the children.

I personally preferred to be 100 percent present when I was with my young children—and 100 percent focused on work when I was away from family. It took a few years to work out what was best for me and my partner, but that is how we have operated. It is always challenging when I am exhausted from work and come home to active kids. During these times, it is hard to be totally present. It helps that my partner is active in the parenting role with me. Usually, I will go home and try to take 30 minutes to unwind with a cup of tea, then I check in with what is going on. When I am very late at work, I come home and start cooking the evening meal, which actually can be unwinding time for me.

When my girls were younger and I was working in a head coach role in a local club, it was challenging in the evenings, as I would need time to organize the next day's practice each evening. This involved checking in on individuals and organizing crews for the next morning. This was a source of angst at home as it was also family time. Over the years, I figured out how to minimize the amount of time I devoted to coaching tasks while at home, but given the nature of running a local club, it was not possible to eliminate it altogether. Now that I am coaching full-time with the national team, this is no longer an issue, as most work is completed at work.

Becoming a mother changed my perspective on the world. It was not just about me and my own goals anymore. I became aware of a distinct shift toward enabling the goals of others. This was a revelation to me and made a significant difference to my coaching. I have found qualities of motherhood, in general, to be very rewarding: Compassion, caring, service, strength, and creativity are all qualities that have made me a far better coach. Athletes and coaches are usually driven, and they can sometimes forget to appreciate the support available from the people around them.

ORGANIZATIONAL SUPPORT

Organizations supporting female coaches need to be proactive in checking in where they can help. Particularly when a team is traveling it may be necessary for young children to come with their coach. It takes a lot of the stress away if the organization can ask what is needed for an individual coach. Do they need a family room for a child and support? Is there child care available where needed? Can flexibility around work hours be organized? When children are young sometimes it is necessary to take time out for doctor's appointments, looking after sick children, and so on. This is not a long-term situation for the organization, and having their coach feel supported reaps benefits in the performance of their teams.

It is also important for senior coaches to be supportive of female coaches with young children. This is not just in supporting them in a practical sense, but making sure athletes are aware of the benefits of having a female parent as a coach. My own mentor, Tim, who worked with me for many years at the club, was very proactive in reminding athletes of the roles of a mother in running a family—their organizational expertise—and how lucky they were to have me at the club. This verbal support goes a long way in encouraging respect from those around us.

Remuneration is a significant issue that often limits opportunities for women. In general, women have received less pay for the same role. They have even received less when required to assume additional roles, such as administration as well as coaching—which was the situation I faced when I started working at our university club. Some coaching jobs in women's sports are often offered on a part-time basis, and the length of contract does not provide security, making it difficult to leave another line of employment. This was the case for me early in my career and caused much angst at home with my partner, who viewed this as me not being valued for my time. However, this is a reality for many women and a particular issue for women with children. Often, we are asked to do additional work to make up a salary (this too was the case for me, for many years) or to be paid part-time when we are working full-time hours.

On a related theme, relocation also comes into play for women. There have been roles offered to me that I have not taken because of my partner's work commitments. My current role involved many years of traveling 45 to 60 minutes (sometimes longer) to get to work and then return home. We have recently moved closer to my work since the COVID-19 pandemic, and Adam has made the shift to work from home.

The culture of an organization is also a consideration for female coaches. Early on in my coaching career, it was common to be in a work environment where there was a "blokey" or alpha male–oriented culture. This can be quite challenging for a woman, and it is not a comfortable, supportive, or an attractive workplace to be in. On many of my early national team experiences, this was the case for up to a 12-week assignment. I would not have considered a long-term position

Courtesy of Rowing Australia.

in that kind of environment. If there are no signs of any shift in culture or support among other staff or the organization itself, then I would not consider the role.

The need to be constantly proving yourself can be draining over a long period of time, and it was a reality for me in some of my national team appointments. I was fortunate to have a supportive partner and family, including a brother who also coaches at the national team level, along with supportive mentors.

Other sources of support are available to women who are coaching and raising children. Informal online chat groups are an option. There are many married women with families who are coaching and can give advice and counsel to young coaches with children trying to figure it all out. *Moms in Coaching* is an online group in women's basketball in the United States with a podcast to help guide moms on and off the court. It was started by a young coach who found she needed to reach out to others for advice on how to be successful as a mother and a college coach. There are many women in various careers who are raising families and would be willing to share their stories of success if you will take time to ask them. In Australia, we have a number of mothers now in our sport at the national level, and we all support each other.

CHILD CARE

Options for child care can include family members if they are nearby, *au pairs* if you can afford them and have the space for them in your home, family day care with a caregiver you trust, or day care centers. A useful strategy is having a team of friends that can help with carpooling to get your children to different commitments. I found that mothers in particular are usually very willing to volunteer to help other mothers out. I would offer to drop other mothers' daughters at home when I could, which meant that I had people to call on when I needed them. Of course, you need to know and trust the families that you ask for help. One important consideration is to know to ask for help early, before everything implodes. But in the end, it is OK if you don't manage to get your child to their commitment every time if it means keeping your own sanity. Sometimes, there must be sacrifices on both sides.

In my family, I usually organized all the after-school activities and carpooling, even when I was away traveling with the team. This is what worked for us. My partner would organize the girls getting to school on time. On the plus side, both my daughters became very self-sufficient, as from an early age they would get breakfast and be ready for school, and my husband would take them to school and head to work. As he works in information technology and often late into the evening while I leave home early, we found individual routines that worked for us over time. For example, when I am in town working, I come home and cook the evening meal. When I am traveling, my husband cooks and organizes all day-to-day family activities while I will still organize the girls' after-school activities. Once they graduated to senior high school, they were self-sufficient.

In closing, I would encourage all coaches who are mothers to manage their time well and to be present for their children when they are with them. Demonstrate love and patience and be a good listener with both your team and your family.

It is absolutely possible to be a wonderful mother and a successful coach, and I have found this is genuinely achievable. Children are enormously resilient, and as long as they are loved and cared for, they will end up being good humans. I am so proud of my two daughters and how grounded and independent they are. They are both capable, strong, and organized and grew up with an understanding of the need to contribute to the running of the family and the world around them.

Make sure you have a supportive partner to take on the task of raising a family while supporting you in a coaching career. With good planning, everything will work out fine.

I have very much enjoyed coaching and raising a family and will continue to be a dedicated coach, mother, and partner into the future.

TAKEAWAYS

- Combining motherhood and coaching is challenging, but with enough determination and the right conditions at home and at work, it can be done.
- A healthy separation of coaching from family will serve everyone well—especially the coach.
- Partner and organizational support are essential to a mother-coach's success and happiness.
- Capable, dependable, and caring child care can take an immense weight off the shoulders of a coach who is trying to juggle a busy home and sport schedule.

CHAPTER 6

MANAGING YOURSELF

Roselee Jencke

When I was in my 20s and still playing netball in Australia as an active athlete, my boyfriend at the time gave me a coaching book entitled *She Can Coach!* Unbeknownst to me, I was going to get an opportunity to meet the editor many years later when I was attending an NCAA Women Coaches Academy in the United States. Dr. Cecile Reynaud, former head volleyball coach at Florida State University, was a featured speaker at that academy held in Denver, Colorado. When Dr. Reynaud mentioned the book to the 40 women coaches in the audience, I thought, "I have that book." *She Can Coach!* was one of the first coaching books I had ever read. Published in 2005, this book was so interesting, and from it I learned many great stories about how these 20 successful women approached coaching in various areas.

Indeed, we—women—*can* coach and be very successful. One question, however, is whether in doing so we are going to follow the model that precedes us or whether we need to subscribe to a different approach, one that allows coaches to have a more well-rounded, balanced, and healthier life. I contend that we better serve and set a positive example for our athletes by balancing our commitment to coaching them as well as we possibly can without resorting to behaviors that aren't sustainable or conducive to our well-being. We can and will be better coaches by taking better care of ourselves.

STRESSORS IN COACHING

One of the first things you must accept when you become a coach is that it is anything but a nine-to-five job. Yes, you have schedules for practices and games, but other than that, time and the tasks you need to perform at any moment are often determined by factors beyond your control.

Just try and set rigid rules for when players and the coaching staff must do this and that and see how effective it is over the course of a season. What if your best athlete is a minute late for the team bus? Do you leave her at the curb? Kick her off the team? Or what if your top assistant coach has car problems and makes it to practice five minutes late? Do I demote or fire her? Tardiness is one of my pet peeves, but I've learned how to deal with it, and in the rare instances it happens, I try not to get bent out of shape about it. And just as importantly, I do not inflate it to the point where the penalty exceeds the crime.

Another challenge in coaching that I find stressful is when staff members are not able to manage their moods. I have an expectation that my athletes, when they come together as a team, are in control of their emotions and prepared to give their best. Sometimes staff, because of what is happening in their world, don't always present themselves as being in the best mental and emotional state to work. When that happens, then you are not only dealing with what you are working on with your players, you are also having to monitor and sometimes step in for an assistant who is "having a bad day." That shouldn't be the case, as it is both a diversion of your attention and a drain on your own energy to have to do so.

Another stressor for any coach is when friction develops on a team, either between individuals or groups of players or between coaches and players or even between coaches and coaches. If we aren't united, coming together in a unit that puts aside differences and feelings to cooperate and complement one another to be the most effective collective we can be, then we are in trouble, and the entire season will be a struggle of discord and disappointment. I believe we are all in this together. Certainly, there will be times of disagreement and comments that are stated or interpreted in a negative context, but at the end of each practice, game, and day, we need to be together and loyal to one another and the program.

A final stress point I'll mention is the almost inevitable second-guessing that goes on among players, staff, yourself, fans, and the media. Organized sports competitions are almost always public events in which evaluation, by oneself and others, is constantly occurring. I would advise not paying attention to outside criticism from someone who hasn't been a coach. After a game, you are always thinking about what you could have done differently or how you could have been of more help to the team. When you take time to reflect back, you might think about something you may have missed, and that is important to consider moving forward. You need to evaluate your coaching decisions after the game and give those your undivided attention. Identify what you did well and what and how you can do better the next time. Also, evaluate the key performance indicators (KPIs) and whether you met the goals associated with each of them. But don't dwell on the outcome or performance for more than 24 hours. You and your players need to move on because there is another contest coming up.

EVALUATION OF SELF AND PROGRAM

Success in the knowledge economy comes to those who know themselves—their strengths, their values, and how they best perform.

Peter Drucker

Most fundamentally, a coach must know her core values and ensure they are in alignment with values held highly by your organization. If not, you may not be working at the right place and will most likely be continually frustrated and disappointed. It is important that your coaching staff and athletes' core values are also congruent with the core values of the organization. And remember, it is important to show respect for others in your program as people. They are going through many of the same things you are in trying to manage themselves.

Oftentimes, we as coaches are so focused on the day-to-day responsibilities that we get stuck in the patterns of behavior that we have established, and we develop a skewed perspective on what and how we are really doing. We may fail to see flaws or potential opportunities when we become set in our ways, our hearts, and our minds. You need to make time daily for a brief reflection on how you managed the day.

Self-Assessments

This can be quite daunting, but filming yourself at practice and games is important to do. I did this early in my career, and it was quite revealing. I received some very useful feedback from this experience. Not only did it show what I was doing, but there was also an audio recording of what I was saying during practices and games. I could see and hear that I was talking too much. I could see the players were standing around listening to the coaches and not doing any activity. We went back and changed our training to make sure there was limited downtime or nonactivity, with less talk and more coaching on the move—so giving the athletes feedback while they were in a drill instead of stopping the drill.

I have spent some time observing one of our basketball coaches, Andrej Lemanis, who coaches the Brisbane Bullets. He is the former coach of the Australian National Team and coached in the Australian basketball professional league, the NBL. As I watched the practices, I saw the players never sat down for a drink break; they simply went over to the drink station to have a drink and they were back out on the court. When I talked with him about this, he told me he had all the times in training mapped out to simulate what happens in an actual game. The tempo of the training followed the tempo of what happens in competition. Players didn't sit down. Feedback was on the go, breaks were the same time as allowed in a time-out, and it was a good lesson in the importance of specificity of training.

When I compared that to some of our past practices, I could see the wasted time as I let players sit down to have a drink for two minutes here, three minutes there, and when you add all that up it ends up being quite a bit of time that we could have been using more effectively. We were wasting too much time, which made the training time too long.

What it forced me to do was to manage the time better and be much more effective and efficient in the time we had our players on the court. Training became more game-like, and our team really responded well to that change. We always spend time evaluating athletes, but the most important part of being a successful coach is knowing yourself and what you are doing first.

How do you want information given to you? Do you want it in writing? Do you want to listen to a report or a podcast or a book on tape? Organize your office so you can work without distractions at the best time of the day for you. Do you need it to be quiet, so you work alone, or can you work with other people popping in and out of your office? Be aware when you are most mentally sharp and plan your most challenging work during that time. It may be before everyone else arrives in the office or late at night at home.

Find a certified expert who can administer and analyze a personality assessment such as the Predictive Index, DiSC, or Myers-Briggs. These assessments can be extraordinarily useful in helping you better understand yourself, improve interpersonal communications, and connect with colleagues and athletes more effectively.

Time and Task Management

Being able to manage your time and all the tasks you need to accomplish as a coach is important. It would be valuable to use something like the Eisenhower Decision Matrix to organize your day, your focus, and energy for the day. This was a system designed by U.S. President Dwight Eisenhower to help him prioritize and manage the many duties and decisions he had as a U.S. Army general, then supreme allied commander of NATO forces, and ultimately president of the United States. It is also known as the management matrix or the four quadrants of time management.

The matrix organizes tasks by urgency and importance (see figure 6.1). What do you need to be dealing with, what can you put on your schedule to work on, what can you delegate, and what is not important or a priority? Taking the time to plan and organize your time can relieve you of many of the stressful items that pop up throughout the day.

Athletes' Feedback

Some players are open books and want to tell you everything about their entire life, while others can be quite closed off. They can also inform

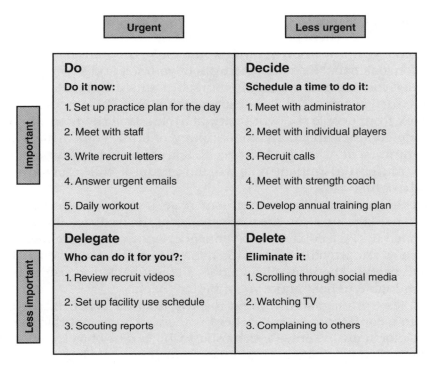

FIGURE 6.1   Management matrix applied to coaching tasks.

you of how you are doing in managing yourself and the program if you will encourage them to do so.

Checking in with the players prior to training is important for us. We have a 20-minute "good to go" period where they do all their pre- and post-rehabilitation work and check in with the physio, the sport scientist, and the strength coach. During that time, I am there too, so I can touch base with each one of our athletes asking them how their day was, but also the other two professionals are good at picking up signals that there might be something wrong. Athletes will let the staff know if they are sore or anything that needs attending to, and then the staff can come to me and let me know of anything I might need to be aware of. This is also an opportunity to get a sense of how they feel about how they are being coached, or you can get more formal feedback through the 360-degree evaluation explained in the following section.

Outside Feedback

There are various ways to get feedback. More and more coaches at many levels are realizing they need an executive coach or some type of feedback from outside their program. If a high school, club, or college coach can't have that consultation service paid for out of their budget, they are realizing that they may need to invest in their own personal growth.

Learn your strengths from a feedback analysis. You can do this yourself or have others help you. Think about your decisions as a coach for the past year and analyze if you would make the same decision again when you look back. Knowing more about yourself and how you operate will assist you in better managing yourself, your staff, and your athletes.

You can also conduct a 360-degree evaluation. This involves getting feedback from people you work with at all levels of the program. Have someone conduct an anonymous survey of staff, your athletes, and your administrator to get their feedback on your performance as a coach. You can also identify a trusted group of colleagues and ask their thoughts.

There are a variety of ways to gain more self-awareness. Here is a word of caution. Make sure you are ready to accept the feedback if you ask for it. Be open to the feedback, and remember not to shoot the messenger when they are providing you with honest and constructive feedback. You will need to thoughtfully evaluate the feedback and use what you feel is valuable to help make you a better coach.

Coaches are not usually going to have another coach in the same sport as a confidante because there is too much competition, so they will look for someone outside their sport who can be objective. Coaches should seek out advice and counsel from other coaches in different sports at their university or high school. Those acquaintances who are coaches would be more of a mentor than a professional executive coach.

If coaches are really serious about their career and professional development while dealing with strong competition and ongoing recruiting, I would strongly recommend coaches look for outside feedback. I still have my coaching mentors—some I played for or have coached against—but they are retired and happy to listen when I need advice or encouragement. I also use former coaches of people in the league, and we can have strong, robust conversations, which is what you are looking for. Sometimes I have found I have blind spots, so it is important that you have other people who can actually see everything. I think I am doing everything I can, and I think I am treating other people fairly. However, I may not be.

It is also important that the coaching staff around you can be honest with you. Sometimes that is really difficult for them. Even though you are wanting to make the best decisions for the team, they may be reluctant to speak up. You have to make them feel comfortable enough that if you ask them what they are seeing you do or say, they will let you know if they see it differently. Obviously, they don't want to upset you or hurt your feelings.

When you begin coaching, you need to understand that you are not always going to hear what you want to hear from others about yourself. There is a lot of criticism in coaching by people thinking you should do it this way or that way, but if you can change the thought process around and the way you ask questions and problem-solve, then that should help you with those relationships—and that honesty goes both ways.

Outside Expert Evaluation

When I first started coaching the Firebirds netball program, I was a young coach and raring to go. It was about that time I was introduced to Bo Hanson, senior consultant and director of Athlete Assessments (www.athleteassessments.com). He had been hired to do a review on netball in Queensland, and I was scheduled to meet with him to go over that review. After that thorough process, I decided to continue to have him working with the program and working with us on developing the Firebirds team culture. One of the first things we did in developing the culture was to get to know the athletes and coaching staff better through the well-known DiSC (Dominance, Influence, Steadiness, Conscientiousness) profile.

That assessment is practical and easy to understand. It helps identify areas that might need attention. Bo worked with our program and became a mentor to me for those first six years of my coaching. It was a trusting relationship and respectful because of his knowledge and experience as an athlete and a three-time Olympic medalist in rowing. Having an executive coach like Bo who was able to advise, support, and give me critical feedback when I needed it was useful and important in my growth as a coach. If I had a difficult situation to manage, I was always able to consult with him on how I should think about this issue, or look at it differently, or what questions I needed to be asking to handle the situation more effectively.

SELF-MANAGEMENT AS A COACH

Over my long career I have developed good routines, become very well organized, and managed my time effectively. That wasn't always the case. It is important to remember that if you don't take care of yourself, you can't take care of your athletes and staff.

I learned how to plan and to prepare my team to create efficiencies that allowed me to have breaks during the day, even if only brief ones, without in any way diminishing my efforts. It is amazing how simply taking time to enjoy a cup of coffee and a short stint of solitude can recharge my batteries so that when I return to my coaching duties, I am fully energized, my concentration is high, and I am enthusiastic to give my best to those activities.

The best way I have found to manage things as a coach is to be as organized as possible in all areas of my life. That is sometimes easier said than done, but I make it a point to get practice and game plans devised, key messages written down, tactical strategies planned out, and so on, to ensure some structure and direction in what we do every day. I try to foresee the unexpected—the "what ifs," if you will—if things aren't going according to plan, and anticipate possible changes that might need to be made. All of that planning happens well before game day.

By the day of competition, the preparation should have been completed; all I have to do is review those key messages with the team and check the athletes are in the proper headspace for the game. I also try to build in some downtime in the schedule prior to going to the game. I'll sit somewhere quiet, have a coffee, no phone, but prepare by going over my notes and thoughts for the game, making sure I'm in a really good space so that when I step out into that sporting arena, I am fully focused on the players and the game.

During the game, I am usually pretty calm. What is really important, and what I have learned from my players, is that they don't like me being too emotional or demonstrative because it affects them. One of the beliefs in coaching is that if you are wasting energy and being overemotional, then you are not clearheaded enough to make good decisions. Also, you want to set a good example for how you want athletes to handle their thoughts and emotions during competition. If they are getting annoyed by things out of their control, such as officiating decisions, or they are making mistakes and getting emotional, then they are not going to be able to make good decisions. Just like the coach, if they are too emotional, it is taking away energy from thinking about what is really important in their game. So, staying calm as a coach is critical.

James Worsfold/Getty Images

In general, I manage my mood, because that is what my players expect. To help with that throughout the week during our training, I'll make time to have a little nap. I can actually step away from everybody because I live 10 minutes away from the training environment. I can come home, have lunch, switch off, nap for 15 to 30 minutes, and then I'm ready to go. It has all been preplanned anyway, and all I have to do is get back in plenty of time before our training to go over my notes again, catch up with the other coaches, and check in with the athletic trainers to make sure everyone is available or to see if I need to adapt any of our plans. Making sure I factor in some downtime for myself—like a little catnap during the week, during the day, and then on game day—helps me make sure I am really prepared with the game plan.

You have to know yourself really well to maximize your energy and stamina throughout the year. Some people may have the ability to be switched on all the time, and that is OK for them. Hopefully, they know their personality profile and what makes them tick and how to be most effective. For me, I need to be able to switch off and step away so that I can rejuvenate and look after my well-being. If I am on call 24/7 for an extended amount of time, I am afraid I would burn out. Every coach needs to find the right strategy for themselves.

Proper nutrition is very important. You must eat well and not just nibble on snacks and drink coffee. You need to fuel yourself efficiently enough to maintain your energy and focus as a coach. Make sure to include good nutritional habits for yourself and your staff in your daily planning.

At the end of the season, I have another window of planning and list management, and I finalize all of that while it is fresh in my mind. Then I get away from regular coaching activities for several weeks to switch off from the sporting world, get in a different environment and mindset, and assess my health, fitness, and nutrition. This is an important window for a deeper self-reflection.

ADVICE TO YOUNG COACHES

To those of you who are new to coaching, I encourage you to be well organized and to plan ahead for all of your training. Don't leave things to the last minute or try to do things on the fly. Have good structures and processes in place. That helps you manage the training environment, and also helps you manage yourself.

Seek advice from a mentor or an executive coach. Support the people working around you. Continue to develop your communication, technological, and other skills that are so important in today's coaching. Make time for your professional development. Look around at other sports to get different ideas. Study yourself early. You really don't realize how much you talk and athletes tune out during those long talks.

As a new coach, you might feel like you have all this information and experience to share and you just want to do it all at once. But you might be spending too much time telling, when the way athletes learn is by doing and problem solving themselves. We need to tell athletes less and ask them more questions. We can help them to become better by posing questions and steering them in the right direction, allowing them to problem-solve themselves. They will make mistakes, but that is how they learn.

If you are an assistant coach looking to move to a head coaching position, make sure you are prepared by maximizing your strengths and improving your weaknesses. Know your core values. Know the environment and political terrain in which you work best. Look for and ask for more and more responsibilities as an assistant so that when a head coaching position opens up, you are ready and prepared for the opportunity.

TEAM CULTURE

Team culture is what you live and breathe every day. It needs to be organic and authentic. The culture of a team tells a story about who you are and what your program is all about. Your ability to weave those stories together through your daily work allows players to come in and have an understanding of the history of the program. Culture is about your values and your behaviors as a group, and living those values day in and day out. One example of having a positive team culture means having impeccable standards. This year our team watched film clips on YouTube about group expectations and *above-the-line behavior.* That concept means that in your program, you have a line. Above the line are all these vibrant colors and high energy and behaviors that are "open, curious, committed to learning or ownership, accountability and responsibility" (Conscious Leadership Group 2014). Below the line is gray, negative energy, and behaviors are about "being right, defensive, and closed, or about blame, excuse, and denial" (Conscious Leadership Group 2014).

When we talk about above-the-line behavior expectations, it means to be successful you should have good energy, be positive, and have fun. This is the behavior for everyone all the time. People do slip down into the place below the line, but it is about bringing their attitude back up again and having those standards. If you are not doing things right in the locker room as a team, don't expect a positive team culture to transfer onto the court on game day. If you are not wearing the right uniform, if you are tardy and not being positive to your teammates, if you are not encouraging your teammates, if you are not cleaning up after yourself in the locker room or are leaving the bench a mess with chairs all over the place, what does that say about our team? Those might be little things, but little things matter in a team culture.

Albert Perez/Getty Images

Such standards and expectations of meeting them need to be woven through the program from when the season begins to set the direction for where you are going and what goals you want to achieve as a team. You have your values and behaviors and standards, but you also need to have your framework and your processes. It will be very important for the players to be able to have that system in place and have structure. They know what the requirement is. If they don't know the requirements and the expectations, then that is when you can get below-the-line behavior and have a less than positive team culture.

Early in my coaching career, we were talking with our players about how we wanted to be seen by the opposition. Adjectives came up such as tough, competitive, and fair. We continued to work on it as a group, and we finally gave it a name. The acronym "PURPS" stood for Passionate, United, Relentless, Professional, and Standards. It turns out that our team color was purple, but we didn't think of that until we wrote it on the whiteboard and the players pointed it out. That culture was created organically. We spoke about those values often on a daily basis. I had a phone call a few months ago from some former players, and they just wanted to tell me they were reminiscing about their past experiences as players in my program and how much fun they had, and they said, "We think of you and wanted to tell you we love you to bits." That is what culture means to me. It never leaves that group of people.

TAKEAWAYS

- Develop self-awareness. Take time to really study your actions and language as intently as you study your team. Get input and feedback from others you trust who can observe you coaching in practices and during games. This could even be your administrative supervisor if you have a good relationship. If you are on a college campus, look for graduate-level sports psychology students who can come in and evaluate your coaching style and communication to give you private feedback. Know who you are and how you work best. Are you an early-morning person, or do you work better late at night? Plan the most critical thinking sessions during your best time. Think about if you need a mental break sometime before practices or games to be more effective. I encourage you to outline some guidelines for your staff. These might be developed from knowing what your nonnegotiables are and how you like things to operate. These are your expectations for the staff. You share them with potential staff members before you hire them to see if they will be compatible working within your system.

- Practice self-care. Plan ahead and make sure there is a place for you and your staff to store lunch, snacks, meals, drinks, or anything you need to keep your energy level high throughout the day. Schedule the day so that you can get in some type of exercise or workout, even if it is just an hour walk with a staff member around the campus relaxing and enjoying the fresh air. Some of your best ideas will come out when you are on a treadmill or on a run. Make sure you are getting the amount of sleep you need to be your best self, whether it is eight hours, six hours, or 10 hours. Set a consistent sleep schedule and go to bed at the same time every night. Turn off your electronics, read a novel, and relax. When you wake up, have a routine that starts you off energized. Set up your 24 hours so that you can get everything done and still take care of yourself—the most important person in the program.

- Begin with the end in mind for your career. Invest well, think about another career from time to time, maybe as an administrator, a consultant, a private coach, or a teacher. You want to be in control of your coaching career and how long you plan to coach.

PART II
PROGRAM DEVELOPMENT AND MANAGEMENT

CHAPTER 7

WORKING WITH ADMINISTRATORS

Melissa Luellen

The year after winning the women's NCAA Golf Championship in 2009, my Arizona State University golf squad had only two student-athletes on the roster. This dire situation resulted from a perfect storm of events leading to the departure of team members: I helped two walk-ons get full athletic scholarships and more playing time at a less competitive golf program, two seniors graduated, two student-athletes were dismissed from the team, and two others decided to turn pro early.

Having achieved a huge goal in capturing the national title, you would think I'd have an easy road ahead. Yet, there I was, the coach of the defending champions, with only two players left in our golf program. We were unable to enter tournaments because we could not field a full team. If not for the good professional relationship I had established with my athletics administrator over the previous few years, I'm fairly certain that I would have been dismissed.

RELATIONSHIP BUILDING

Relationship building is vital in all areas of life, but it is especially valuable when unexpected challenges present themselves. Fortunately, I have had excellent relationships with my athletics administrators during my 20 years of college coaching. I have worked for four different administrators, and three of them had numerous years of experience in college athletics. They all loved to help the student-athletes and coaches succeed.

Your athletics administrator or supervisor can have a huge impact on your success, but it's definitely a two-way street. Building a relationship is about your ability to identify and initiate working relationships. It is about developing and maintaining relationships in a way that is mutually beneficial to both yourself and the other party because good relationships are critical to getting things done and essential when your success depends on others.

I realize not all coaches may have a good relationship with their administrator. I spoke to my previous athletics administrator to find out what administrators expect from a coach and received in return the following list:

- *Be honest.* Number one on the list is always tell the truth and do not leave anything out.

- *Communicate frequently.* The coach should be proactive in communicating with her direct report on a consistent basis. Regular communication is extremely helpful, even when things are going smoothly. Communication may be easier if you can get to know your athletics administrator outside athletics. Get together for a meal away from the office, and learn their interests and about their families.

- *Be budget accountable.* In the area of budgeting, do the research on what you need to be successful in your sport. Be specific about how this will have a positive impact on your program. Identify ways that you can fundraise for things you may want or need for your program. Make sure your expense reports are accurate, and do not use university funds for personal use. Experienced athletics administrators who oversee several programs have more knowledge than the coach does about the resources the athletics department can provide.

- *Follow the rules.* No responsible administrator is going to be very forgiving if you get into hot water by breaking rules and regulations of a national, state, conference, sport, or school governing body. Never give your athletics administrator a reason to question your integrity and honesty.

We, as coaches, often forget that athletics administrators have enormous and wide-ranging responsibilities. As head coaches, we have responsibility for one team and a few student-athletes to manage. In most athletics programs, athletics administrators are responsible for several teams and, more often than not, hundreds of student-athletes and lots of coaches and support staff—not to mention all of the other administrative responsibilities, such as budgeting, student-athlete support services, and rules compliance.

It also helps to learn how your direct supervisor makes decisions. How does the administrator want to receive information so they can reach a decision concerning your program? It will make the process smoother for both of you if you know how the director of athletics makes decisions. Take time to get to know the other athletics administrators and staff in the department. I am fortunate that as a golf coach, I can play golf with my athletics director periodically.

Off to a Good Start

When you are being interviewed and are considering taking a position, spend as much time with the athletics administrator as you can since this is the person making the recommendation for you to be hired. Be prepared with questions. Ask them why they're in this position and how long they have been in administration. Find out what they did before and what other sports they currently oversee. Learn their vision for the program, and ask to see the operating budget. Determine if the operating budget includes fully funded scholarships and if the financial support matches their vision for the program. Inquire about any fundraising expectations they have for coaches.

Once you are leading the program, there will be times that you may need additional financial support for your program. Know the exit strategy for you as a coach. What do I need to do to stay here, and what would get me dismissed? Make sure you know the expectations.

Make sure you understand administrators' thinking on critical situations that you may face in the future. Would they help support you in formulating a plan and developing benchmarks for a student-athlete who is not satisfied or progressing in the program? The administrator may feel that you recruited that athlete and invited them into your family, and now you want to get rid of them. As you well know, relationships with prospective student-athletes are built over a period of time, and unfortunately in recruiting, you don't always have enough time to get to know them as well as you would like to. Once the athlete gets to college, you truly find out why they compete. If an athlete loves what they are doing, they will do everything they can to improve. If they are playing for their parents, that shows up in college.

Even if things didn't work out with an athlete in our program, I believe it is important to find another place for them to pursue their education and athletic career. In the end, I want them to be successful, and hopefully my administrators understand that philosophy. Tough decisions will need to be made, and you need to understand whether support from your supervisor will be there.

Nurturing the Relationship

From my experience as a head coach for a number of years, having an effective working relationship with my athletics administrator is paramount to my success and job satisfaction. It requires a commitment from me to be open, direct, and engaged in ongoing and frequent communication. It means building a relationship of trust over time. This requires me to know myself and be open to coaching from my athletics administrator just as I want my student-athletes to be open to coaching from me.

Every athletics administrator is different in their leadership and management style. Try to adapt—manage up—to make the situation work best for your athletics administrator. *Managing up* is building and sustaining a productive working relationship with your athletics administrator. It means caring about and respecting how your athletics administrator takes in information, makes decisions, structures their day, and likes to communicate.

Develop an objective understanding of your athletics administrator's strengths. Meet or exceed the expectations for the quantity and quality of work. Be honest and keep your athletics administrator informed so there are no surprises. Don't just show up at your athletics administrator's office only when you want something. Keep your athletics administrator informed of the good and bad.

In building a working relationship with your athletics administrator, it is important to be authentic. Being authentic is being honest and open about who you are and what you value most. Being authentic is at times being vulnerable, taking responsibility, and acknowledging mistakes.

Consistent communication with your administrator is key. Provide a weekly update, either through email or in a face-to-face meeting, explaining how things are going and informing the administrator of any issues of concern.

Have regular monthly meetings with your athletics administrator about your team. At first, I thought it was a little bit too much, but then I realized it was really important to have regular communication.

Have your administrator conduct an anonymous survey of your athletes at the end of every season. I get a copy of the results to see if there are any issues or trends that need attention. One year, most players felt the expectations of the team were not clear enough. The next year it came back that the expectations were very clear. Surveys are helpful, but feedback is difficult to take, and you must be vulnerable, especially when you think you've got it all figured out.

Often the more successful we are, the harder it is to listen to feedback on our performance. And without critical feedback from our athletics administrator, colleagues, and student-athletes, we can make mistakes that damage our team, our institution, and our reputation. What we do with the feedback is critical. If we act on it, it can improve our performance. It can make us better at what we love to do. Equally important, we will take big steps in building trust and laying the groundwork for a channel of continual feedback.

Athletes have been known to go in to see an athletics administrator with complaints about you as a coach. Sometimes athletics directors will side with the student-athletes. A coach should document various

Courtesy of Auburn Athletics.

conversations and situations with all players. Sometimes a comment can be taken the wrong way, but it is the impact and not the intention that matters. It would be a good idea to schedule individual meetings with athletes every two weeks. While I only have six athletes on a golf team, those individual meetings take up a lot of time, but the value they provide to your relationship with the student-athlete is tremendous.

Even though we are fortunate to have real golf scores to decide who qualifies, sometimes I might want to make a change for various reasons. It is important that a decision and how it may affect the athlete and the entire team are understood. Each athlete has a developmental plan to follow that they have written in their own words and that says how they want to get better and what they will be doing to get better. When I talk to them about their plan, I find it important that they have used their words, and this was their plan to continue to improve. The more you can have in writing, the more it protects you as a coach.

GETTING SUPPORT WHEN CRISES OCCUR

When I came to Arizona State University (ASU), I had only coached for two years and had never even been an assistant coach. My new boss was Don Bocchi, who was a longtime football coach before stepping into an administrative role. His support of me started the day of my interview at ASU and, fortunately for me, never changed. Don has a huge passion for people, for all his coaches, and for the student-athletes in the program. I told him that I would look to him to be my mentor since I was so inexperienced. This created a bond and friendship that has lasted to this day.

Don's support was essential in helping me overcome the challenges of that 2010 roster situation I mentioned at the beginning of the chapter. Here is what happened.

It had always been my philosophy to have at least one walk-on on the team roster to provide her with an opportunity to earn a scholarship and to remind my scholarship golfers how fortunate they are to be receiving athletically related financial aid. I encourage the walk-on to take full advantage of being on the team. She should be the first to arrive and the last to leave practice. She should do everything she can to improve her game and lower her score. If that fails, it's OK, but she knows she will no longer be in our program. Don knew and approved of my philosophy on walk-ons and was fully supportive in my decision to help the two walk-on student-athletes gain scholarships elsewhere.

I also recruited two young women who, I soon learned, I had not studied and vetted effectively before bringing them into the program. They became fast friends but were clearly not capable of living up to the responsibilities of team membership. I shared my concerns with Don, and he gave me some good advice. I talked with both student-athletes, disciplined them, listened to them, cared for them, and gave them the benefit of the doubt. Nonetheless, while we were hosting a team event, both golfers blatantly broke the rules. I was finished with them, and my athletics administrator was 100 percent supportive of my decision. The two student-athletes were provided releases and transferred to other NCAA Division I golf programs, where they were quickly dismissed from those teams.

So, now I was down to four returning golfers, but I met with Don and reassured him that I would find a good player or two during the fall, and we would continue our competitive success. Then, in mid-July, only a few days apart from one another, I received calls from two golfers who said they were so sorry, but they had decided to turn professional, effective immediately. I called Don in a panic, and he set me at ease. He told me that we would overcome this serious roster-shortage situation, that he never doubted my integrity, and that he fully supported me and believed in me as a coach.

The fall season was spent taking our only two golfers to a few tournaments so they could compete as individuals. I helped them continue to develop their games and focused on recruiting. Fortunately, by January, I had six new golfers on the roster. We competed frequently using 21 of our 24 competitive dates in the spring. We won a tournament and qualified for the NCAA Women's Golf Championship. My job was secure. I had weathered the perfect storm, primarily because I had tremendous support from my sport administrator.

Alternatively, coaches can feel like they are stranded alone on an island when things go badly and they have not developed a good rapport with their administrator. You will need all the support you can get if you find yourself in a caustic relationship with your direct supervisor. Have you ever given your athletics administrator a reason not to trust you? Have you ever shown a lack of respect? If so, take the necessary steps to repair the relationship. Make deposits to your account to build trust and apologize, if needed. We expect a lot from our student-athletes, but sometimes they make mistakes. We are all human, but we can get through the rough patches if you follow your core values to make decisions and work closely with your sport administrator.

Other obstacles can make it difficult to have a good relationship with your athletics administrator. When you get a new administrator, it can sometimes be a challenge because maybe you had a fantastic relationship with the previous administrator and now you must work at it. If you have not built the relationship both ways, it can be tough. Initially at least, it is good to meet with the new administrator or direct report early and often, asking lots of questions and keeping track of answers. Make sure you keep notes from those conversations so that when issues arise, you have documentation about the expectations and guidelines that were understood from those meetings.

Also, it is sometimes a challenge for a coach to connect with a sport administrator who has never coached. When you have sport administrators without coaching experience, you should understand their job is about finance and management. The coach's job is management and performance. The two of you can work harmoniously, respecting the value of what each of you bring to the collaboration.

SHARING THE TEAM CULTURE

We, as coaches, are usually very protective of our team culture. I learned the bubble concept from the former golf coach at ASU, Linda Vollstedt—one of the greatest golf coaches of all time. You, like Linda, may prefer to create a bubble around your team and determine who comes in your bubble and who is out of your bubble. Your sport administrator and the athletes' parents may not always fit comfortably in your bubble, but it is hard to put up those boundaries.

Here is how we have dealt with building and protecting our team culture. I was never an assistant coach before becoming a head coach, so I really did not know that much about team culture except from my own personal experience. Golf is an individual sport and a team sport, and "team" is very important, so our athletes need to be good teammates. You must learn how to be a good teammate—how to be supportive yet hold each other accountable.

In the past, our best teams from an enjoyment standpoint were the teams that got along well. Those teams were always the ones that held each other accountable. If they can get the respect and they hold each other accountable, that is the ultimate place you want to be as a team. You can still have fun, work hard, expect to do well in the classroom, expect to follow the rules, and have excellent etiquette, which is big in our sport and very important to me as a coach.

During competition they do not see their teammates for four hours, so they must really focus on their own game. When we start a round, the number five player tees off, then eight minutes later the number four player tees off, so they are seeing their teammates, but you don't know how they are doing the rest of the round. We talk about how important positive body language is, so they give a fist pump after they hole out, which lets the next players watching back on the fairway know they have scored and can see their reaction. Some other teams will give hand signals like giving a heart sign with their hands. All teams try to come up with their own signals to each other on the course.

Courtesy of Auburn Athletics.

It is an interesting phenomenon when you have a connected team because it seems that when one or two players start making birdies, they all start making birdies. I have seen four out of five birdies happen in the exact same place around the same time. I have seen a definite connection when they all love and respect each other as a team. Most of them come into college not playing on a team, so they have to be taught how to be a good teammate. The players really relish their teammates because being on a team is such a small window in their career.

So, when we travel, we try to maintain that close-knit group feeling by limiting those on each trip to just two coaches and five athletes. Once you start adding more people into the bubble, it can get messy pretty quickly. However, it is also important to be respectful of the athletics administrators and the athletes' parents when they want to be involved.

If I have communicated frequently with my direct-report administrator, I might invite him or her to go along with us on an early season trip. That way, if the administrator wants to join us when we travel to the national finals, the team already has some familiarity with that, and it is not disruptive to our approach. But I don't want an administrator on every trip, either.

As for parents, during the season we will typically have a "family night" at tournaments on the evening of the first round. The director of golf operations sends all the parents hotel information for each tournament well in advance so that they can stay close to the host hotel. We always thank the parents for coming to the tournament to support the team. Maintaining a positive relationship with parents can go a long way when you need support for your program and with your administrator. But ultimately, you must decide when and how often you want outside people in your team's "bubble."

One more point about communicating with others in that bubble. When meeting one-on-one with your athletics administrator, assistant coaches, or athletes, turn the electronic devices off and devote full attention to your people. Being fully present, being demonstratively interested, and being a good listener goes a long way in building and strengthening relationships. It shows you care and that you have prioritized them. It makes a difference.

In closing, based on my experience as a head coach for a number of years, having an effective working relationship with my athletics administrator is paramount to my success and job satisfaction. It requires me to know myself and to be secure in and committed to being open, direct, and engaged in ongoing and frequent communication. It means building a relationship of trust over time with my players, staff, and others who are essential to the success of our program, including my AD.

TAKEAWAYS

- Having a great working relationship with your athletics administrator can have tremendous benefits for you, both as a coach and person, and for your program. Do all you can to strengthen that connection, including being honest and communicating frequently with your administrator, being accountable with your budget, and following the rules.

- Strengthening and maintaining your working relationship with your administrator entails being open and direct in your communication, earning trust between the two of you, and adapting in a positive way to the administrator's management style.

- The value of a strong working relationship with your administrator is most apparent when you need support during challenging times.

- If your relationship with your administrator is strained or goes off the rails, first assess your role in the situation. If appropriate, apologize, try to make amends and set things right, and convey your appreciation for the administrator's role and responsibilities.

- Your administrator should be informed and supportive of the culture you want to establish and maintain in your program. Elicit that support by demonstrating the positives such a culture manifests, such as better scholastic performance by student-athletes, great discipline and enthusiasm by players and staff, an athlete-centered coaching staff that prioritizes players' holistic development, and backing by players' parents and the community.

CHAPTER 8

BUILDING AND SUSTAINING A WINNING PROGRAM

Amber Warners

There are several elements to a successful sports team and program. Winning is certainly one aspect, be it the number of wins achieved compared to the number of losses, conference championships, regional championships, or even national championships. But there is much more to the definition of a successful program than winning.

Success in a program also entails realizing team goals, creating and maintaining a positive culture, and developing strong relationships between all members. And all these factors have a cause-and-effect relationship with each other. Consistent winning happens only in the presence of those other things, and those other things are enhanced and reinforced by winning. Let me give you a few examples.

In my experience, when a team is playing for a championship, there are times when things go really smoothly on the court during that run and it is pretty easy competing because everything seems to be going their way. There are also at least a few times when things aren't going well and the season is on the brink of ending. It is during that downtime in a season that the star players or "point-getters" start to feel even more pressure to produce because the outcomes lay on their shoulders. It is during this time that those players usually act out against their teammates or get very upset and place blame on their teammates for not performing better, and then there tends to be a collapse physically, emotionally, and mentally.

In 2010, we were playing in the NCAA Division III Volleyball National Championship Semifinals and we were down 0-2 sets and down 16-21 in the third set. Our back-row passers were passing poorly, and we just could not get the ball to our best player who was a middle attacker. When I called a time-out, I fully expected our outstanding middle blocker to get all over our passers for not playing better. Instead, she told the back-row players that she would do a better job blocking for them so they could position themselves better on defense. It was like the back-row players immediately became more relaxed and more confident. Now I don't want anyone to think we are afraid to show our emotions or get on each other to push one another, but this collapse did not happen because of the trust, accountability, and culture that we have worked so hard for in our program. We went on to win set three and won the match in five sets. There is no way that we would have pulled that match out without Becca reacting to the situation how she did.

COACHING PHILOSOPHY

My philosophy as a coach is twofold. First, I want to win. Winning is fun. Winning is way more fun than losing, but we don't even talk about winning much with our student-athletes. What I mean by wanting to win is that I want our program to do things in such a way that we can look back and say we did everything in our power to get the result we wanted.

Someone once asked me how I measure success in our program. My first reaction to that question was to think about the number of wedding invitations that are given out to the teammates when one of our players gets married. You only invite people to your wedding that you truly care about and have a great relationship with. And if you think about it, a player will usually graduate with only a few other teammates each year. But a player has seven years of teammates—their class as well as three years of players older than them and three years younger than them. Most player weddings I go to have 15 to 20 teammates attending. I consider that measure to mean we have a successful program when I witness all those teammates being at one of those weddings.

I firmly believe we have won a great deal of matches because we focus on more than just volleyball skills and court development. Don't get me wrong. We still focus a lot on the volleyball, but doing that alone will not bring out the very best in our players on the court. It is only a part of it. Adding in all the other things we do in our program is an important reason why we have had so much success over the past decade.

Players' experiences matter. It matters for longevity in the program, retention rates, attracting recruits, motivation, and win or loss outcomes. Having a great team culture will not only give you more wins, it will also be an additional factor that will draw better talent to want to come and play in your program.

Building and sustaining a winning program can be interpreted in different ways. I think of myself as a coach who wants to win more than anyone she knows but at the same time wants her players to have the best experience of their lives because of the culture that was relentlessly pursued day after day and year after year. Sure, I care about all these things because I want to win, but it is a great deal more than that to me. It has to do with building and maintaining something so special it will transcend the results you will see on paper. Not only will your team have more wins and maybe even add some championships for your school, but it will give your athletes an experience that will teach them how to work hard to be their very best in everything they do. They will carry that work ethic with them into their lives after college—into their family life, careers, and relationships. I want us to have the best team chemistry we possibly can have. Players will play better and push themselves harder if they love their teammates and enjoy being together. Being in our program will give them an opportunity that many say was some of the best time of their lives.

The second part of my philosophy is I want every one of our players to become the best they can be on the court, in the classroom, in their relationships with others, and in their faith. I acknowledge that in the big picture of life, this second part is bigger than the first part. I am a coach that holds both parts to the highest standards, and I know this is why our program is special and has helped us maintain our success in all aspects.

Every coach has their own philosophy. No matter what the level of athlete you are coaching, it is important to get players to buy in to your philosophy. If you are coaching at the collegiate level, you must recruit players to come and play for you. It will be important that you find student-athletes who are not only talented but also are looking for the type of program you are selling. If you are coaching at a middle school or high school level or club environment, you will get players to want to play for you if you are doing things in such a way that they want to be a part of it.

I was fortunate enough to observe six of the best volleyball coaches in the country for three to four days and get a look inside their programs. There were many similar things they did, but there were also a lot of things they did differently. Each one had a very different style and interaction with their players, and they were all incredibly successful on the court. I took away a few things from those visits. The first one was each coach had players that fit their style and philosophy. I believe those coaches recruited based on that as well and were very clear to recruits about who they were as coaches and how their program worked.

I also learned that there seems to be no one way to do things to achieve success. There is no magic potion, and there are multiple ways to teach skills, do drills, and handle players.

In addition, I came to understand that I needed to be my authentic self but still improve in certain areas. I never should try to be someone I am not because it won't work out in the end. When I talk to recruits, I am very transparent about who we are and what our program is like, because if I am not honest with them, players won't know what to expect and may not last long in our program.

PLAYERS ARE PRIMARY

We look for players who are very talented and extremely competitive but care more about the team as a whole than about themselves—players who are willing to invest in others and willing to work through disappointments and challenges to help them get better, rather than bailing at the first sign of conflict.

Coaches can have a huge impact on the team's culture with the way they manage their players and their team. If a team has a bad culture, there will be athletes who will not play as hard, try as hard, care as much, and will possibly even quit. Building a great culture will enable you to get the most out of your players' talent.

When athletes feel connected, have a positive experience, have fun, and love their teammates, we know they will fight harder for each other on and off the court. They will dig in and push themselves more when things are not going their way because they have something worth fighting for—their teammates.

Creating and maintaining a great culture is not easy. It takes commitment, time, consistency, and passion. It takes fighting against egos, insecurities, selfishness, and superficial relationships. It means setting standards and expectations that transcend any one player or person. It takes work on a day-to-day basis to show that you care, holding people accountable, expecting high investment on and off the court, being consistent in the way you treat players, knowing how players treat one another, and maintaining good communication both verbally and nonverbally. Once you have a good team culture, you have to continue working on it every day to keep it going. If you stop paying attention, you could have the team culture slip back to a point that it isn't productive anymore.

In our program, we have expectations of players to contribute to the growth and maintenance of our culture:

- Accountability
- Work ethic
- Communication that is ongoing and honest
- Service to one another
- Relationships built on caring, love, and vulnerability
- Gratitude and joy for others

Accountability

It is important to have standards and hold the players accountable. This includes everything from players being on time and working hard, giving full effort, to how they treat one another and how hard they work for the greater good of the team.

Unfortunately, some coaches only focus on their sport and their players' skills and feel it isn't their responsibility to address anything else. If there are issues going on within the team, it will certainly affect what is going on during practice or matches. I often tell our best player that they need to be the best ball shagger to show their teammates that they aren't beneath doing what needs to be done for our team to function to its fullest.

Sometimes, coaches may have different standards for different players, are afraid to hold the better players to the same standards of behavior, or don't care about holding the poorer skilled players to the same standards. They are unwilling to confront day-to-day accountability issues or just don't feel that it is their job to be concerned with this area because they are so focused on the sport stuff. They may also be worried that this may come off as being an "aggressive coach."

Make sure the standards are clear and that your administration is supportive so that no one gets caught by surprise. Not addressing these issues often will break down trust and cause division among team members.

Work Ethic

We demand a lot from our players. They work. Most people would assume that means they are in great physical shape—and they are—but it also means we work hard in all areas: physically, mentally, emotionally, and spiritually. We hold them to a standard in everything, from how hard they work on the court to how much they give to the program and how they treat one another and invest in one another.

One example of how we do this is through our off-season/summer workout program. We give them nine challenges that they need to be able to complete when they report back to campus for preseason training. Some of the challenges are physical and others are not. The physical challenges are geared toward different types of fitness—anaerobic, strength, core, and agility. We also have them write a letter of recommendation about themselves in the third person, outlining why they should be a member of the team and what they can bring to the group. Each grade level answers different questions.

First-Year Students: What qualities will you be able to bring to the team? What things will you do to be a giver and builder to our program? How will you improve our program? Please comment on things that are on the court and volleyball-related as well as things off the court. How do you overcome adversity and setbacks?

Sophomores: Why should you be promoted and brought into a more reliable role? How will your contribution be different from last year? How will you come into the season this year that is different from your first year? What will you be able to do for the newcomers to help them adjust to being members of the team?

Juniors: What can you bring, or how will your role change, for you to now be the face of the program? Why should you be promoted into a leadership role? How has your experience in this program made you ready for more responsibility? What will you do or bring to help make the last two seasons everything you want them to be?

Seniors: Why should you be moved into ownership? What will you do with your experience to own the upcoming season? What are two things you want to see from this team this year?

Another challenge is a partner challenge. They are paired up with one player who they need to regularly touch base with over the summer. This allows for a mentorship between an older and younger player and a sense of community, and they need to answer questions about one another when they come in for preseason.

There is also a nutrition challenge throughout the summer to make sure they eat properly and drink enough liquids. The physical challenges are hard enough that if they don't work at them throughout the summer, they will have a hard time passing the standards when they get back on campus. If they don't pass a challenge area, they get one chance to retest. After that, someone else on the team who already passed that challenge would need to volunteer to pass it for them. These challenges have been very effective because most players come into preseason in great shape.

However, some challenges for certain people are hard to pass, even when they work on them, and this is where the players push themselves emotionally and mentally. They don't want to let their teammates down. They don't want to make someone else have to do the challenge over again because they didn't push themselves hard enough.

Communication

The way a coach communicates with their players is very important for establishing a winning culture. I always try to overcommunicate with my players. My players can't read my mind any more than I can read theirs. I am going to be deliberate and let my players know what I am thinking and why I am doing things, *and* I am going to do everything I can to find out what is going on in their minds as well. I can't assume that they can see the "writing on the wall," even when I think something is very obvious.

My first year as a head coach, I was working with varsity high school players. One of my outside hitters had seven hitting errors in a row before I decided to take her out and try someone else. She either got blocked or hit the ball into the net or out-of-bounds. After the match, while I was

Calvin University Sports Information

walking to my car in the parking lot, I was approached by the hitter and her mother. They wanted to know why I took her out of the match. From then on, I have assumed that my players don't necessarily see everything the way I do. If I decide to make a change in the lineup mid-match, I will walk over to the person I take out and talk to them about the change. It could be saying something like, "Be ready if you get another opportunity," or "We need you to keep the ball in play more and we will work on that tomorrow in practice," or "You did great; I just wanted to give someone else some time." If I decide to make a switch in the lineup before a match, I will always tell the involved players it affects a day before or well before the match, if it is a decision on the same day as a match.

I also tell my players that I can't read their minds. If something is bothering them, they need to come and talk to me about it. It is just as much their responsibility to communicate with me as it is for me to communicate with them. I will have numerous meetings with them throughout the season. These meetings may last only 15 minutes but are used to talk to each player about skill development, ways to improve, things we need more from them, and playing time. I also ask them in these meetings what is it that they want me to know. I am here to listen to anything they want me to be aware of or want to tell me about their personal experience.

I find that when I need to have a tough conversation with a player, it is easy to try to avoid doing it because it is hard and uncomfortable. So many coaches take what they perceive is the easy way and decide not to address issues. I have found that part of why our culture has been so great is because the players know the things that affect the team and that they will get addressed. It helps the group continue to thrive. This goes along with accountability.

When I approach a player I need to address about something, I always do it one-on-one. I do it with my heart in the right place, giving the player the benefit of the doubt and always affirming what they are doing well first. But I am always going to be very truthful about the behavior that needs to be changed. Confronting with truth, but doing it with love, is key. When the players know you love them, you can still get on them about their behavior and they take it better. "I know you well enough to know that you would not intentionally come off like this, but when you do, this is how I perceived it. And it is likely your teammates and the other coaches do too."

Some examples of things I address with our players:

- Being late
- Not being invested
- Not building relationships
- Body language/eye rolling
- Not being focused in practice
- Roles on the team—why they aren't playing and what they need to do
- Individual performances—good and bad
- Behaviors outside of volleyball that are hurting the team
- Changing the lineup or substituting

I coach at a Division III college, and we don't have athletic scholarships that are given for four years. So, at the end-of-the-year meetings, when I know someone has a small chance of making the team next year, I am going to say something like this: "You may have a tough time making the team next year. If you decide to try out, I want you to know I am 100 percent behind you, and these are the things you will need to do in order to improve your chances. And even if you put in the work, there are no guarantees. I am telling you this now so that you aren't assuming anything and aren't caught off guard when tryouts come around." When I do that, it puts it back in the player's lap, and they need to make a decision instead of them blaming me for having no idea they were on the bubble.

One other area that I think about a lot happened to me as a mom, wondering how my sons were treated by their coaches. And I always ask myself two things. Are my best players who produce for us day after day getting affirmation and praise from me, or do I never say anything to them about what a great job they do because I just expect it each day? It is important that your best players are given feedback and praise as well. This will help them stay motivated and hungry to keep getting better. The second question I ask myself is: Am I giving as much attention and communication to our worst players? I know that I do give more attention in practice to our players in the lineup, and that is the way it should be. But off the court, am I giving our weakest players attention as human beings because they are still a very integral part of our success?

While communication between coaches and players is vital, communication between players is also a key to a winning culture. One of our standards in our program is to always tell the truth to one another.

One example of how we do this is an activity we do called "What do you bring, and what do you need to be careful of?" Each team member, including the coaches, will take a turn saying something that they think they bring to the group, and then a couple of other teammates and coaches will feed into them and affirm to them another strength or two that helps the group. Then the person will talk about one thing they need to be careful about overdoing—in other words, one of their weaknesses that they bring to the group. Then a couple of people will bring up anything that they feel this person has the potential to do or that is hurting the function of the group. It is a very powerful exercise, and it really helps bring out and address members' strengths and weaknesses in helping the group reach their potential on and off the court.

Another way I have communicated with our players is to have them fill out a short two-question form after a match. It allows each player to voice their thoughts, give self-evaluation, and communicate with me one-on-one. I then take a couple of minutes after a match and read each player's responses. It allows me to be able to understand who I need to follow up with in person and get a feel for how each player is doing. Figure 8.1 offers an example of that evaluation.

Lack of communication always seems to lead to misunderstanding and misinterpretation. By communicating consistently, even if it is about things that players don't want to hear, there will be a lot less confusion and misunderstanding, which will lead to a much healthier team culture.

Service

We all have a responsibility to serve one another. We strive to be givers more than takers, and this starts from the older members of our team.

In our program, we consider it a privilege to serve, and the seniors want to make sure the first-year students as well as the other members are taken care of. We see this done in our program in a variety of ways.

While everyone is assigned a different job for the season, such as taking care of the medical kit to and from away games, in our culture, the seniors take pride in serving the underclass players. In some programs, the first-year students need to do a lot of the serving because they are the newbies and everyone else has taken a turn in previous years. Our seniors always eat last, and the older players touch base with the younger players to see how each person is doing on and off the court.

We go on a retreat at the beginning of each season. We usually go to someone's cottage, and there are usually not enough beds for every person to sleep on. Instead of giving priority to the seniors, first we draw numbers for choosing where to sleep. One year, a senior was sitting by a first-year student when they drew their numbers. The senior was one of the first to pick and the new student was one of the last. This first-year student was having a hard time being away from home

Postmatch Thoughts 2016

Laura Danhoff #11

Opponent _____

Opp. Set Score _____

Knights Set Score _____

1. What are your overall thoughts and feelings about how the match went for you personally? Analyze your own involvement in the match.

   _____

   _____

   _____

   _____

   _____

   _____

   _____

   _____

2. How did you perform on the six skills that you committed to?
   - Positivity
   - Competitiveness
   - Discipline
   - Unselfishness
   - Humbleness
   - Patience

   _____

   _____

   _____

   _____

   _____

   _____

   _____

   _____

   _____

   _____

FIGURE 8.1   Example of a player postmatch self-evaluation.

for the first time and not sleeping well. The senior switched numbers with her because the senior wanted the new student to have a comfortable mattress, because she knew the new student needed to get some much-needed rest over the weekend.

Another time we came home from a tournament at three in the morning. When we come home from trips, the underclass players drop stuff off in our locker room and then walk to their dorms while the upper-level students get in their cars and drive to their off-campus houses. On this particular night, it was raining and cold, and everyone just wanted to get home to their beds. I found out the next day that one of our seniors waited around for the younger players and drove three different carloads of them to their dorms because she didn't want them to have to walk in the cold and the rain. These are examples of great servant leadership.

When the younger players feel and see how the older players treat them and take care of them, it makes those players want to carry on that same servanthood when they get to be seniors. That is a wonderful part of our team culture and only positively influences things that happen on and off the court with the team. There is no more powerful relationship than that between the older and the younger players.

Reaching Back

When we won our first NCAA National Championship, I wanted to somehow tie in the players who had been a part of our program in the previous years and show them how they helped in what this team had accomplished. I asked our seniors to name one upperclass player who had an impact on them and give me a couple of sentences on why. I then contacted those players who were named and asked them the same question. I traced it back all the way to the 1970s.

There were really impactful things that came out of that exercise. First of all, the earliest person named happened to be the mother of one of our incoming first-year setters. It was really powerful to think that our incoming player's mom had an indirect impact on her daughter in our volleyball program 30 years later. Another observation I made was that in all the comments I received, there was not one word about volleyball. It was all about a senior player taking the time to get to know an underclass player and giving words of advice and encouragement.

Caring, Loving, and Vulnerable Relationships

I get more out of our players and can push them harder because they know how much I care for them and love them as people first. I am not an easy coach to play for. I demand a lot from our players not only on the court but in all that is expected of them off the court, but I also do various things to show them that they are valued and loved.

Doing this takes work, but it is very simple. It is staying in touch with each player to know what is going on with them inside and outside the team setting. It is showing interest in their relationships and their academic life and spending time with them. I try and touch base individually with every person every week. This can be as simple as an informal one-minute conversation before practice, meeting for coffee, or just offering some encouragement in passing. In my earlier years, I would make sure I touched base with the first-year students on Mondays, sophomores on Tuesdays, juniors on Wednesdays, and seniors on Thursdays. Anyone who I felt I needed to follow up with was on Fridays. In addition, I have gone to the dining hall to share a meal one-on-one with players within the first few weeks of the season, and I usually don't talk about volleyball much. I have also done home visits. I go to the players' dorms or off-campus houses for around 30 to 45 minutes. This allows me to be able to see where they are living and to get a feel for their daily routine and living space. Our players love this, but it also allows me a glimpse of who they are, and so I find it far more beneficial for me than for them. I try and care for our players as if they were my own daughters.

We strive to incorporate love, grace, and vulnerability into our daily living with one another as team members. It means meeting people where they are in their life and loving them unconditionally. It means building relationships and spending time with one another and only speaking truth. It means having real conversations and being vulnerable with one another. It means loving someone enough to be able to accept criticism from them, and also being able to confront them when needed.

To start building trust with one another, one of the first group activities we do near the beginning of the year is called "person, place, or event." We take turns sharing something about ourselves that we normally don't talk about in casual conversation. I ask everyone to be willing to be vulnerable and real and to open themselves up to the group and trust. It is talking about a person, a place, or an event that has been a contributing factor of who we are today and how that has affected us. I set a timer for three minutes, and when it goes off that person knows they need to wrap it up. It is one of the best trust-building exercises we do. At the end of that activity, we feel totally different about one another and have a much better understanding about who each person is and some of the things they are dealing with outside volleyball.

This relationship development also takes place throughout the season, involving time with just the players. I had to guide and suggest to the upperclass players some things to do in the first couple of years, but after that, they have taken on many of these things on their own initiative. Here are a few of the things we have done in the past.

- The seniors write letters of welcome and encouragement to the rest of the team over the summer.

- The upperclass players divide up the rest of the players and make sure they are spending extra time and attention on the underclass players they are assigned.

- "Closing down Knoll." This is a once-a-week activity where they go to dinner at the dining hall and sit there and talk until it closes and they are asked to leave.

- Affirmation board. We have tiny baskets (actually from a Christmas Advent calendar) with each person's name on one. Players write a note of encouragement or thanks on little pieces of paper and slip it into the baskets. Every Monday, the players pick up their notes, and it starts over for the week.

- Hot seat on the bus. One person answers any question that is fired at them.

- One-on-one meal rotations. Players have a meal with a different team member each week in the dining hall.

- "Lib night." Once a week, all the players go to the library and sit on the floor and study. They sometimes do this in a room in our fieldhouse and get food delivered.

- We assign bus seating that is different for each away match, so everyone has a chance to talk to other people and cliques are less likely to form.

We also choose to use truth and grace while giving the benefit of the doubt. Anytime you have a group of people chasing down goals and competing, things get sticky. Relationships can be rocky and personalities can clash. One year we had a first-year student with a very type A personality. It really rubbed the upperclass players the wrong way. And if I am going to be honest, it bothered me too. I talked to the captains and told them that they needed to accept Rachel for who she was because she was family now, and though you might not like your siblings, you choose to love them. I also talked to them about how she was wired and how they liked how she always kept score and could keep rules to the drills we did straight for her team. I then talked to Rachel and told her that I knew her heart was in the right place, but it was inappropriate when she interrupted me or tried to tell the upperclass players what to do. She had no idea she was coming off that way. We talked about the things she did that helped the team and discussed a couple of different ways to tone it down at times to allow for the upperclass players to take the lead.

When you show a person unconditional love and walk through life together, it allows you to trust others when they speak truth to you because you know it is only because they want what's best for you. This is true in all walks of life and transfers onto the volleyball court. The players will fight harder on the court for one another and as a group.

As human beings, we need to experience all the emotions—even the negative ones. We live in a world where we are trying to shield our student-athletes from the negative emotions. I am a parent. I don't like it when one of my sons is hurting or experiences disappointment. My first instinct is to try and fix it for him—to be a "steamroller" parent, paving the way for my child's success. But if I do that, I am not helping him deal with those negative emotions. Instead of fixing it, I need to help him navigate through it by supporting him while he deals with it.

More and more of our incoming first-year students are afraid to take risk for fear of failure. We actually want to put them in situations where they experience disappointments and failure. Why? Because teaching them how to deal with that is how they grow and become stronger in all areas, and it allows them to push themselves further out of their comfort zone, which helps them become better on the court and off the court. How they respond to those things makes all the difference in how much they grow and become gritty. I want gritty teams that never give up. I want our players to have given so much of themselves in all these areas that when they are seniors and the season is done, they will have had the best experience of their lives but know they can't play another year because they have nothing left to give.

Gratitude and Joy for Others

We also believe it is very important for our players and coaches to show gratitude. We believe this is important especially because there are a lot of people who help us behind the scenes to allow us to be our best. It is important to tell those people who have supported us and influenced us that we are grateful for them. We have done this in different ways over the years, from individual handwritten cards to text bombs (everyone sending a text of thanks at the same time) to short thank-you videos. As a by-product, research indicates that someone who shows gratitude will experience the following benefits:

- *Physiological:* stronger immune system, lower blood pressure, better sleep
- *Psychological:* high levels of positive emotions; feeling more alert, alive, and awake; more joy, optimism, and happiness
- *Social:* more helpful, generous, compassionate, forgiving, outgoing, determined; less lonely and isolated; better self-esteem and mental toughness (Morin 2015)

Mudita is a Buddhist term that has no pronunciation. It means being happy for someone else's successes. It means putting yourself as sec-

Calvin University Sports Information

ondary when someone else has success. Being happy for a teammate when they get named player of the week. Shaking hands with our opponents after we lose and looking them in the eye and telling them congratulations. Watching our bench celebrate after the players on the court earn a point. I think we have one of the most talented benches in all of Division III, and they have the most joy and fun of all other volleyball benches. These women know that they could be playing more and receiving more accolades if they played for another team, but they aren't jealous—they're joyful and know how important they are, despite others being on the court.

It is hard to be happy for others when we want what they have. It is not easy to look at someone else and be genuinely happy for them. We need to celebrate success more. This is true in all areas of our lives, no matter what our stage of life is. Love produces gratitude and a servant's heart. Sometimes one leads to the other. For example, if I have gratitude and love someone, I'm going to be happy for them when they do something great.

EMPHASIS ON MENTAL FOCUS AND TRAINING

One part of sport that is getting more and more recognition is the mental side of competing. Elite players will often say it is the difference maker in their success as an athlete. I find it troubling that some coaches don't want to spend time away from skill development to work on developing the mental side of the game, even though it is commonly talked about how important it is in performance. In addition, depending on the level of sport you coach, the resources available to help athletes compete under pressure and perform at their best vary. Furthermore, most coaches are not equipped to know how to help their athletes in this area.

We incorporate mental training into almost everything we do. I want to have our players be pushed to the edge not just physically but also emotionally and mentally, so when things get tough on the court, they will be able to handle it because they are prepared. I want our team to be at their best mentally. We don't ever focus on the end result, but instead let the end result be the by-product of all the things we do daily.

We have already talked about the importance of how you manage your team to develop the right culture and how much that helps a team reach their full potential. Adding mental training into the mix has really helped our team with our success. When they become their best in their skills and their best in their mentality competing, and when they love to be around their teammates and coaches, that is when you put yourself in a position to win more championships.

Let me give you an example from one of our seasons. We have a very specific serving strategy that allows us to be aggressive and very offensive with our serves. We train our players on what they should be thinking as well as the characteristics we want them to have when they serve the ball. We want them to serve this way regardless of the pressure of the situation. We were nearing the end of our regular season and starting to get ready for our postseason tournament run, and we noticed that our players just didn't seem to be adhering to all of our guidelines. They seemed less confident in their serving overall, and their serves were not as consistent and aggressive. So, I called them all in during the middle of a practice and asked them all to take a ball and serve once. Once they did that, I asked each one of them to serve again, but before they did that, I asked them to tell me on a scale of 0 to 10 how confident they felt the ball would go in—10 being they felt 100 percent certain the ball would go in; 0 being they felt zero confidence the ball would go in. The answers were from a 4 to an 8. Now, we spend a lot of time on serving, and we equip them with the tools and practice to feel really good about their serving. I was shocked the numbers were so low. I then asked why their numbers were so low. One player, Jenna, who was our setter (she gave a 5 for her answer), said that some days she doesn't think she is a very good server; other times, in matches, it is hard for her to block out what the crowd is saying to her. Then I talked to them about recommitting to the serving philosophy and guidelines, and I said that they had every right to believe they were a 10 when it came to having their serve go in. Being a 10 doesn't mean it will always go in the court, but it means they believe it will go in. For the next several days, between every drill we did in practice, we brought them into the middle of the gym and asked them to go serve one ball and to choose to "be a 10." There comes a time when a person has to make a choice to believe in themselves.

Fast-forward to the first round of the NCAA tournament. We found ourselves in the fifth set down 10-14 with our senior setter, Jenna, serving the ball. Remember, previously she said she was a 5 on the scale of 0 to 10, believing she would put her serve in. She proceeded to serve the next six volleyballs in bounds, which allowed us to win the next six rallies and to win 16-14, and the team went on to win the regional and finish in the Final Four. When Jenna talked to me later that night, she said there is no way she could have served like that if we didn't work on the serving mentality like we did. She also told me that when her back was to the wall and her volleyball career was on the line with her serving, she decided that she was a 10. She said she actually felt like she was a 20.

BENEFITS OF ESTABLISHING A WINNING PROGRAM

Loving and caring for one another and at the same time holding people accountable to high standards, a really high work ethic, service to one another, and communicating well will produce several things in a group. When these things happen there is more buy-in from everyone, there is less ego individually, the experience is much more fun because there is more purpose, and you will win more.

When players feel like they are a part of something special, it gives them many other positive experiences other than what happens on the volleyball court. When players serve one another and are given clear communication, it allows for more buy-in from all the players. They might not be happy with their role and try everything they can to earn a starting position, but they aren't wondering why they aren't playing or thinking that people don't value who they are and what they bring to the team.

In 2010, we had our best player have to sit out three weeks with mononucleosis. We asked our starting right-side to move to the middle for those three weeks because she was our next best middle. We then moved a senior who was on the bench to play the right-side. When our best middle was able to return back to the lineup, we realized that the backup right-side was actually doing better than the right-side we asked to move to the middle. So, the player who was selfless and happily helped the team out now found herself on the bench. I could tell she was disappointed, but I never once sensed she had not bought in to the goals of the team and totally embraced her role during the postseason on the bench.

Here are some more ways that all of these areas are interrelated and build off each other:

- If someone has been vulnerable and is shown unconditional love, they are going to work harder for what the team needs to do to help accomplish its goals.

- If one takes the focus off oneself, is happy for others, loves their teammates, and works really hard, they will experience a lot more fun and joy.
- Love produces gratitude and a servant's heart. Sometimes it reverses itself. Serving produces love.
- If our work is not founded on gratitude and love with a servant's heart and honesty with one another, then our work can't be the best it can be. And that will also affect our results.
- In the example of the nine preseason challenges, when a player can't pass one of them and someone volunteers to pass it for them, we see love and servanthood amid disappointment, grace, and gratitude. This usually causes resiliency and an even better work ethic.
- In the example of Julia, the player who wasn't in the lineup in postseason because she served the team by moving to another position, we saw disappointment, truth and love, servanthood, and mudita.

I believe the higher the stakes and pressure, the more important these concepts in managing players become for a team. We need to stand on something firm when things aren't going our way under pressure. We will not be as effective on the court if we don't live by these core values. This was exemplified in the story described earlier, when our middle, Becca, took ownership for not blocking well instead of blaming others for our team's poor performance.

We don't just win because of the way we do things. The most important ingredient is having talent, and we have had many talented players come through our program. We must cultivate the people on the team to bring out the most in them.

By doing things the way we do, we bring out the best in our players: We play with joy, we have a great experience, we play better, and because of that we win more. I have had coaches tell me we are a hard team to break, and that they feel like we never give up, no matter what the score. I know it is because of the foundation we have in one another. This is how we pack our punch. This is our "secret sauce" that people ask me about all the time. And I can talk about all these things, but what I can't always relay is how much goes into what we do. It goes way beyond the volleyball, and we aren't perfect at it. Some days we get it right, and some days we get it wrong. But nobody gets in the way of hurting the team when it comes to these areas of our culture. If they do, they won't last in our program. Our players won't allow it any more than I would.

And finally, I think things need to be aligned just right for a team to win it all, and that also involves a little luck that things fall your way. Winning is hard. To keep winning is even harder because as a

Courtesy of Calvin University Sports Information/Robert Kurtycz.

coach, you are dealing with all kinds of other factors that come along with winning—expectation, pressure, motivation, work ethic, lack of confidence, and pride.

CHALLENGES IN COACHING

I would love to tell you winning is incredible and has no negatives. Now don't get me wrong: Winning is fun, and it is way better than losing, but winning puts a lot of stress on these culture concepts. Our success challenges us to continue buying in to these concepts, especially when we are winning, because winning tends to hide issues that should be addressed sooner rather than later. They can be easily shoved to the background if we aren't intentional about bringing them out.

Another challenge from winning a lot is not focusing on outcomes all the time. It is easy to put so much emphasis on getting wins that we no longer spend the time developing all the areas in our culture that have helped us win.

In 2011, we were something like 20-0 in October, but there was something missing. We had stopped taking the time to build the relationships that we needed to. We had started to put our focus on the outcomes too much. It was one of the most passionate discussions in the locker room that I can remember.

I often get asked what happens when I have a problem athlete or an athlete who doesn't buy in to the way we do things. My answer would be that it all depends. We don't expect players to always be happy with decisions or to conform automatically. In addition, we don't want our athletes to be the same or want them to fit into a mold. We want our athletes to become a true version of themselves. I have relationships with my athletes where it is OK for us to be 100 percent honest about our emotions with one another. The rule that I have always gone with is that if I have an athlete who is hurting the team, and when they are made aware of what they are doing they refuse to change, then that is when I need to take action to stop that behavior or the person. Nobody gets in the way of the team and its performance. I have the control to put someone on the court or keep them on the bench as well as keep them on the team or remove them from the team.

Another challenge I have faced in the past several years is doing all these extra things to build our culture and facilitate team chemistry, while doing other things like recruiting, being a mom, and having family obligations. I find that there are times during the calendar year that I have to put my family before the program and times the program comes before my family. Sometimes I don't feel I do a good enough job in either area.

Finally, I find that the more we win, the harder it is to lose. The more we win, the more pressure I put on myself, and the wins become more a sense of relief instead of joy. I really don't know how to manage this sometimes, and it is a very lonely place to be in because there aren't many people around that understand the way I feel or what it feels like to be going through it. When these feelings surface, I try to do exactly what we train our players to do, and that is to not think about outcomes and focus on something that is in my control. I also have to constantly remind myself that I need to have more fun and enjoyment with our players.

Winning is not easy. Managing people is not easy. It takes a lot of work to communicate well, to build relationships, teach the right mentality, and prepare a team to play at their full potential, but the bottom line is getting the very most from the talent you have. Focusing solely on the physical skills will not put your team in a position to reach its potential to win; you have to do so much more.

TAKEAWAYS

- The best programs develop generations of athletes who associate with and sustain a program, and instill a sense of responsibility in senior and veteran players to continue the work and culture that has allowed the program to be so successful over the years.

- Every coach needs a philosophy that is true to who they are, emphasizes the well-being and development of the athletes, and is effectively communicated and demonstrated by the coaching staff.

- Working with and nurturing players in a positive manner is the single most important responsibility of a coach. In doing so, strive to promote these behaviors in your athletes.

- Coaches must appreciate and attend to the mental side of their players' development as much or more than their physical skills and conditioning.

- Benefits of creating a winning environment include a sense of shared responsibility and work ethic among coaches and athletes to maintain it; making service to others a priority and doing what's best for the team rather than having selfish goals; players learning how to deal with pressure and expectations; and a resiliency and confidence among players to meet the challenge when the going gets tough.

- Challenges associated with winning so frequently include a tendency to overlook cracks in the system until they become big problems, recruiting players with talent who want to be on a winning team but not make the sacrifices necessary to contribute more positively than negatively to it, immersing yourself in outside commitments that make managing and overseeing the program diligently very difficult, finding losing increasingly difficult to accept, and focusing on how not to lose (and the outcome) rather than the process being a fun journey of striving to win.

CHAPTER 9

ESTABLISHING A HIGH-PERFORMANCE CULTURE

Carla Nicholls

It was 10:45 p.m. on Christmas Eve, a time when many families are in a jolly mood and setting out milk and cookies for Santa Claus. Instead, our medical team was in a trauma operating room tending to a young teenager who had just suffered life-threatening injuries in a motor vehicle accident and was in need of immediate surgery.

The emotional response during this event was extremely intense for every member of our trauma team that night for multiple reasons, but the one that hit home the most was that we all had children of our own and couldn't bear the thought of what if this was our child. The pressure we were feeling was indescribable, especially knowing the girl's mother and father were waiting just outside the emergency room department's doors wondering if they would ever see their child alive again. The team remained focused on one single purpose—saving that teenager's life. Throughout the night, as the hours passed by, every team member's senses were on high alert, reacting swiftly to each other's needs, letting only the very important voices and requests ring through the air, and avoiding any confusion or mindless chatter that could interfere with the priorities that needed to take precedence.

Over time, this team had learned how to react to each other's needs, and we clearly understood and respected each other's roles and responsibilities within our group. Just by looking into each other's eyes, we were able to communicate our thoughts and predict each other's needs. This ability to communicate was particularly critical since we were required to wear protective masks that covered our mouths and noses at all times. Our team's mandate was to save lives, and to do that we needed to be unbelievably high performing as individuals and, even more important, as a team.

The nurse in charge led the preparations of the surgical suite as well as assigned the roles and responsibilities of the other nurses on the team. The anesthetist took the lead when it was time to anesthetize the young girl and provide the life-saving measures to keep her alive during surgery. The surgeon then took the lead of everything related to the actual surgery. We were all very much in sync that night, and not one single team member questioned who was in charge or who was accountable for what. Twelve hours flew by, and no one gave up, no matter how tired, hungry, and emotionally drained we all were.

As challenging as such experiences were during my time in the medical field, they benefited me significantly when I made the move into my coaching career. I didn't realize it at the time, but soon I gained an appreciation of the importance of an effective team and how creating a culture is so paramount to the team's ability to succeed! A culture that nurtures cohesiveness, respect, understanding, clarity, diversity, and inclusion is critical to perform at your very best.

Throughout this chapter, I will refer back to the experiences that have informed and shaped the leader and coach that I am today, and my hope is these experiences will serve to spark some ideas and actions you can take to enhance and strengthen your program's culture.

HOW A HIGH-PERFORMANCE CULTURE PRODUCES SUCCESS

I loved participating in sports, but especially track and field, before entering the nursing program at the University of Saskatchewan. As I started my nursing career, I found myself desperately missing athletics. Working as a full-time operating room nurse, which included loads of night shifts, just wasn't enough. So, I took a coaching gig on the side with a local track and field club (athletes from 8 to 80 years old), and it didn't take long before I was hooked. I was back in the sport that I loved since I was a child.

Soon after that, I was offered an opportunity to become the head coach of track and field and the cross-country program at the University of Regina in Saskatchewan. Despite being pregnant with my first child and having a secure job in the medical field, I accepted the position, noting that it paid a mere $1,500 per year and the only office space provided was that which I carved out inside my car. To say the least, my parents were horrified that I had made this decision to walk away from nursing. The university team I took on was comprised of 3 women and 14 men and had finished at the bottom of the conference standings. Although the roster included some extremely talented young athletes, they struggled to be successful as a team and unfortunately had a much stronger reputation for partying than they did performing.

Courtesy of Arthur Images.

I've learned a lot about coaching since taking that first job nearly 20 years ago. Now I am employed full-time with our national sport federation, where I served as a national team coach at the 2008 and 2012 Olympic Games and multiple world championships. I then took on the role of team leader of both the 2016 Olympic Games and 2017 World Championships. Just recently I accepted the position as head coach and lead of performance for Athletics Canada's Para Athletics team. We returned from the Tokyo 2020 Paralympic Games tied with swimming as the top two Canadian para teams at the Games.

Looking back on all of it now, whether I was in the operating room tending to a victim of a traumatic injury, leading the university track program, assisting Team Canada at the 2016 Rio Olympic Games to earn the most Olympic podium performances in the history of athletics in Canada, or achieving the success we just recently experienced in Tokyo, I realized that each one of these experiences had common elements in place that led to success. No matter how high the stakes are and no matter how intense the pressure, high-performing teams are able to accomplish unimaginable achievements. A majority of the time, these teams are led by trusting and transparent leaders who have built and prioritized diversity and inclusivity throughout their team. These teams have built cohesiveness and have a clear understanding of everyone's roles and responsibilities. They are guided by a well-defined vision—a vision that every team member believes is achievable—and because of this buy-in, all decision making, planning, and preparations are created to achieve that vision. Once a team gets to this point, pressure becomes a privilege. It's then that a team knows they are well prepared and have done everything possible to prepare for that moment. With this knowledge, an athlete or team can direct all their focus on the execution. No matter what your arena looks like, an operating room or a packed Olympic stadium, if you can prepare your team to respond to whatever is thrown at them with confidence, that in itself is success.

Peter Drucker, the father of modern management, was claimed to have said, "Culture eats strategy for breakfast." I never really understood that phrase or thought I could relate it to sport until I experienced working with teams and groups of individuals who had achieved success through prioritizing building team cohesion. He was right, and it became very evident to me that as coaches, it doesn't matter how hard we plan and strategize. If we don't invest in the people and the culture of our team, achieving success will be sporadic and in some cases impossible.

In his book *The Culture Code: The Secrets of Highly Successful Groups* (2018, p. xviii), Daniel Coyle stated, "Group Culture is one of the most powerful forces on the planet." If this is true, then no matter what level of sport we are involved in, if performance or improved performance is ultimately the end result of our efforts, taking the time and attention to build a winning or what some would refer to as a high-performance culture within our own teams is critical.

Unfortunately, you can't purchase a high-performance culture on the Internet or buy it in a store, you can't touch it, and you certainly can't smell it, but you absolutely know it is there because you can feel it in the air within training environments that have nailed this culture. You can hear it in the voices of the athletes and staff, and you see it in the eyes of their teammates. Team culture shows itself through your team's cohesiveness and then, ultimately, your team's performance.

ELEMENTS OF A HIGH-PERFORMANCE CULTURE

Being a part of a high-performance culture team is exciting, yet these environments can be extremely vulnerable and cannot be taken for granted. Your culture needs to be continuously fostered and challenged to ensure it remains intact. One moment of success does not mean that the pattern will continue. A true winning culture achieves performance outcomes and goals as the norm, not the rarity and certainly not by accident. Creating sustainability in beliefs, behaviors, and expectations truly defines a successful culture.

Remember my first university team that was comprised of 17 athletes and was at the bottom of the conference standings? By the last year that I was head coach of that university team, it had blossomed into a full competitive roster of 40 men and 40 women athletes. That year we had missed winning the conference championship by a single point! *One* point behind one of the strongest teams in the country with a history of winning over the past 30 years! I wanted that win more than life itself at the time, even though I knew what we had done was a huge accomplishment for our team, to get as far as we did. What happened the next year after I left the university to take on the role at our national sport organization was even more impressive. That next season, and multiple seasons after that, the team continued to bring home the conference banner. Throughout the years of making changes that mattered and committing to focus on the culture that needed to be changed within the program, a legacy was created in which the sustainability of the culture, with expected behaviors for all team members, created continuous performance gains.

So why does culture eat strategy for breakfast? Creating a successful strategy or plan is incredibly important for coaches as we rely heavily on our planning and our goal setting and identifying the areas to improve to ensure the success of our athletes and teams. We use these plans to stay on task and to ensure we don't lose track of the list of items that need to be accomplished. Sadly, all your hard work may be for nothing as these strategies and plans quickly become worthless if you did not take into consideration the strengths of and input from your team members. Your team and your approach become very targeted toward solving immediate problems and less about what can you actually achieve together as athletes and support staff alike. If you commit to targeting and building your team's culture as a priority, you gain the opportunity to build a solid foundation of excellence created through a shared sense of values, respect, and input from individuals. The belief of what truly can be possible begins to become more clear. Strategies tend to shift directions, often to address current needs, whereas your team's culture really becomes that driving force behind achieving sustained success.

Within this performance culture, as the bar of expected performance potential begins to rise, you will learn very quickly that achieving goals as a group of individuals far outweighs the potential of each member of that team. The team members build off each other's strengths and successes. It takes an effective leader who is able to bring a diverse group of individuals together and extract the very best out of everyone to build this foundation and to create that powerful sustainability to be great.

LEADERSHIP IN A HIGH-PERFORMANCE CULTURE

According to author Brené Brown (2018, p. 4), "A leader is anyone who takes responsibility for finding the potential in people or processes and who has the courage to develop that potential." Leadership is not an easy task, but it is one that you as a coach must take on to ensure the success of your program.

I was honored to be enrolled in a professional development opportunity for coaches, supported by Own the Podium, called the Coach Enhancement Program (CEP). I was selected along with other Olympic and Paralympic national team coaches from multiple different sports throughout Canada. This program targeted our top coaches to focus on and develop our leadership skills and provide us the knowledge needed to lead our programs to podium success on the world stage. Never once did we talk about technical or tactical aspects of our sport; the program was 100 percent focused on building effective sport leaders.

At the beginning of the course, we took time to discuss eight competencies that are critical to being a world-class coach. Those competencies were technical, tactical, aptitude, adaptability, communication skills, critical thinking, vision building, and emotional intelligence. Added to these competencies was the role of ethics and values. You will notice that many of these competencies also represent what defines a strong leader. Yet unfortunately, most coaching certification courses that prepare our coaches today tend to focus highly on the technical and tactical aspects of our sport and rarely touch on preparing coaches for the role of being a leader.

Creating a culture or changing the direction of a culture requires a lot of risk-taking, perseverance, and above all, effective leadership. As a coach, I believe this may be one of the most difficult tasks you take on, depending on the current culture and environment you find yourself in. Taking the time to work through some critical steps, some of which are extremely time-consuming, is well worth adopting as a part of your plan as it sets the stage for you and your team's performance to begin to thrive. You should be defining core values, establishing your own coaching philosophy, creating a vision, engaging with the right people, taking the time to clarify roles and responsibilities, and clearly setting out expectations (what is acceptable and what is not).

Define Core Values

Defining and instilling your team's core values will ultimately create the road map that guides them to their goals or destinations. Your team core values become the "rule book" of behavior and expectations that defines what it means to be a part of a team or group. I have had the honor to be a part of and witness successful teams working together to build out their core values. This approach requires a good amount of time set aside in a schedule with no other agenda item but to identify the values that will define who they are as a team and as individuals on the team. Their values will define how they will act, communicate, commit to working hard, and work together as a team. This gives an opportunity for each member of your team's voice to be heard. Bringing the athletes together and providing them an opportunity to create their team values means they are more likely to truly embrace the values, not only for themselves as individuals but also self-policing their team-mates to ensure that everyone remains true to what they had agreed was important. Taking the time to create these core values creates an opportunity for your team to embrace change when change is desired or necessary. This approach works tremendously well as a team-building project for your athletes as an added bonus.

I also was involved in building out core values within our own national coaching staff. We spent an entire day in a conference room discussing and debating what we all believed was the appropriate list of our coaching values, defining how we as the national team staff agree to conduct business in a way that leads to our national association's vision. It was quite the production, with loaded whiteboards, reams of paper, and sticky notes all over the conference room—including notes stuck on us! At the end of it all, we came up with a list of values that we agreed were important to us and to the success of our program.

We were able to whittle down this list and capture them as a "one pager" that all of us could easily refer to as needed. It defined how we would communicate and respect each other and reminded all of us of the reasons why we were hired as coaches of the national program. Our job is to put as many of our Canadian athletes on the Olympic and Paralympic podiums as possible, to improve the number of athletes who achieve top-eight results, and to increase the number of athletes who achieve personal bests and seasonal bests on the world stage. We currently use these coaching values as our guide when we are leading our teams or athletes or debating with each other. If we lose our way or get sidetracked with good old white noise, it doesn't take much time to get us back on track once we take a pause and review our core values that we all agreed to uphold.

Establish a Philosophy

Taking the time to identify and reflect on your own coaching philosophy and values is a must. Identifying these essentials creates the fundamental foundation that you build your program from; it guides all choices and pathways of decision making and directs how you react to the people on your team.

I highly recommend writing your coaching philosophy and values down somewhere so that you can revisit and reflect on them often. Every time I start a new notebook (where I keep all my information and coaching notes), I take the time to review my coaching philosophies and values. I then select one word that represents my values, and I write it on the inside of the front cover so that I see it every day. Today, the front cover of my little notebook reads in bold letters "INTEGRITY." This reminds me that I will make decisions and lead my team with the utmost integrity first and foremost. Nothing less will be acceptable.

Create a Vision

Creating a clear vision identifies that reason why you, your athletes, and your support staff show up every day on the field or in the gym. If your team is unclear about the vision and folks do not know why they are coming to practice every day, chaos will surely be hiding around the corner.

Key to building out your vision is the belief that your team can achieve greatness. If you don't believe in what is possible for your team, no one will.

There will be people who think your goals are foolish and your vision is outrageous and even impossible—I know this from experience! Your job is to convince everyone around you—your team, your staff, and your stakeholders—that this vision is achievable and then start making the necessary changes to achieve that success. "We cannot change what we are not aware of, and once we are aware, we cannot help but change" (Sandberg 2013, p. 156).

Your vision must be clear and concise, and it must have a destination. An example of a vision I had set out for my university team was "University of Regina Cougars will be the top-ranked athletics team in the Can West Conference by 2008." Another vision I found that was created by a local volleyball club was simply, "We are dedicated to teaching our athletes the skills they need to be successful both on the court and in life."

Once communicated, you and your team are now accountable, as this vision defines what your team's intentions are. Not only does it create accountability, but your vision also creates the direction that everyone will build their planning and interventions upon, keeping their "eyes on the prize."

There will be times when distractions, or what I like to call "white noise," will sneak in and try to derail your progress to achieve greatness. Gossipy conversation and people trying to cause undue destruction make a lot of the white noise that tends to cloud your ability to see that vision clearly, and soon you are sidetracked and forget where you are going. The best approach is to remove distractions and clear the air as soon as you can.

It is easy to get caught up in conversations that are meaningless and sometimes destructive. When you find yourself in these types of situations, ask yourself if what you are doing in that very moment is leading you closer to achieving your vision. If the answer is no, change it. Every approach and decision you make as a coach, make it with intent and commitment to achieving your optimal goal. This will plant the seeds for sustainable and repeatable performances of excellence.

Surround Yourself With the Right People

As you are building your strategies to create success within your team, make sure you surround yourself with people who have the willingness and desire to achieve the same goals you have. Do this while embracing diversity throughout your team. Having a diverse group of individuals, especially within your support staff, will bring to the table challenging conversations and different ways of thinking, planning, and making decisions, all for the greater good of the program.

To get the very best out of your team, it is essential to provide a safe environment for both athletes and staff. In a safe environment, team members feel confident to respectfully challenge each other, challenge the direction, and challenge decision making, because everyone knows it is for the betterment of the entire program. In an unsafe environment, where athletes and staff feel uncomfortable to share views or concerns for fear of being reprimanded or penalized, a perfect storm of betrayal and untrusting actions are sure to follow and spread.

All individuals from your team bring their own backgrounds and daily experiences to practice every day. This is the beauty of diversity. However, keep in mind that there are probably close to 20 hours a day that you don't have influence on your team. There will be times when athletes and staff members will show up for practice and not be at their best and find it tough to focus on the task at hand. Before pointing fingers or blaming, take the time to recognize that your team members have lives outside of your practice, and there may be multiple challenges that they are facing that you cannot possibly be aware of. However, if you can find the time to take them aside, ask them how they are doing, and listen with empathy and curiosity, this will help you unravel and appreciate what they might be going through that is causing concern.

Showing athletes or staff members that you have noticed a change in their behavior, and taking a moment to listen to them, will help gain their trust. There will be times when you realize that those who appear to be acting out are actually having some real challenges or struggles in their personal life. Do your best to give everyone a chance and the time to come around. Just taking the time to be empathetic and curious to their current situations will make a large impact.

Building trust takes time, but providing a safe environment and leading with transparency, integrity, vulnerability, and empathy will make a huge difference on how your team responds to your leadership. We are leading people first, performances second. Getting to know your team and understanding their weaknesses, building on their strengths, and managing differences will have a positive impact on your program.

Clarify Roles and Responsibilities

I can't stress enough the importance of clarifying roles and responsibilities within your team environment. Providing clarity within your team of who is responsible for what is the first step for your team to be able to function effectively. When there is confusion of roles, you can lose control quite quickly, and then the good old "white noise" starts to creep in and throws you off course.

Prior to our conference championship, I had selected an athlete to be on our travel team roster even though she had not achieved the performance standard to travel with the team. We desperately needed her because we would not be able to qualify our relay team for the national championship without her, due to recent injuries of other key players. I made the decision to bring her at the last minute. I very quickly needed to convey my intentions and define exactly what this athlete's role was on our team to the athletes and staff. If I did not clarify her role soon, gossip would start about why she was on the travel bus. There would be suggestions that it wasn't fair that she was able to join and others were not, or that she must be one of the coach's favorites. When this happens, athletes can become resentful, coaches are confused, and white noise begins to get louder, and before you know it, the team's focus is lost and we don't qualify for the national championship. With immediate communication of my intentions and clarity on the role this athlete played on our team, we were able to settle in and focus on the relay and not the gossip. The good news is, we qualified our team for the national championship that year.

Our Olympic and Paralympic teams have large numbers of staff members with multiple roles and responsibilities. It is very easy to lose track of who is responsible for what, and without role clarity, jobs either get duplicated or forgotten and blame becomes ammunition for a good fight. It is incredibly valuable within any project that you take the time to ensure that all the different tasks that need to be completed are identified and laid out, listing them as "who is responsible" versus "who needs to be informed." If this is well communicated, even the most complicated projects should flow smoothly. Here's an example.

The intricacies of what seems to be a very simple task at the Olympic Games could, in fact, actually end up being quite complicated and, if miscommunicated, an athlete's performance may be on the line. One of our top-ranked athletes was competing in the decathlon at the Olympic Games, which is a two-day competition that consists of 10 events that the decathlete must compete in. The first day of competition goes very late into the evening, ending around midnight. Considering all the recovery modalities that needed to take place after the first day of competition to ensure he was ready to compete early in the morning, we had to make a plan to ensure that we could get food delivered to him while he was receiving therapy versus wasting valuable time going to dine in the cafeteria. Our plan was created with the priority being this athlete would be recovered as soon as possible, fed, and in bed by 0200 hours (2:00 a.m.). At first, this doesn't seem like such a big deal; however, if he did not get his food, he would not recover well and would not be able

to compete at his best for his second day of competition. This seemingly small task consisted of the following roles and responsibilities:

- The head coach was responsible and accountable for assigning everyone their duties to ensure this task gets completed.
- The lead nutritionist was responsible for selecting the appropriate recovery meal for the decathlete, after discussions with the decathlete on types of food choices.

- The lead nutritionist was responsible for sharing with the team manager exactly what was needed to provide our decathlete with the proper nutrition to fuel his recovery.
- The national event group coach was responsible for informing the team manager what time the athlete would be finished with his competition and therefore what time the team manager needed to have the food ready for the athlete.
- The team manager was responsible for informing the cooking staff about the needs of our athlete and the time the food would be picked up.
- The cooking staff was responsible for ensuring the proper food was prepared and ready to be delivered on time.
- The team manager was responsible for ensuring that the food was picked up and delivered to the athlete on time to the agreed location.
- The entire sport science and sport medicine team providing treatments for the decathlete needed to be aware of this plan so that they could organize their recovery modalities around his nutritional intake.

You can see how important it is for the smallest of details to be defined and assigned, or else confusion will be the end result. Just to finish off the story, the food was delivered smoothly, the athlete got to bed on time, and the next day he finished with an outstanding podium performance.

Set Standards and Expectations

Setting standards and expectations is another concrete stepping-stone for athletes and teams to achieve success. An example can be as simple as creating "performance standards" that are measurable and achievable. These include setting a minimum performance standard required to be considered on your team, creating a minimum performance standard that athletes must achieve before they can travel to a competition, or setting standards that must be achieved to compete at the conference championship. All these types of standards begin to define an expected pathway of performance that will challenge your athletes but ultimately take them closer to their goals. In my experience, athletes thrive when expected standards are clearly laid out. This provides them a clear pathway to achieving their own personal goals as well as the team's goals.

Other standards that are not necessarily performance-type standards but more expectation standards are also essential for your team. When I led the university team, I insisted that everyone must wear an appropriate practice uniform when they practice; they must be respectful to teammates, opponents, and officials; they must wear the appropriate travel uniform when on the bus; and for heaven's sake, they must be on time, if not early. All these behaviors were key pieces that were missing within the team when I first started with them. Previously, there were no expectations set out and because of this, team members did not feel accountable to the team or actually even respect being on the university team.

When I created these standards for our group, there was a huge uproar and worry that athletes would not be able to achieve them and that they would not want to continue to be on the team. The absolute opposite happened. The more I challenged the athletes, the more the athletes would respond and achieve my expectations.

I will never forget an incident that at the time seemed minor, but looking back, I realize it was a real game changer for our university team. I had just led a team meeting the day before we were to go on the road for a major competition. I laid out the expectations regarding performance but also the behavior expectations—including being on time! The departure time was set for 1:00 p.m. sharp. The next day, after we loaded up the bus, at one o'clock I told the bus driver to head out on the road because we were ready to go. Wouldn't you know it, after four minutes on the road, I got a call from a very agitated coach asking me where the bus was! I told him we were on the road. He responded, "It's only four minutes after!" and I responded, "You are late." We left him behind. Although I knew it would be a bit of a struggle to do what we needed to accomplish that weekend without him, I had to keep my word to the team on the importance of being on time and, even more important, being true to our standards. The athletes were never late again when they realized that if I would leave a coach behind, I would leave them behind!

It is important that everyone on the entire team and staff is treated with the same respect and expectations, no matter what their role is. Who would have known that a simple act of leaving a late coach behind would be a turning point for our team in terms of buy-in and team cohesiveness! We were one coach short that weekend, but we ended up with one of our best performances of that year.

Be an Example

As the leader of a team or group of athletes, it is critical that you lead by example in all that you do. Strive every day to bring the best possible you to every practice, competition, debrief, meeting, and get-together.

As an athlete, I had a coach who was notoriously late and sat on a chair through most of the practice yelling at the top of his lungs while filling himself with unhealthy snacks. I never felt that he fully engaged in what we were trying to achieve. I then moved on to a coach who came to practice on time, dressed in our team apparel, spoke directly to and made eye contact with each athlete, and was absolutely engaged in our practice. He asked how our day was going and truly cared about us as people. Guess which coach got the best performances out of me?

Your team is watching you all the time. They look to their coaches for guidance and cues, and whether you realize it or not, you are a mentor for them during their sporting career and, in most cases, life after sport. The previous coach that brought the best out of me was also the coach who encouraged me to take on the role of coaching in athletics. I wanted to be able to provide positive opportunities for others and help them to believe in what could be possible for them, as he had done for me.

Learn and Improve

I can't stress enough how important it is to ensure that you take care of your own needs for learning. Days become busy and we lose track of time; before you know it, all your attention has been given to others, and you have completely avoided your own needs. Commit to challenging your own professional development because your team will most certainly benefit. In doing this, you also create and encourage others to continue to learn and access new knowledge as they themselves strive for excellence. Great coaches continuously ask themselves how they can improve and build on their approach to achieve better results for their team.

With continued learning also comes the ability to embrace feedback. Constructive feedback is key to developing yourself as an effective leader as you continue to drive your athletes and team to success. One of my favorite quotes from Brené Brown is, "If you are not in the arena getting your ass kicked on occasion, I am not interested in or open to your feedback" (Brown 2018, p. 20). Be sure that the feedback that you are receiving is coming from reliable sources—ones that you can truly trust have your best interest and the best interest of your athletes and team first. Receiving feedback in a constructive way will show others your openness to collaboration and will foster that willingness in others to accept feedback from you.

Celebrate Even Small Wins

Tracking achievements and celebrating those small wins can highlight what is actually possible and help athletes realize that achieving long-term goals may not be so far away. Celebrating smaller achievements builds that fire and passion to achieve greater success, but it also creates buy-in that the process you have put in place is working.

Having athletes believing in and trusting your process is just as significant in their development. Training and preparing can be grueling at the best of times, and with minimal glimmers of hope and achievement, athletes can begin to lose their way and wonder if the work they are doing will truly achieve their dreams. There will be days and weeks and sometimes even months when athletes may not see improvements. As coaches, we can be guilty too often of being so focused on the ultimate goal that we may forget that for others, the road may seem quite daunting and almost impossible to manage.

Breaking it down and celebrating the stepping-stones and not just major milestones along the way will help them to realize that the process is working and that they are improving and getting closer to their ultimate goals. Creating a sense of moving forward and that you are on track as a team and program is a very effective way to build that key trust.

Debrief

At the completion of every project, game, and tournament, committing to and leading a debrief with staff and team members, no matter the outcome, is critical for ensuring improvement and ongoing success. Allowing team members the time to share their thoughts and experiences, reliving and accounting for what went wrong and what went right, is critical. It may appear that a game or a tournament or championship was hugely successful; however, high-achieving teams continuously identify what they did well alongside what they could have done better. Identify areas that are in need of improvement; record them, learn from them, and create strategies to ensure improved execution for the next time. Having staff and team members involved in the debriefs is vital and allows all voices to be heard. This input gives everyone the feeling that they are a part of the process, which again builds on that very important foundation of trust and ultimately ownership of their destination.

Troubleshooting Culture Killers

Try as you may, you will find yourself in situations that just cannot be resolved. It might be that someone from your team may have clearly done something outside the expectations, such as broken team rules or been involved in an inappropriate incident, or it might be a situation where a team member is just not adjusting to your culture or environment. These difficult conversations must be dealt with swiftly because they aren't going to simply disappear.

The longer you leave things boiling on the back burner, the stronger the heat gets. Before you know it, your house is burning down and all that you have built is destroyed. You must learn to deal with issues head-on.

Mike Robbins, the author of *We're All in This Together* (2020), identifies this as "embracing the sweaty palm conversations." If there is an issue that can't be resolved without inflicting damage to your team culture, you need to make a change. Be clear with your communication, outline what is acceptable and what is not acceptable, document and document some more, and then release them from your program if there cannot be resolution.

In 2016, right after our national federation achieved the highest medal count at the Olympic Games ever in our history, our team gathered for a very intensive three-day debrief. It began with, "Congratulations on winning the most medals ever at the 2016 Rio Olympic Games," but very quickly went on to, "We missed achieving three more potential medals." We dove deep into discussions on what went wrong, what was missed, and what we could do better next time around as we prepare for the Olympic and Paralympic Games to ensure those medals came back to Canada with us. Take notes on the debrief and share your findings with the rest of your team. This is the opportunity to reassess, make some adjustments, validate your plan, and then execute again.

CLOSING THOUGHTS

There is nothing more powerful than a team with a common vision and values, strong leadership, clear roles and responsibilities, and the willingness to succeed for the greater good. Refer back to the story I opened the chapter with.

We saved the young girl's life that Christmas Eve. It took 15 bags of infused blood, 50 packages of sutures, 40 screws, and 8 metal plates. But more than that, it took 12 hours of skilled and focused performance by a surgical team operating within a culture of excellence. That night, the entire surgical team stayed after and shared a Christmas Eve meal together consisting of fake turkey, boxed stuffing, and soggy frozen vegetable mix that had been set aside for us six hours previously. During dinner, we took the time to celebrate what we had accomplished and actually had some good laughs together, eventually agreeing that night was the best Christmas Eve we had ever experienced. We all left for home that night exhausted, yet knowing we had achieved something great together. The next time we were all back together after a little rest, we debriefed the entire procedure and made notes about where we could have been even more efficient.

Team culture can be extremely vulnerable. Recognize and understand the importance of leading and working with others and treating them as people first and as staff and athletes second. Effective leadership is achievable if you can lead with a high degree of emotional intelligence and integrity. Be self-aware as the exemplar of what you wish your program to be; and also be sensitive and responsive to the needs of those you are leading. Reflect the discipline and dedication needed to stay true to your purpose and your goals, yet be willing to adapt as circumstances change.

Creating a positive team culture is not a new concept, by any means; bringing it to life and actually creating it is the exciting challenge. Now, more than ever, athletes need to be surrounded by a culture that is built on a foundation of trust, hard work, and commitment to one common cause. In the sporting world, we are measured on performances, but there is so much more behind the performances that will inspire generations of not just athletes but great people, thanks to the environment you create and the direction you lead with your teams.

We could continue to dig deeper and deeper into the role of a coach as you establish or enhance your program's culture, but I thought I would end it here with a favorite quote of mine often attributed to Maya Angelou: "I've learned that people will forget what you said, people will forget what you did, but people will never forget how you made them feel."

TAKEAWAYS

- Decide on the vision, core values, and expectations for the staff and athletes in your program.
- Keep your coaching philosophy up to date and review it from time to time.
- Think about the core competencies you need as a coach, and work hard to excel in all those areas.
- Define roles and responsibilities for each staff and team member. Communicate clearly when and why there may be changes.
- Recognize and celebrate improvements as part of the daily process.
- Set the standard for expected behavior, have integrity, and continue to learn.
- Take advantage of debriefing after events as part of the continuing climb to get better.
- Remember, you are coaching people.

CHAPTER 10

DEVELOPING AND IMPLEMENTING A STRATEGY

Melody Davidson

I grew up in a small town of about a thousand people, and my family always volunteered in the community. In small towns, if you play the sport, you coach it. I played volleyball, basketball, softball, hockey, and swam, and then I coached them all. I first started coaching ice hockey when I was in eighth grade and my brother was in the seven-and-under age group. I'm not sure how I got to be the coach, but I suspect that the parents who saw me watching practices with my face up against the glass felt sorry for me because at that time girls didn't play hockey, so they invited me onto the ice. And once I was on the ice, I never left. It was a trait that people learned about me as time went on. If I got my foot in the door, I wasn't letting the door close.

When my sister was in sixth grade, I went with my mom to register her for softball, and they asked my mom if she would coach my sister's team. While pointing to me, she said, "No, I won't, but she will." So, I coached a lot of teams while growing up, and through that time period I learned a lot. Most of all, I learned that planning, organizing, and working with parents would prevent crises, and that it was essential to deal with them when they did occur. After that time, I became a recreation director for 10 years, and that was the perfect petri dish to learn all about planning on a broader scale, looking after a whole community with various ball and hockey teams.

I didn't have any formal training in strategic planning, but I learned a lot about it through trial and error. All of the volunteer coaching jobs I took while growing up and my experiences as a recreation director for 10 years taught me a great deal about what needed to be planned for and how to adjust at a moment's notice. I think it was Mike Babcock, the very successful NHL coach, who said, "You don't value experience until you have it and realize how much it teaches us."

I did my undergraduate work in physical education with an emphasis on coaching and sport administration, so that was always helpful giving me a good background in the sciences. I was also very fortunate growing up in Canada and gaining experience through the Coaching Association of Canada (CAC) and our national coaching certification levels. I dove into all of those really deeply. I completed all the tasks and was Level II or III certified in just about every sport I coached, and I went on to the highest level of certification in ice hockey. The CAC provided structural foundations and guidance on coaching.

I was fortunate to combine all of that—the experience of coaching since eighth grade, the college degree, and the coaching certifications—to learn how to coach *and* how to plan as a coach. The value of effective planning cannot be overstated.

FORMING A PLAN

A good strategic plan will give you the foundation you will use through good times and bad times. That plan should include goals and objectives, time lines, budgets, facilities, staff, athlete identification, scheduling, and much more. It will be a master list for your program, serving as a valuable guide when you need to make various decisions. Having a good strategic plan will also ensure everyone involved is aware of the direction of the program and what they need to do to accomplish those objectives. When you think about your year and talk to the staff, athletes, schoolteachers, and whomever else might be involved in the athlete's lives, it allows you to take everything into account.

While I can't say I really enjoy putting the plan together, I do enjoy the creative process and collaboration it entails. This is the time to think outside the box and put in innovative ideas to keep your program fresh and getting better. A well-thought-out and thorough plan is necessary if a coach is going to get the best out of the athletes and create the best environment for them as people. To me, that is why planning isn't just a good idea—it's a critical duty of a responsible coach. In my early years as a coach, I would brainstorm and come up with what I thought was a good plan, but I didn't involve enough people. I soon learned that collaboration with staff and other key stakeholders helps to avoid problems that I, alone, could not foresee.

In longer-term planning, I start with the end in mind. This type of planning makes us evaluate where we are now and where we want to go. If our goal is to go to the Olympics, I put that in the schedule and work backward four years from there. In women's ice hockey, obviously we have to qualify, but in Canada it is not about qualifying—it is about being in the gold medal game. If I were coaching a club sport, it might be a provincial championship or a national championship.

Once you identify the end point or goal for a time span that is determined by your type of sport, level of competition, and the assets you have now and expect to have in the future, you can start to fill in the pieces, such as team building and technical and tactical development. Other areas to consider would be establishing a team identity, setting team standards, performance measures, lifestyle considerations, and any other components you want to add.

Review the plan carefully to ensure that you haven't omitted an important factor in progressing toward the target you have set. Working through this planning phase will ensure that you are clearly laying out the activities for everyone and will keep them from wasting time. If you haven't planned for everything, it will be hard to add things at the last minute because you may end up overloading your athletes or staff, which is the last thing you want to do. Even though we have a detailed plan of where we want to go and how we are going to get there, we have to be ready to adapt to unpredictable events that may come up. The worldwide pandemic that began in 2020 is a good example of how every organization had to pivot to keep moving forward. Make sure you are ready for change, and adapt as quickly as possible.

The annual plan is more structured and specific. It is never the same from year to year because you don't have the same personnel or schedule, and circumstances are constantly changing the challenges ahead of you. We usually start with the yearly plan and the days off. Coaches are notorious for not giving days off, so I always put those days in to make myself accountable, whether it's mandated days off like in college or vacation days. There may be special days or times coming up in your athletes' lives that you have learned to plan for over time because they are useless if you plan to have them at practice. It could be midterm exams, which make it tough for them to concentrate on athletics, or you need to give them a week off for final exams. I also try to look at my own personal life and plan around family time, weddings, or other occasions. However, I am a bit more flexible with my own time off.

It is important to have a very global vision in your planning. For example, you should be aware of national and religious holidays. Creating an environment that respects diverse cultural beliefs fosters a strong environment, and by building time off for or acknowledging these holidays, you are supporting that diversity. Your plan is a big jigsaw puzzle. Your master plan on paper should show commitment and a foundation that you can fall back on in tough times.

The next step is to put in the competitions and what the schedule is going to look like. Then I'll build the segments out with so many contests and so many weeks in my segments. I start to fill it in from there with practices and off-ice training, mental sessions, nutrition education, and all the other pieces that will be going on with meetings at the national level for our coaches. There might be meetings planned on media training, drug testing education, respect in sport, and many other subjects. I try to place all that in the schedule. We also include the important rest and recovery days. While it is critical to get those planned days on the schedule, you have to pay close attention to your team's needs as they go along and adapt to days off as needed.

Everyone has a different method of drafting or documenting a plan. Computer-based planning is most popular now, I suppose. Those of you tech-savvy coaches will probably wince when I admit that I still use one of those big desk calendars to design my plan. I know many of you use Excel and other software programs and are able to merge everything together, and that is great. I wish I could do that. I often get asked if I have a template or something others can follow. I can provide templates for people, but it will look like the large calendar on my desk because, honestly, that is what I use to put our plan together and refer to constantly throughout the year.

PIVOTING FROM THE PLAN

Within your plan, you should have built-in checkpoints. Some people use the terms *micros* and *macros* as checkpoints. You should have weekly check-ins and debriefings with your staff. That can be as simple as making time after practice to talk about where we are, where we need to go, and what we have coming up. You look at the entire picture, think about whether you foresee anything coming—which may be something like bad weather, if you are coaching an outdoor sport—and then make sure you and the team are prepared for that.

With the weekly and monthly segments, you should have built-in times for one-on-one check-ins with all your staff and players to talk about what you have coming up and how the plan has gone so far. Maybe you overestimated what they would have learned and you need to do more skill development, so you will need to back off your tactical and systems segments and revamp it from there. Making modifications doesn't mean you are scrapping the initial plan; you still have that foundation, that road map, that you can return to once the crisis or setback you've encountered is conquered. That foundation will remind you of how you navigate such diversions and get back on course.

As each year goes by, you learn more and more about where you could go sideways. An international pandemic has added another layer to that thought process. You will know it is parents' weekend and be aware of the possible aftermath, when the parents have told all the athletes they will be doing something different in the sport. Maybe you are coaching a younger team and you set up birthday celebrations, and then you

AP Photo/The Canadian Press, Jacques Boissinot

happen to forget someone's birthday. While it may seem like a small thing, it is a big thing in that relationship. There may be a death of a loved one in someone's family, so you have to really think things out. You won't have all the answers initially, but as long as each segment and year goes by, you can continue to stockpile all those things that you may need to think about and include them in the plan next time or consider them as you move forward. It helps your plan become more complete every year.

Sharing the Plan

Some coaches are very protective of their plan and keep it close to their vest, sharing it only with their staff and athletes. When I was a volunteer coach at the youth and club levels, I would share an overview of the plan with parents so that they could see that, yes, the practice sessions, competitions, and social experiences for their children's development were all taken into account.

When I coached at Connecticut College and Cornell University, I would develop the plan and tie it into the budget. That helped the administrators understand why I was asking for a certain amount of financial support.

When starting out in a paid coaching position, I strongly recommend having a five-year plan. You can't really enact sustainable change in under five years. Of course, that is something that you will want to ensure that those who hire you also believe in, as well as making sure they understand your vision for where you want to take the program. If you can get support on those important points, then it comes down to how effectively you plan, allocate the resources available, and perform your duties. That's all any coach could ask for.

BENEFITING FROM A PLAN

To this point I have tried to help you appreciate the necessity of a strategic plan, get a sense of how to develop one, and understand that, at times, you will have to temporarily veer from or amend the plan as circumstances dictate. Now I want to get into a couple of side benefits of effective planning.

Developing Team Culture

The significance of a positive team culture has become more appreciated in recent years. But creating such a culture doesn't happen by accident. It will happen only if your plan promotes it. If you keep in mind your team culture and build on it throughout the planning process, you will be setting the stage for what I call "memories" to happen throughout the year that unite your team.

I am a big proponent of psychologist Bruce Tuckman's (1965) stages of group development and try to follow those stages of forming, storming, norming, performing, and adjourning. It was developed in the mid-1960s, but it is still very helpful today (see figure 10.1).

So, how does that model affect your thinking when you are planning and considering team building? Well, for example, I'm always very

Forming	Storming	Norming	Performing	Adjourning
• Getting to know one another • Excited about the team • Anxiety about the unknown • Unclear purpose • Best behavior or the honeymoon phase • Independent roles	• Conflict about roles or process • Competition with who will lead • Individuals, not yet a team • Emotions are high • Resistance to emerging leaders • More clarity on purpose • Frustration with process • Cliques form • Power struggle as leaders emerge	• Team is a respected concept • Engaged in the process • Supportive of everyone • Cohesiveness with group • Relief to know process and goals • Common goal as a group • Acceptance of role • Clear roles for each person • Confidence in the team • Commitment to the purpose	• Vision of success • Motivation to compete • Consistent behavior • Interdependence and connection • Balanced power • Focus on team goal • Trust within the team • Team needs before individuals • Happy with the process • Results are achieved • Confidence in process and teammates • High functioning • Synergy is strong	• Sadness with end of season • Recognizing efforts with awards • Change is inevitable • Task completed • Letting go of this team

FIGURE 10.1   Phases of team development.

mindful of when the storming phase is going to happen. I try to ballpark when it is going to happen within a week or so. Some years it comes earlier, and other times it might come a bit later, but it's imperative that you get your team to and through that phase fairly early in the season. If you don't, it can be very detrimental as the season goes along.

Note that in Tuckman's model, anytime your team has been apart, you start again. Anytime you lose players, you start again. Your plan should reflect that. At the beginning of the year, when building your identity, your vision, your purpose, your mission statement and values, the way you choose to put those pieces together is going to drive the development of team culture.

We used to have team rules or expectations, but how those are formulated and what is negotiable and nonnegotiable and how you hold people accountable to those pieces are all a part of the culture of the team. That needs to be a part of the planning. When the athletes leave for a holiday break or time off, the team starts again, even though it has only been five days. You are starting again because they have gone away and they all had individual memories, events, and opportunities with people outside the team. Now when they come back together, you have got to reset them with your team. Those pieces are crucial. Whatever you do will create those memories, but when someone creates conflict, you are going to have to manage that.

In 2020, we saw there can be a lot of uncertainty and conflict among teams with social issues. How you go about handling these types of issues that come up will say a lot about the culture within your team. The team culture is the legacy you are going to leave behind. What is that going to look like? How does your team conduct themselves? What do you want people to say about you and your program? You have to teach lessons to your team such as, "This is what we stand for or what we look like." How quickly and how you handle that might be a big factor in determining the team's success and its culture in the future.

A key element in having a positive culture will be your staff. They have to model a culture of excellence in their day-to-day actions. There is such a gray area now with the way athletes are raised with their parents possibly being their best friends. The athletes tell them everything, and they bring that into a team setting where some of your staff might be only one or two years older than the athletes. You have to make sure to let the staff know that it is fine to be friendly with the players, but you are not their friends. There are many pieces within the culture of a team, and it takes time to develop.

If you are coming into a new environment as a coach, you really have to work hard to establish a culture or build on the culture if it was a good one before you. One of the good things, or bad things, about coaching in a high school, college, or club program is that you will have players for four or five years. If you can get the first-year students and sophomores understanding the culture, then as they become juniors and seniors, they start to do a lot more of the teaching on what is expected in the program. However, if you get some bad eggs in there and you can't trade them or release them, it makes it a little bit more of a challenge at times. You really have to work to get the team culture in a good place.

The culture of my teams always focus on competing, passion, intensity, communication, skill, work ethic, and I like to say fun. I believe that if you are in the program, it is because you enjoy it, and hopefully throughout practices you would see some smiles and some comradery and athletes supporting each other. Fun looks different for every person. You could look at me and think I didn't have any fun, but I could walk off the rink and think that was the best practice ever.

I always question my coaches when they say the players were not very good today. I tell them, "Start with yourself first, and if the athletes didn't get something, then you probably missed a step as a coach somewhere. If they weren't ready to execute it, then that is on you as a coach. So you have to back it up and figure out where the gap is and fill that in."

We have to be so careful not to make assumptions or try to read into people's feelings. That is where head coaches really have to get to know their players on and off the field. Not so they can be involved in every part of their lives, but so that their players know they are there for them. As a coach, you need to know what to check in on and what not to worry about.

When we are training full-time with the national ice hockey team, we have 28 players and 15 staff. That's a lot of people to keep up with and check in on. I used to write all the names on a whiteboard, and my goal was always to have a touch point with each one of them about something every two days. At the end of our on-ice practices, I would circle them up, I would give out some logistical information, and then I would high-five them or give them a fist bump. I would look into their eyes and if they didn't make eye contact with me, I knew that was someone I needed to check on right away. Generally, if they are in a good place, they will look up at you and say "Thanks, coach" or something, but if they don't make eye contact or it is short or curt, I paid attention to that. I generally will wander around and make sure I check in with them. If I miss connecting with them one day, I'll follow up the next day to see how they are doing. It is hard work to be a head coach, but knowing and caring about everyone in your program is important.

We don't rise to the level of our expectations, we fall to the level of your training.

Greek lyrical poet, Archilochus

AP Photo/Scott Gardner, CP

Maintaining Success

There are a lot of people involved in keeping a sports program at a high level. There were many people before me in the Canadian ice hockey system that fought a lot of battles. Winning breeds success and breeds a good culture. And effective planning is needed in establishing and continuing both.

Early on, the success of the system set up the accountability pieces. Now, as we have moved forward, I would say the planning, the "leave no stone unturned" work ethic, and the type of people we have in the program demonstrate the accountability and the expectation to win. We would always say to the athletes, whether they were 12 years old or 50, "We are not looking for ice hockey players who are athletes; we are looking for athletes who are ice hockey players, and they are good citizens." We are fortunate that we are a high-profile sport in Canada, so there is a strong expectation of winning a gold medal all the time.

We lay out the expectations right away and are fully transparent that everything we do is toward becoming champions. We are fortunate to have an incredible system with club teams in ice hockey; however, it might still be one of our gaps in connecting. While they all know what it looks like at the top with the Olympic and senior team, we could do a better job of educating the coaches and connecting the dots with those coaching our future national team athletes, because the system is so big.

There is still a lack of understanding around the women's game because many of our coaches and young athletes have not seen a high-level women's hockey game in person. They seem to be more familiar with the NHL or the men's game, so we have some work to do to fill in those gaps, and the young players are hungry for that knowledge. Many of our national team players run hockey schools and development camps where the girls attending get to meet those high-level female athletes and follow them. We still need more work around the leadership and coaching of those young athletes.

TAKEAWAYS

- The art of coaching is never mastered. Teaching technical or tactical aspects is easier to perfect than planning or team building, but the latter are just as important.
- Part of becoming a better, more artful coach is gaining self-knowledge and confidence, and being able to be completely transparent about what you know and don't know—all while investing in learning in areas where you have knowledge gaps.
- Your team is going to go through different phases each year. Make sure you are familiar with those various phases and how to help get your team through them.
- We, as coaches, are developing members of tomorrow's society. How well we do our jobs will help to shape their future.

CHAPTER 11

RECRUITING, ORGANIZING, AND MENTORING A STAFF

Tara VanDerveer

I thought I could teach myself to play the piano, but thank goodness for my piano teacher. She was so awesome. I learned a lot from her as a student. She could take me to a place of understanding and performance that I couldn't get to by myself. That's what I want to do for our players and our staff. I want to help our staff become great head coaches. I want to help our players become great players and reach their goals.

When I think back to my experience in learning to play the piano, it reminds me of the important role my staff and I can play in developing our athletes and the responsibility we have to do that. So, as a head coach, assembling and leading a coaching staff is one of the most basic and critical aspects of the job, and there are certain fundamentals I ascribe to in this process.

ASSEMBLING A STAFF

When I took my first head coaching job at the University of Idaho in the late 1970s, I didn't have a very large budget, so if someone wanted to volunteer, they helped out with the team and it was great. However, I soon became more systematic and discerning in recruiting my assistants.

Finding and Screening Assistants

I had only one brief experience as an assistant coach. When I started coaching at Ohio State University, I was an assistant coach for the varsity team and the head coach for the junior varsity team for two years.

Although I was not an assistant coach for long, the things I learned in that role have stuck with me throughout my career.

As a head coach assembling a staff, you must first determine the number of assistants you need. I don't want an entourage. I want to have a very efficient staff and people who work hard, are really into it, and can get a lot done. I know a lot of people come to the gym with 15 people on their staff. I can't do that. The staff size is relevant for the situation you are coaching.

Again, at my first job at the University of Idaho, I didn't have a video coordinator or a director of basketball operations. If you are coaching at the high school or junior club level or at a smaller college and you don't have a large budget, look for volunteers who are interested in being a part of your program and give them responsibility for things that need to be done.

I want to hire people with integrity—people who are honest and trustworthy. I want to work with people who complement me, so they have different strengths and weaknesses than I do. I want to work with people who are collaborative. They can have a strong ego, but the team is above the individual.

Our program needs coaches who are hardworking and have a specific skill set. Many people may think that in basketball, you just roll out the ball, but there is a lot that goes on behind the scenes in planning. I am looking for coaches with great communication skills who are compassionate and passionate about the sport of basketball. For me, I want a player's coach. I look for people who will make the players' experience in our program a great one.

What works best for me in identifying potential assistant coaches is word-of-mouth information from other people whose judgment I trust. A lot of my hiring success has been hiring people I know. I call people I have worked with in the past, or someone like my sister who is a coach, and primarily people I really rely on. After I get a base of potential candidates, I arrange to meet and talk with them online, consult the head coaches they have worked with, and then do a lot of background reference checks.

Our basketball camps are a place where I get to watch young coaches and their work style. Summer camps are a good way for young coaches to get involved with the college game and to get to know college coaches. It is a great way to get your name out there. Coaching in the various USA basketball programs is another good way to get exposure to other coaches who may be looking for assistants.

I have made mistakes in hiring staff members. The mistakes I have made were hiring people I really didn't know well enough. I wanted to think they were someone they weren't. While you may not believe this, sometimes I have a little trouble in being direct. I can beat around the bush really well. I don't want to hurt people's feelings. I want them to do well, but there are times when I just think, *Hmmm, I have to understand my own shortcomings and be more direct*, but not in a hurtful way.

> ## Seeking Out Women Coaches
>
> Women's basketball is played by women, so having women coaches is important. We know what it is like to be a woman and a female athlete.
>
> You want to get someone with good experience, and you want to find well-trained candidates. From what I see in this basketball world, women need to have good technical skills and understand basketball, but still need to be trained and mentored to be successful. Women seem to be so harshly judged and not given second chances. Somewhere the ball gets dropped, and we don't do a good job of training coaches. We have to make sure we mentor each other better on how to be successful.
>
> The way it is right now, there are very few women that coach men, so I feel a double obligation to hire and promote women. I try to mentor women so that we can balance the scale a little bit and young women can see that women can coach. In the NBA as well as a few other professional sports, women are getting the opportunity to coach men. Hopefully down the road, women are applying for jobs and getting opportunities to coach men in college sports. The NBA may be ahead of collegiate sports in terms of women coaching men through looking at their skill set isolated from their gender. They don't have to worry about recruiting athletes. I think there are some progressive male collegiate administrators who might be interested in hiring women because a lot of our student-athletes grow up in single-parent homes and are raised by women. In fact, I think women could help a men's coaching staff a great deal.

Breaking in New Staff Members

I have two new assistants this year, which is unusual, but I'm not concerned about it at all. I knew going into the hiring process that I would have two positions open, but I only struggled with the decision about one of them.

Right away I knew I needed someone with a lot of experience—and someone with a lot of "Stanford experience." In some ways that limited the choices to two people for me. One of the qualified coaches had just settled in at another job and had her young family to think about. I ended up hiring the other person who knew Stanford. She had a great experience playing basketball here, and she already had some good coaching experience as well as excellent recommendations. She was working at a university nearby and could move quickly and not miss a beat. I was done with hiring for that first position basically in one day. While I have never gone into it thinking I need to hire a former player, what I found is that I really need to have people who fit the profile of Stanford-type students who are unique to Stanford University. Make sure you know the type of person you need to hire and if they will fit into the culture of your university.

For the other position, we wanted to bring diversity to the staff. I struggled with this hire for over two months because there were so many really good candidates. I had the various candidates jump through a lot of hoops: writing a recruiting letter and being on an hour-long Zoom call with myself and two former assistants asking a lot of "what if" questions. "What if a player forgot their shoes? Do you tell Tara?" We gave them various situational things to talk through with us. I spoke with several people who had worked with them in the past and began checking with the people they listed as references. I tried to listen to what they were saying. I then got it down to three candidates, then two. I struggled with those final two people for a couple of weeks. Then when I made the decision, I knew this person was going to be a great fit in the program. It was a matter of knowing what I'm good at and thinking about what these people could come in and do in their position.

LEADING A STAFF

Whomever you have, make the most of it. Be efficient with your time, and be specific about what you want to do and how you want to do it. It is important to communicate your expectations to everyone in no uncertain terms. The head coach has to have a vision for everything and the staff has to buy in to that vision. They don't have to agree with it totally, and they might not do it that way, but they have to understand your vision. With recruiting, it is about what kind of players you want to coach, not really the players they like. On the court, it will be the drills you want to do and the offense you want to run, not what they want to run.

Discussions need to be open and transparent with your staff—here is what we are doing and why. I don't say it is my way or the highway because we are going to talk through things. I really want a lot of input from my staff, but there are times I have to finally say, "Look, I am the head coach. We are doing it this way, and that 18 inches of where you sit versus where I sit is a lot farther than you think."

In our basketball program, I am the head coach and I have three assistants. One thing I have learned to do is have a hierarchy of assistants. I have a number one assistant, number two assistant, and number three assistant. I think it is helpful not to act like all three assistants are equal, because they are not. My number one assistant is paid more than number two, and number two is paid more than number three, who is usually the newest assistant. I have developed job descriptions for each of those positions. That's not to say that it is strict, but the way I look at it, the easier jobs are usually for the number three assistant. This year when I hired two new assistants, I asked them, "What are you good at? What do you like to do?" At the same time, to develop them as coaches, I asked them, "What do you need to be doing?" I try to mix things up and change up the workload so that people are successful fulfilling their specific responsibilities, but they are also challenged.

Mentoring the Staff

I think of mentoring as an "organic process," although my assistants would laugh at me for using that term. It is not like I have a specific process, but we meet every day as a staff. We plan our practices together every day. We sit together in a room and I am involving them in everything. We watch video and talk about game and practice philosophy, as well as everything that is going on in our program. I think that is critical because they are learning about every aspect of the program.

Our meetings are a minimum of an hour and a half and are usually two hours, so they are exposed to everything. They might have certain tasks they do before or after our meetings, so we'll talk about what they are doing, such as preparing recruiting letters, parent letters, or scouting reports. I'll touch base with them about their other specific responsibilities, but they are involved in everything we are doing. I also encourage interns and assistant coaches to keep a notebook so that when they become a head coach, they will have copies of how you develop practice plans, how you divide up your day in terms of your workload, and all the other aspects of the coaching profession.

In practice, I have assistants run drills; in games, they take owner-ship of out-of-bounds plays and all the time and score situations. But I

Courtesy of Stanford University.

can always overrule them if I feel I need to do that. If you hire the right people and they are doing the job well, it works. As the head coach, I can't do everything. I don't want to be in charge of every single thing, and I'm not a micromanager. If you are one of my assistants, I am not going to be looking over your shoulder or telling you how to do your job. In fact, I tell them, "You come up with the way to do it." I want them to take ownership of things and not look back and just say, "Well, that was Tara's dumb idea."

So far, there is nothing I could ask for that the new assistants are not doing. They have been great. They get a lot of positive mentoring from the other top assistant, which is key to our staff being successful.

Coaching and Reinforcing a Team Culture

During the recruitment and screening process for assistants, it's critical that you talk about the culture of your program and ensure that any candidate you offer a job to has bought in to the type of environment you have created to be successful. There are certain beliefs that underpin our culture at Stanford that must be supported and promoted every day, by each member of our staff.

We play basketball and coach basketball because it is fun. It is really important that we work hard but also that it remains fun. I want our players to say at the end of practice, "It's already over?" They have fun and improve. I want to take them somewhere they can't go by themselves, whether it is through the drills we do, the mentoring we do, or the videos we watch together. I cherish helping players be the best they can be.

At the same time, I get along best with players who are hardworking and unselfish. Basketball is a team game and was invented as a team game. If a player wants it to be all about their stats, I say take up tennis.

We are old school. Our kids tuck their shirts in. We're on time. They jog going from the court to get water. We are always coaching them in everything we do—how to come out of the game and how to go into the game. These are the types of things that have made our program successful over the years.

I want them to be great teammates. People talk about how what you learn in basketball are your life lessons. I don't talk about that with our team, per se, but I don't want them to just be Xs and Os basketball players but great teammates—and people we want to be around and they want to be around. The culture is one of love: love the game, love each other, play hard for each other, be unselfish for each other.

We bring in former players to talk about their experiences and how much they loved being on the team and what they gained from being a part of the program. The sisterhood is the strongest part of our team, and our staff does everything we can to sustain that aspect of our culture on a daily basis.

Assigning In-Game Coaching Responsibilities

The way I divide up the responsibilities during a game depends on who the assistants are. I have always had a lot of different assistants; I even had two sets of assistants in my Olympic coaching experience. It starts with where we sit on the bench.

I have one assistant who sits on the left of me, along with the director of basketball operations (DOB), near the official's table. She is in charge of making sure that the fouls are recorded correctly and basically double-checks everything at the official's table, including time-outs, possession arrows, and the overall logistics of the game. She knows who the officials are and keeps up with the scorebook.

The assistant on my right is more about what is taking place on the court. I am actually talking strategy with them both, and some of it depends on their experience, but the two people next to me are my most experienced assistants.

The assistant next to the players on the bench has her primary responsibilities, which include when the players come in and out of the game. She gets to them first and talks with them. The player substituting out will go get water and then come back and sit next to her for any feedback or instructions.

During time-outs, we don't have a formal meeting out on the court because we talk constantly during the game. A constant conversation can go on during the game since I stay seated on the bench most of the time. It is a constant conversation because all of us are watching and talking about various things that are happening on the court. Sometimes I can work well in that commotion and sometimes I tell them, "I just need to think for a second."

Quite honestly, for years I had the same staff and we were on the same wavelength, and if one of them told me to get out of the press, we were out of that press. I think sometimes assistants can see things better during the game because they don't have to make all the decisions. They can watch specific things and give me feedback on what is really happening out there.

Evaluating the Coaching Staff

Obviously, we have the official annual evaluation form that is required at universities. My informal evaluations are absolutely situational and minute by minute. That ongoing assessment has, at times, dictated very hard conversations with some young staff members, reminding them about the way we want things done here and if they aren't meeting those expectations.

I don't know that I am easy to work with. I don't know that I am hard to work with. But this is who I am, and I can't change. Basically, I let them know this is what has worked well for a long time. This is what I know, so I am going to communicate to our staff this is what I need you to do. For the most part, the train is going down the track pretty fast, and the people I hire get on that train and get with it. Most things are already set in place, so they just slip in and understand this is what I need them to do.

I try to give new staff members a lot of specific feedback early on. I am a little bit like my dad. Both of my parents were teachers. If my dad wanted me to do a job, he would show me what to do, watch me do it, and then say, "Get it done." That's how I tend to do things. For example, when we have our first recruiting letter getting ready to go out, I'll say to the new coaches, "Here is the letter I want written. Do you have any questions? OK, get it done, and get it done by this time." I have confidence that it will be done, and done correctly.

In the 35-plus years I have been coaching, I have had very limited problems with staff. If you are having problems with your staff—you have got real problems. There are so many issues going on with the 18- to 20-year-old student-athletes on your team, and those are the problems you have to deal with. My staff issues have been short and few and far between.

I have never necessarily had to fire someone, but I have told people I think another position would work better for them, and they got the hint. Loyalty, integrity, and trust are important for me to have with people I am in the room with. If I can't trust the people I am in the room with, I don't want to be in the room with them. I'll deal very directly with them and say here is what I heard or here is what I understand.

If they don't follow the rules, that is a problem. We are very strict about following NCAA rules and Stanford rules. Sometimes young coaches struggle, and when that happens, I count on my more experienced coaches to help me see things. They will step in with the young assistants and say, "Hey, this is your position. Here are your boundaries, and this is what you need to be doing." They make sure all the coaches are representing the culture that is important to our program.

Nurturing Relationships in the Women's Coaching Community

I have had the opportunity to work with a lot of different coaching staffs, and the staffs that are the most successful are the ones that are the closest and have fun together. Our staff laughs a lot. We sit in our staff meetings and we play games, like putting money in the cup if we get off track in our meetings. We put a lot of money in the cup.

My sister spends a great deal of time outside of practice and games with her staff. I don't really do that, since I don't consider the coaching staff my social group. But whenever we are together, we have fun, work hard, and enjoy each other.

To my staff and to female coaches at all levels, these are the four things I encourage you to do in your coaching roles:

1. Be positive.
2. Be encouraging.
3. Be honest.
4. Be direct.

My very first coaching job was not by my choice, but my dad made me coach my sister's team after they had lost the night before 99-11.

Elsa/Getty Images

What I learned was that everyone on that team is someone's sister and to make sure you take care of them. Young coaches are so anxious to run a tight ship, but they just really need to care for the players they are coaching and invest in them as people.

There are some great women coaches out there, and we need to take care of them. I feel a responsibility to help people. At Stanford, we call ourselves the recycling bin. A coach may be fired, and we'll hire them and help them get back into coaching. We have done that several times. It has been great. Those coaches have often gone on to other jobs and been successful.

In the Pac-12 Conference, and by the way I have coached in our league longer than all the other coaches combined, I really try to keep in touch with the young women to talk to them, encourage them, and help them as much as I can. I feel that way about all the coaches out there. I am not saying I have all the answers, because I don't, but I still have a job at the same place after 35 years, and Stanford is not an easy place to win. Obviously, to win and be successful, it is the people you have around you. You have to have great players, and you have to have a great coaching staff.

TAKEAWAYS

- In assembling a staff, find assistants you can trust and who will work collaboratively. Find them through dependable references and networking.
- When onboarding and mentoring assistants, ensure that they are in sync with your vision, and assign them roles that accentuate their strengths and augment what you do.
- Enlist your staff to prioritize and reinforce the team culture you want to create and maintain in everything they do.
- Evaluating a staff is an ongoing process. Put emphasis on providing lots of feedback to your less experienced assistants to set them on the right course.
- Invest in present and potential women coaches. It is very important that we provide them examples of how to be positive, encouraging, honest, and direct in their roles.

CHAPTER 12

PLANNING, SCHEDULING, AND DELEGATING

Felecia Mulkey

The first couple of years coaching at the University of Oregon were an eye-opening experience. My assistant coach and I were both new to the Pacific Northwest, having recently moved from Georgia, and one of the tasks I delegated to her was to arrange the travel itinerary for our team's road trips. Our travel roster totaled around 34 student-athletes and staff at that time.

One of the first trips was to the state of Washington. So, after we arrived and checked into the hotel, we all headed out as a group to dinner. My assistant coach had planned for us to dine at a steakhouse that she found online. When I looked over the itinerary for approval prior to the trip, I saw the restaurant name and assumed it was part of a chain with a variety of dishes and a range of price points. It wasn't until we pulled into the parking lot of a casino that we both began to get nervous. My assistant had unknowingly booked a reservation and private room at a high-end restaurant inside a casino.

We walked into the restaurant in our team travel gear and were shown to our private room. The hosts serving us pulled out each chair for every individual in our party so we could take our seats. I remember our athletes' expressions as they realized how outside the norm this type of dining experience was going to be for us. I also recall the look of terror on my assistant coach's face as she was trying to calculate how much this meal was going to eat into our budget. As we all received and opened the menus, you could hear gasps and whispers from the student-athletes. The price of the least costly steak—not even including sides—would have typically fed four student-athletes an entire meal.

I assured my assistant coach that this was in no way her fault. I had approved the plan; the fault rested with me. I then told our student-athletes to make sure they were well-fed, and if they could be cost-conscious and share a side, please do so. The team finished the meal like they were all queens for a day.

My assistant coach and I learned a valuable lesson that day: A little extra research can go a long way in avoiding major errors of judgment. We learned that to stay within budget when traveling to a new area, you should not only find restaurants that can accommodate a large group but also check that the menu items are affordable and within our budget structure. Assumptions are no substitute for careful planning; it pays to be thorough in your research.

I have been coaching college athletes for over 20 years, and my organizational and planning skills have improved considerably since I took my first job. Admittedly, much of that improvement resulted from learning from many mistakes, like the dinner at the expensive casino restaurant.

Moving forward from that moment, our travel itineraries became something entirely different. Not only did the planning help us stay within budget, but the extra attention to many details helped us be much more efficient in how we practiced on the road and the time we spent in restaurants, which allowed more time for studies, rest, and recovery.

Planning and organization for team travel is essential, but that is only the tip of the iceberg when it comes to managing a program. The head coach must take into account all areas, determine how and who is best to cover them, communicate and delegate those assignments accordingly, and then be sure to monitor closely and adjust if needed.

CHARTING A PATH TO GREAT THINGS

One of my favorite things about coaching is the process or journey that the student-athletes go through each year. As a coach, sitting back and just allowing the journey to happen can present many perils and pitfalls to players on that path, making it unlikely they will be enriched by the experience or reach their desired destination by season's end.

Stop for a minute and consider what that annual journey looks like through the student-athlete's eyes. The athlete shows up for the first team meeting. Then progresses into practices. Practices lead into the season, which will require travel. The season will also bring about starting lineups, moments of excitement and accomplishment for each athlete, and moments of disappointment. The role of the coach is to help each athlete progress through the season's journey with the most positive experiences as possible along the way, rather than experiencing a roller coaster physically, mentally, and emotionally.

Through the journey, the student-athletes are growing physically and perfecting their craft. They are growing mentally, learning to cope in some situations and to take the lead in others. The season may result in a postseason experience where the athletes peak as individuals and as a team at the right time.

If you step back a little further, you realize what is directly affecting that student-athlete's journey is the path of the entire team. The team will go through ebbs and flows; they will grow through the four stages of team building and hopefully continue to become one strong, cohesive functioning unit.

Take another step back and you see that the success of the individual and team journey will depend on the skills that are taught during those practices. The mental journey will be set in motion by the boundaries that are set in that first team meeting and then upheld during those practices. What about injuries? Rainouts? Sicknesses? What are the contingency plans for those athletes? You can help shape the journey of your athletes by carefully planning your year to the best of your ability. Also, you can encourage if not arrange opportunities for invaluable off-court experiences, such as time spent talking on road trips, chatting with teammates in the locker room after practice, and so on.

All those organized and spontaneous activities need to be considered in a coach's annual planning. The task is, in essence, to maximize the use of all resources available to optimize the journey that your athletes and team will take that season. How can I plan road trips so that travel is most efficient and the athletes are dialed in to the task at

Trip Planning Tips

Over the years, I have found these key activities very helpful in ensuring successful team travel:

- Check and double-check. Once the reservations are made for the restaurant, hotel, and bus, mark your calendar for days you will call to confirm the plans. Check and double-check the addresses associated with the trip. When the plane lands in a city, our staff has a list of calls to make. There is a call to the bus driver to make sure that the bus is there to pick us up. There is a call made to the hotel to tell them that we are on our way. We call the restaurant or catering service that we are using that day. The next morning, we do the same thing—calls to restaurants and so on—to confirm that they are ready for us. I used to think that this was annoying to places of business, but over the years I have caught many mistakes by using this tactic. It is worth any annoyance that it may cause! Plus, most people and businesses appreciate the organization.

- Take notes and debrief. During the year, make sure to note things that work and do not work with each trip or event that you have planned. We have a folder for each trip where we will keep confirmations. After and sometimes during the trip, the staff will make notes on a restaurant, hotel, or even a planning concept. Did it work? What went wrong? What could we do different next time? Or the note might say, "This was great! Let's do it again!" In the moment you think you will remember all these things, but you won't. By taking time to debrief, when you sit down to plan your next year, you will not make the same mistakes and will not have to reinvent the wheel.

hand, while also enjoying themselves from departure to return? What activities, lessons, and challenges can I provide them each week to be stronger physically and mentally? These are just some of the thoughts that a coach must consider in charting the best possible course for the season's journey.

PUTTING THE PUZZLE PIECES TOGETHER

How do you ensure that when a season is over, all your athletes have appreciated the ride enough to tell you, "Coach, I would gladly do it all again." After all, that is really the goal, right? Of course, we all want to have a winning season—a conference, state, regional, or even national championship would be nice—but when we are planning at the beginning of the year, providing our athletes the best experience through the season ahead should be foremost in mind.

At Baylor, I am fortunate to have two full-time assistant coaches and a director of operations, and the entire staff is involved in planning. We meet and begin to put together the puzzle pieces of the year. We reflect on the previous year using notes and records we kept from the prior season, determine areas in which we must improve, assess the resources and tools that we have, acknowledge the challenges we are likely to encounter, and clearly define each of our responsibilities. At that point, we are ready to assemble the puzzle that is the master plan to "win the year." We will meet several times a week for a couple of weeks to hammer it all out, and then we meet weekly to discuss changes and modifications.

Since scheduling is such a big part of what we do, we take a calendar-based approach to help structure the planning process. For many years, I was old school and simply used a blank wall calendar, a pencil, and colored pens to chart things out and denote different categories of activities and events. But we have since converted to a computer calendar format in Excel that is free and available online. Each month is a different tab. I am sure there are even more high-tech alternatives these days, but I like the ease and simplicity of the basic calendar that allows us to make changes easily.

If you are coaching at an educational institution, one major consideration is the academic calendar for that year. First and last day of classes, midterms, school holidays, finals, and so on. Enter them all on your master calendar, as those dates are not likely to change.

Then note all the dates on your competition schedule and include conference and postseason tournaments. Also identify any preseason tournaments or exhibitions that you have committed to or plan to attend. Be sure to note recruiting periods and any plans or commitments in that regard. And, if you have any plan for professional development, like coaching clinics or conferences, include those as well. While this master season calendar is most beneficial to you and your staff to stay on course, it will ultimately be of great service to your student-athletes and team throughout the year.

Once your calendar is set up, it's time to drill down on specific areas that must be addressed: budget, equipment, compliance, recruiting, academics, practice schedule, skill instruction, evaluation system, travel, fundraising. Every program and sport will have different categories that are more or less important in that regard, so tailor the areas of focus to what fits best for you.

Budget

Budget will affect much of your planning and organization. When you begin to plan the other areas, you will constantly refer to your budget. Questions to consider when planning your budget: What is the fiscal year for your school or organization? Do you submit information for your budget to be considered during the business office process? If so, when is that due? If you are planning a purchase, are there bid processes you will have to go through? Are there fundraising opportunities to supplement your budget? How much will you need to recruit effectively?

In my situation, we submit travel information in June, and our budget is presented to us by the end of July. If you know you will need to fundraise for a special trip or a team-building activity, a new uniform or a team gift, this can be a different line item and will require some planning all its own.

Practice Planning and Skill Instruction

Each sport will be different here, but the common denominator is that every sport will want to improve a team's skills over the course of the year, with the goal of peaking at the right time. I go back to my master calendar and mark when our first day of practice will be. This will be based on NCAA or governing body rules. From there, I make a note of the first allowable date of competition. Then I work backward. My sport, acrobatics and tumbling, has start difficulty values that are related to the risk and difficulty of the skills performed. I will sit down with my coaching staff and create a strategy of where we would like to be at the beginning of the season and where we would like to be at the end of the season.

Using that as a guideline, we plan out our practices, noting monthly goals. For example, we start practices around the beginning of September. We will note that by the end of September, everyone competing at a certain position will have mastered these particular drills and skills. We work closely with our strength staff to ensure that

Baylor Athletics

our monthly goals for skill progressions will align with the strength progressions in the weight room.

Once the monthly goals are determined, we will go back and set weekly goals. These weekly and monthly goals will serve as a guide. Some teams will progress faster than others. The plan is a guide that can easily be adjusted and will likely become fluid as athlete personnel flourish or underachieve.

Practice Scheduling

Our staff has always planned our practice dates out months in advance. We are a semester school; the team will receive their fall calendar in July and then their spring calendar in October. This works for us because there are no questions about the time requirements. The athletes can take that calendar and plan extracurricular activities and trips and so on. If you are a college coach, you are familiar with the time management plan (TMP) calendars. Our staff operated this way even before the TMP requirement. We have found that this type of planning leads to accountability across the team.

The amount and length of practices at the collegiate level are determined by the sport's governing body and national organization and the division of competition. With those guiding rules in mind, I set out to design the practice schedule for the entire fall around the middle of June. If you are a veteran coach, you can spout off the playing and practice season without blinking an eye. If you are a new coach, some questions to consider before you begin the practice scheduling process are: When are you allowed to start practice? Is there a preseason practice or conditioning time frame that is allowed? Will you be able to keep the team following finals and bring them back prior to the first day of school? Do you have to house and feed them if they are practicing outside of the academic calendar? That last question will also take you back to your budget. Once you have determined the parameters that you have to work with, you set out your practice days.

When I was a young coach, I thought we had to go hard from day one of practice until the last day. Over the years, I have come to appreciate days off. It is not only good for the student-athletes' bodies but also good for their minds.

I have found it beneficial to "ramp up" frequencies of practices and intensity over the course of a semester. Since we are a spring sport, we can afford to ramp up over the course of the fall semester. For college coaches, just because we are allowed 20 hours of athletic-related activity during our season doesn't mean you have to use it! I usually start with practice or weights four days a week. Through the first month, make sure that the athletes are getting adequate rest. I try to give them two days off back-to-back if possible. This allows them to figure out the physical piece and get used to college life—which is particularly important for first-year students or first-time team members. Over the course of the semester, I try to maintain two days off a week, but there will be weeks prior to the end of the semester that we will go six days a week to make sure that we reach all the goals that we have set for the fall semester.

Something to consider: If you feel the need to practice more days than not, consider significantly shortening one or two of the practice days. You will likely be surprised with the result. When it comes to effective practice planning, days off are more important than days on! Consider putting the extra practice on the calendar so it's there if needed, but mentally mark it as a likely day off if things are going well. That way the student-athletes don't have a practice pop up on them. Instead, they get a surprise day off.

Recruiting

If you are a college coach, you should take ample time to identify your recruiting calendar. This will vary from sport to sport. Once the team calendar is identified, dig a little deeper and think through times that you will travel and host official visits. Add those to your master calendar. For smaller staffs, this will allow you to succeed in recruiting and spend some time focusing on it, even when you are in midseason, preseason, or skill instruction. Make sure to plan out this budget for the year with events to attend, travel costs, official visits, and so on.

Travel

Think back to my story of the team dinner at the beginning of this chapter. How much better will your team's experience be if you put in some extra time to plan your travel? Not to mention your own personal mental well-being! Some questions to consider as you plan travel itineraries: What about your travel is nonnegotiable? Game times? Athletic training treatment prior to the game or meet? Is this a flight or a bus trip? Is it a day trip or an overnight trip?

Plan the travel to and from the event first. This could be a huge portion of the expense of each trip depending on your mode of travel. Nail this down first for peace of mind. If it is a flight, look at flights well in advance. This will play into budget because the longer you wait, the more expensive the flight. If it is a bus trip, will you be chartering or using an institutional vehicle? Can your team use vans? A note: I have found that with flights, it is worth the little extra expense to use a travel agent. There are so many other things to consider for team travel, this could be one thing that you can delegate to an outside professional. You may spend a little more but will make up for it with simplicity and peace of mind.

Lodging will also be important to consider if it is an overnight trip. We like to find hotels near to the competition site but also centrally located for restaurants. It is important to do the research on the hotel as well. Read the reviews! The pictures on the website can be misleading. We look for hotels that have meeting rooms that we can use for team meetings, athletic training treatment, and potentially team meals if catering is an option. Many times, schools will have a travel packet that they offer to teams who are visiting for competition. If not, we will call a coach at that school and ask for references on lodging.

Dining is always a bear to tackle when you have a large roster. It is tricky to find a restaurant that can seat our entire team. Sitting in the general seating area and ordering off the menu is a nightmare for a large group. What could have been an hour meal can easily turn into several hours of waiting, with everyone eating at different times. If we are going to use a restaurant, we ask for a private room and a limited menu. If we can get enough variety with a buffet style in a private room, we sometimes do that. However, I like for athletes to eat what they want, especially for a pregame meal. If the restaurant is open to the idea, we will preorder the food. We call the restaurant 30 minutes ahead of time, so the food comes out soon after we arrive. Again, this all works better with a private room and the prearranged meals.

Rest and recovery are a priority for my staff and team. I like for the team to get an adequate amount of sleep. With that in mind, we take an unusual approach to breakfast while on trips. We will either cater breakfast in the hotel meeting room (sometimes the hotel can offer this service), or we give the team a two-hour window where they are required to wake up and come down to eat. This allows flexibility for morning and non-morning persons. Another option is to take groups that do not want the hotel breakfast to a local restaurant, although the people in that group usually have to wake up earlier and will spend more time away from the hotel where they could rest. But it is up to them how they want breakfast in the mornings.

We will plan study times during our trips to make sure that the athletes can keep up with schoolwork on the road. These times are clearly designated on the itinerary so the athletes can plan accordingly, in case they have a test coming up or a paper due.

We distribute the itinerary to the travel team a few days before the trip. We include what travel gear to wear, the uniforms needed, if they need to bring extra clothes, and even a weather report for the area so they can pack accordingly. Ideally, the itinerary will be so detailed a stranger could come in and lead the team trip.

Roommate assignments always create excitement as we review the itinerary with the team. We divulge the roommates the day we discuss the itinerary. We have a large roster and will rotate roommates each trip. If athletes live together daily, we typically split them up. The coaches decide who rooms together on each trip.

The coaches and administrators have an itinerary that is much more detailed with phone numbers for restaurants and lodging. The athletes' itinerary has only times and details pertinent to the athletes. Parents do not receive a team itinerary. However, if we can, we will try to allocate family time when parents can come to the hotel or meet us for dinner. This is typically after we compete. If time and budget allow, we try to visit something fun that is unique to that city. We have gone to museums, parks, shopping malls, cool restaurants. At the end of the day, the experience is what matters!

NURTURING A CULTURE

Culture is everything on a team. As a coach, we either create a culture or we allow it. There are some coaches who will blame their culture on one or two athletes or on a certain class. There is always the hope when that athlete or class graduates, the culture will automatically be better. If you do not take a role in creating a positive culture, you may never get the culture you want. When I think of team culture, I automatically think of my first team at Baylor. I had just left a championship program at the University of Oregon and came into an existing program at Baylor that had consecutive losing seasons.

The culture on this Baylor team was different from what I was used to at Oregon. When competing against them prior to coaching there, I could see the culture on the sidelines and how it reflected in their performance on the mat. The first thing I noticed when I got on campus and interacted with the team was that there was zero communication and zero accountability to one another. It was an "every man for himself" mentality.

My staff and I were intent on changing that, and that is one of the reasons we spent so much time creating a detailed plan for the year. From practice and weights to detailed travel itineraries to mandatory study hours, their year was completely planned. Once we had the plan in place, we shared it in detail with the team. We explained the expectations and the consequences if someone missed a session with a tutor or wore the wrong practice shirt on a certain day. Once we presented the plan, we stuck to it as a staff and held people accountable each time a mistake was made. We held up our end of the bargain.

Before long, the team started taking pride in the little things. They liked that they were more disciplined than other teams on campus. Other teams on campus recognized it as well. The team started to take pride in this—and in who they were. The discipline and attention to

Baylor Athletics

detail became part of the team identity. They began to hold each other accountable in every aspect. Holding a teammate accountable leads to conversations and dialogue that will allow the team members to become closer and gain respect for their teammates. This communication carried over into their performance. You could see confidence build individually and as a team throughout the year.

That team went on to an undefeated season, including a national championship over the reigning champion, the University of Oregon. It was a dream season. Baylor was not the most "talented" team in the country, but they were the best "team" in the country. Before the end of the year in April, the team that wanted nothing to do with rules and guidelines in August had now begun to ask for specific details about what to wear on the plane, and they would request to review the travel itinerary as a group prior to the trip. It always made me smile because they had no idea about the steakhouse at the casino or the time that we had to change hotels in the snow because we booked the wrong number of rooms.

TAKEAWAYS

- Taking adequate time to plan and organize every aspect of your season will not only make your life easier, it will drastically improve your student-athletes' experience within your program.

- Season planning is not a perfect science, but then again, neither is coaching. The time that you spend preparing on the front end will be time well spent for you and your staff and will drastically improve your year.

- Be ready to pivot. Rarely will the year go exactly as you plan. There are too many variables for things to work out perfectly every time. The ability to think on your feet and make a change will be crucial. If you have thought through the original plan in detail, thinking on your feet will be easier. Many times, with practice planning, we will have a plan A and plan B. You can think through possible scenarios and have a plan in place, no matter the obstacle.

CHAPTER 13

SELLING YOUR PROGRAM

Carolyn Peck

When I was in high school, Pat Summitt, women's basketball head coach at the University of Tennessee, spoke at our girls' basketball banquet. During her talk, Pat made a statement that made a real impact on me. She said, "No one person is ever successful by themselves." That simple statement always stuck with me as a player, a coach, a professional businessperson, and a professional sportscaster. Anything that you ever do, you are never going to be great or successful because of what you do alone. It is going to require a team effort.

When I think about high school and what we were able to accomplish with that girls' basketball team, what we did when I played at Vanderbilt, what I did as an advertising account executive in pharmaceutical sales, it all required a team—a collection of individuals working together. I was able to coach with Pat as a restricted earnings assistant coach, then at the University of Kentucky, then win an NCAA Division I Women's Basketball National Championship at Purdue, and go on to coach in the pros and even be a broadcaster in television. Everything was a team effort. But, as a coach, to get that team buy-in to become champions requires something very fundamental.

Every great coach I know who inspired me, and those around them, has one thing in common. None of them tried to be someone they were not. They were comfortable in their own skin and conveyed themselves in a way that was perceived by everyone as genuine and authentic. That is why my first recommendation to any coach who is finding it hard to get the full support of those associated with her sports program is to be authentic. Be your true self. Some coaches take on an artificial persona that they believe will endear themselves more with the media, boosters, and recruits, but it never works in the long run. A coach isn't a "brand" like Nike, Adidas, or Puma that can be designed and packaged to appeal to certain audiences. In coaching, you can't fit a mold. You have to be your authentic self and that will become your brand.

RELATIONSHIP BUILDING

Coaches are the critical component in presenting their program, gaining others' interest and support for it, and then creating and maintaining those bonds with stakeholders. Yes, it's a sales job, but one that is authentic, not contrived or filled with false promises.

You market it not only to the players you are recruiting and want to coach, but you're also marketing to the media and your fans, who you want to have watch your team play. You are marketing to the boosters who you want to support and donate to your program. You are marketing to your athletics administration so they will have buy-in and supply the resources you need for your program to be successful. And you are marketing to the media, so they might possibly gain an interest and cover your sports program.

But what should a marketing job look like from a coach? It sure isn't like trying to move a used car off the lot. You can't simply turn a switch and expect reporters at the local newspapers, the television and radio stations, community members, or prospective or current athletes to simply buy in. Instead, you must constantly work at developing and investing in those relationships. You must find the customer and what the customer's needs are, and you have to know what it is that you have to market and how you bridge those two together. Instead of just going in and talking about what you want them to do for you, you need to form a bridge—a connection, a common bond—between your needs and theirs. You must make a connection between their interests—in the case of media, selling more subscriptions or programming—and your own.

Media

It is very important to establish strong rapport and mutual respect with the individuals responsible for covering your team. That doesn't mean just shake their hand or say hello and think about what they can do for you. The type of relationship you need to develop is a two-way street that is based on honesty and trust.

You must be honest. When you lie, deceive, or manipulate, the media is going to try to get that "gotcha" moment. But when you are honest and straightforward and, in turn, find who you can trust, it is a home run because you are working together. You have to understand that if you want media to cover your sports program, you have to allow them to cover you and your team when it is going well and when it is not going well.

I learned a lot of that when I was coaching at Purdue University. Mike Harmon was a beat writer for the West Lafayette newspaper, and he had a vested interest in our women's basketball program. He wholeheartedly and genuinely cared about the team. When you meet a person who cares that much and can relate to how much you care, you can tell a better story to the public about your sports program. One of the things that we did with Mike was give him full access to our women's basketball team. He was invited to practice. He got the inside story, the inside scoop. And when it was legal according to NCAA rules to release names of players who had made a commitment to our program, we gave him those names, so he got to write those first stories. That investment in him created an even greater vested interest by him in our program.

When you talk about working with the media, college and high school coaches need to carve out a particular space in the media landscape because your sports program may not be of interest in your particular geographical area. You have got to make it of interest and educate your media on why it is interesting and why it is a compelling story. When you look at different markets, where some sports are covered in the media more than in other areas of the country, you ask why. It is probably because the coaches took the time and effort to educate the media on the sport. The coaches gave the media full access to their program, coaches, and student-athletes.

Community

I remember when I was a player no one knew anything about the University of South Carolina women's basketball program. You look at that program now and see what head coach Dawn Staley has done for South Carolina's program. Dawn has made women's basketball a national story. She took a vested interest not only in building a winning basketball program but in the community and the state of South Carolina. She knows everything that is going on in Columbia, South Carolina, even outside the walls of the University of South Carolina and in the city of Columbia. She is a contributing and interested citizen of that community, and the citizens have become invested in her and the women's basketball program.

We were able to do the same type of thing in West Lafayette, Indiana, when I was coaching at Purdue. A small group of people knew on Sundays that I was going to be at Harry's Chocolate Shop playing Ships and Sailors with some of the older men who supported our program. They were the members of the local community, and they got to know me as a person. That was important to me and to our women's basketball program. The community must know who you are and what you are trying to accomplish coaching one of the local college or university teams.

The best way to develop those important relationships is to be actively involved in the local community. Don't just be there with a hand out asking for their support. "Do this for us. Do this for me. Do this for our player. Do this for our program." What are the players doing for the community? It is a two-way street, and when there is buy-in, that is how you develop a caring and committed relationship. And when there is a genuine relationship there is a commitment—and that is where you get support. The community wants to see the team do well, and the team wants to perform well for the community.

Athletics Administration

The support of those who hire you and pay your check is also imperative. Make sure you have open and transparent communication with your athletics administration, and make it frequent so there are no surprises.

Communication with your athletics administration is giving them the good, the bad, and the ugly. Don't just tell them, "The team is looking good and all is fine" when it is not. Share with them when you have a player who is not fitting into the team chemistry or your system, so when there is a complaint that comes to the athletics administration, they will have the necessary background and won't be surprised. When you are forthright with the athletics administration in advance, they can help you circumvent some of these problems before they reach a serious level that puts you or your program at risk.

Student-Athletes

Otto Greule /Allsport/Getty Images

My college head basketball coach at Vanderbilt was Phil Lee. He taught me the value of relationship building. When he recruited me, I was not a basketball player. I was a person. He, his wife, and his two children recruited me. They treated me like a third daughter. I grew up 35 minutes from the University of Tennessee in Knoxville, and I decided to go to college and play basketball in Nashville. It was because of how intentional Phil was in developing that relationship with me—as a player and as a person. And after I got to Vanderbilt, I saw the same thing in every young woman he and his staff recruited to Vanderbilt. He had the ability to build and sustain that relationship.

Pat did the same thing in developing relationships at the University of Tennessee. It was very misleading for people to watch Pat on the sidelines during a game and see that direct stare. Many people thought she was so evil. That stare was only part of Pat's large personality. She was like a parent who you did not want to disappoint, and if you brought about that stare from her, it meant you had truly disappointed her. Everyone wanted to please her because she made sure you knew that she cared about you.

What allowed me and my staff to be successful is that we were honest. Coaches who are honest with their players are not telling them what they want to hear, but they can deliver the truth even when it is not exactly what the players want to hear. You have to be honest and consistent so your players will trust you. When there is trust between players and coaches, then the foundation is built. When there is no jealousy or distrust or a breakdown of chemistry and you know a coach is going to be honest and consistent, then there is a strong relationship that will get you through the ups and downs of a season.

I look at our team at Purdue. We had tremendous leadership in our players, Stephanie White and Ukari Figgs. Sure, they had tremendous talent, and we had other great players, but the leadership was fantastic. I could talk with that team and be honest with them. I had the leadership on the team to back me up. "Yes, coach is right. This is what she says and that is what we should do. This is what we stand for, what we believe in, and what we are doing."

When I look at other successful teams, the same things happen. There is consistency. You look at Kim Mulkey, head women's basketball coach at LSU. She tells the truth to her team. It is honest, and it is not always sugarcoated, but she loves those players. Wes Moore, head coach of women's basketball at North Carolina State, is honest with his team, and it works.

All relationships are about honesty, communication, and trust. And that's not just the player–coach or coach–administrator relationship, but across the board, including the coach's relationship with student-athletes' parents. Dawn Staley assigns her assistant coaches the responsibility for a certain group of players. The coaches have relationships with all of them, and they have a relationship with Dawn. But one of Dawn's priorities is with the parents of the team members. The assistant coaches do not deal with the parents, she does. Dawn keeps them up to speed. She is not trying to appease the parents, but she lets them know this is what is going on and this is how she manages her basketball program. They know that coming in, and you see the support and respect she has earned from folks associated with her program.

I was fortunate at Purdue and had supportive parents who bought in to what we were doing. I have also been at a program where I did not have that same support, and parents thought their daughter should be playing more—every parent would feel that way. I didn't handle it well because I assumed every parent was going to be like the parents of other players I have coached, whose parents were supportive of the entire team. They believed whatever we were doing worked and the players were all on the same page.

When you are recruiting, you must know the type of person you can coach and the type of families you can deal with. When you sign a player to an athletic scholarship, you do not just sign the prospective student-athlete, you sign the family, too. Make sure that is what you can deal with, and make sure they know what they are getting into as well. Have that communication and understanding that when it doesn't fit, it just doesn't fit, and be OK with that.

STUDENT-ATHLETES AND THE MEDIA

Inviting the media into your sports program means they have access to the student-athletes. I highly recommend before you allow media access that there is a value in media training for your student-athletes. You have to teach your players how to engage and not engage with the media. They need to understand the questioning coming from a group of reporters. The media can ask the same question two or three different ways, and if it is a question you don't want to answer, you have to teach your student-athletes how to "not answer the question they don't want to answer" with an answer. "No comment" is not an option and not an answer. We need to remember there are some great stories about student-athletes, but you have to help them understand how to tell their stories—and tell it the way they want it to be told, without exposing ultra-personal details, but with enough of a personal connection that the fans can relate.

During the COVID-19 period, I helped put together a documentary on the University of South Carolina called "For the Culture." Within that documentary, Aliyah Boston, a first-year forward on the women's basketball team, had lost a professor who was very close to her. She did not play well in a tournament, and there were questions about her performance. There had to be a strategy on allowing her to talk about how the loss of her professor affected her without upsetting her. That was a delicate dance, but with the help of an experienced head coach like Dawn Staley, who has exhibited great leadership, as well as the sports information director who trained Aliyah on how to talk to the media, Aliyah was able to tell her story and find the heartstrings that appealed to the fans.

You look at the University of Arkansas student-athlete Chelsea Dungee, a senior guard on the women's basketball team. She and her mom were homeless. She could talk about not taking a day for granted because she watched how her mother worked so hard to provide for her and put a roof over her head. These are the kinds of stories that teach your student-athletes that it is OK to be vulnerable. It is OK to demonstrate how you persevered because you have used that as motivation and you are determined to be successful, on and off the court.

When possible, it can be helpful to give others glimpses of your team's culture through the media. A program's culture is developed by the players and the coaching staff coming to an agreement on standards that everyone buys into to help reach your common goal. When the media has a sense of those culture-defining factors for your team, it can help them understand why you emphasize certain things and how those priorities affect your decision making.

When I coached at Purdue, our approach was that we did not just want to win a season, we wanted to have a winning program that was sustainable. It started at Purdue with head coach Nell Fortner, and I was her assistant coach. We had a rope that had knots in it and each knot stood for something specific, such as accountability, responsibility, loyalty, and commitment. The last knot was the biggest one, and it represented your higher or supreme being—whatever spiritual or religious connection someone had. It was a heck of a lot easier to climb up when you had those knots to grab on to. That was the idea we used to come up with the rope concept in our team culture. You may not take responsibility seriously when you are sliding down the rope. You may not take accountability seriously, or you may not take commitment or loyalty seriously as you slide down. But that large knot at the bottom was forgiving and prevented most athletes from falling off the rope. It allowed them to climb back up the rope if they were able to reconfirm their commitment to meeting the standards that had been set. Our culture did not cut someone out for missing curfew or a similar minor transgression, and we didn't have a bunch of picky rules. But what we had, and enforced, were the program standards.

If members of the media covering your team are aware of those standards, it can help them understand why you chose to handle disciplinary issues and other matters regarding the team as you did. This will provide a context from which they communicate such incidents and decisions.

Determining exactly what to share and what not to share with the media isn't always clear-cut. The key is to know your players. Make sure you have developed that relationship and have the discussion about their backgrounds and stories. You must understand what your players are comfortable sharing with the public because as a coach, you do not want to put them in an uncomfortable situation or undermine your trust with them. You really need to have an appreciation for what they have been through, where they are now, and where they are going. You want to do anything you can to help them be successful, but it is the relationship piece that you must have, and that requires mutual understanding and trust.

ORAL AND WRITTEN COMMUNICATION

Communication skills are essential to effective leadership. Oral communication means being able to speak in an organized, succinct, and coherent way. It is important that you are able to verbally communicate in a manner that the recipient(s) of your message will readily grasp and appreciate. When you say things clearly and concisely, others will follow. It is also important for coaches to know when to stop talking. Rambling does not sound impressive or professional, nor is it effective. Often the less you say gives each word more impact.

When it comes to written communication, there is nothing that means more to people than a personal note. Text messages and emails are fine, and they are certainly useful for quick responses, but it means so much more to the recipient when you send a handwritten note. A simple "thank you" or "I was thinking about you" is the best. You are giving someone your time when you write a note, and that leaves people feeling special.

Darrell Walker/Icon Sportswire

Speaking on Social Issues

Communicating with your athletes and those in your community about matters important to you and your team, such as social justice, isn't something that should be left to social media. The WNBA did a great job of constantly educating their players in summer 2020. It was not just reacting to what they saw someone else do on social media. There was a strategic approach and a reason and rationale behind the strategy. They had conversations with the specific people they were trying to help and who were affected.

College and high school teams need to be intentional as well if they want to have a positive impact in social justice matters. We know how much a community can look up to our athletes, and what we say and do matters. Conference leaders can certainly be supportive, but a coach needs to take a strong position for the sake of her own program and those connected to it. Young players are watching sports and accessing views on social media, and they can be misled. It will be important to provide strong leadership and guidance to have a positive effect on our society. I think asking the question about an issue is a huge start, but then take time to listen—to really listen—then narrow it down to talk about what we can specifically do together to support one another.

I think back to working with Pat Summitt and how many letters I watched her write. She would have me drive on recruiting trips or to speaking engagements because she was busy writing notes. Once, when rummaging through a drawer, I found a congratulations letter from Pat from a long time ago that said, "We are so excited about you joining our Lady Vol staff. We look forward to working with you. Our staff retreat is Tuesday. Be sure to be on time at 7:30 a.m." It is a handwritten note and I still have it. I will cherish that note forever. I think of all the people around the country that were blessed to receive personal notes from her.

When I received the Nell and John Wooden Excellence in Coaching Award, I was able to observe Coach Wooden as he interacted with people. They were lined up and down the street to get our autographs, but it was really his autograph everyone wanted. He was sitting next to me, and when people got to him, he took the time to speak to each person, relay a personal story, and write a personalized message on whatever they handed him to autograph. The time he took to write a short or long message was something that meant so much to each of those people, and it did not cost him anything but time.

Written communication demonstrates that you are valuable because I am going to take the time to pull out a piece of paper and a pen and write something to you. It ties back to building relationships, even with people you may not know very well or will never see again.

I urge everyone to go look through that drawer, cabinet, or box where you have put all those handwritten items you have received in your career and think about the person who took the time to write that message to you. We should never replace the cherished art of handwriting notes and letters to people we care about. Those will live on forever.

TAKEAWAYS

- Be real. Authenticity is the only way to be successful and respected by those inside, following, or covering your program.
- Put stock in developing good relationships within the community and media, and it will pay off big-time.
- Effective, frequent, and honest communication with your athletes will gain their trust.
- Coaching your athletes on how to conduct and express themselves to and through the media is now an essential part of every coach's role.
- Written communication that is timely, well crafted, and genuine can be as impactful as any verbal message you might send.

PART III
ATHLETE ENGAGEMENT AND GROWTH

CHAPTER 14

RECRUITING ATHLETES TO YOUR PROGRAM

Missy Meharg

When I first started coaching field hockey at the University of Maryland, the associate director of athletics, Gothard Lane, said to me, "Missy, success in the position comes down to recruiting and scheduling. The coaching piece is important, but these two things are the game inside the game at the NCAA Division I level." That has always stuck in my mind.

Thank you, Gothard Lane.

I was fortunate to get the head coaching position at Maryland at 24 years old. Right place, right time, I guess. I worked as a graduate assistant coach for Dr. Sue Tyler, who was the head field hockey and lacrosse coach. She was simply amazing—the G.O.A.T. and a pioneer for women's sports and for the advancement of the industry. I had never felt so empowered by someone in my life. Not a month goes by that I don't think of Sue and my initial years in College Park.

Pure love of teaching, with creativity and equity and with laughter at the core, is how I think of her. When she moved into the administration, she shared with the athletics director, "I think Missy can coach the field hockey team." Twenty-four and taking over a *national championship program*? Really? Yikes!

RECRUITING TO A CULTURE

Taking over for Sue Tyler, I did not need to define a culture of my own, because it was already laid out. I fit her mold, so I basically inherited it. I was so grateful that she believed in me and took a chance with me. Thankfully we were very much aligned in our teaching methods, thinking, and energy.

Maryland won the 1987 NCAA National Championship. I was Sue's graduate assistant coach, so I thought I knew what it would take to be successful. Two seasons later we did not make the NCAA tournament. That was the juncture when I realized I needed my own brand, and I had to figure out what I stood for since Sue was no longer there. It was a daunting task. She was a tough act to follow—one of the most intellectual and charismatic leaders I had ever met. Players really *played* for her.

University of Maryland Terrapins (Terps) are hardworking, competitive, and humble. They thrive on bringing up the weakest link. I was fortunate to have great, strong female leaders who believed in equal opportunity and accentuated the strengths of each individual on the team. That concept seemed to be the key to winning.

College coaches need to be aware of the culture on their campus and the perception other people have. High school coaches, club coaches, and parents need to ask what the coaches' philosophies for leading are and understand the culture of the programs. As coaches, you work hard to make sure your programs are well known within your communities. With that comes the pressure of knowing all eyes will be on you and how you lead your program. The media are everywhere in this part of the United States. In this region, people are always watching what you do as an athlete and as a coach. I take great pride in knowing there's a lot of responsibility in that and seeing to it that the athletes we bring onto campus, and into the program, live up to high standards and avoid problems and recruiting scandals. We make it clear to prospective student-athletes that we want to get to know them and them us. I must say that this contact period makes it much better.

Successful recruiting is essential for our program's success. Our conference is the top conference today, and we want to always be in a position to win NCAA National Championships. We had a streak of top-four positions and several national championships for quite some time. We were able to hold this spot for all those years because of our tradition. The top players brought up the bottom players, and the bottom players yearned to compete at the level of the top players. Since moving into the Big Ten Conference from the Atlantic Coast Conference (ACC) we have had to redefine our image and definition. We seem to be on task.

Sustaining talent starts with recruiting talent who love the program and share its vision and culture with ease, excitement, and pride. The players know better than my staff does who is a good fit and who is not. Maryland has always been a place of natural diversity, equity, and inclusion. I have great pride in the university and the region for this.

I think of recruiting as a triangle. Top players like winning, and they look for that in a university setting. They want to get better at the game while they are there. They also want access to strong, broad-based academic programs. But what I have discovered in recruiting is how important it is to address those things that aren't so obvious: the things they might have underlying concerns about or aren't aware of that could

Zach Bland/Maryland Terrapins

make another program seem like a better fit. So, in addition to offering recruits a winning field hockey team and good academics, I make sure to address that third piece; oftentimes, it's a difference maker.

One absolute at Maryland is people having equality in opportunity and treatment. Throughout their club and their high school experiences, these young athletes have often become accustomed to some preferential treatment because of their abilities and achievements. And, no doubt, some recruits will turn out to be more capable and collect more awards than others during their careers. But I feel strongly that the basic treatment of and caring for one another within a program should be the same. And we make sure that the top players are accepting and respectful of the ones who aren't quite so strong or advanced at the time they come on campus. That's essential in creating the right dynamics—a winning environment—in the locker room and on the field.

Indeed, the culture we strive to nurture in our program has always been serving each other first. It's a culture in which everyone works hard, embraces change, thrives on competition, and accepts the challenge of contributing their best abilities every day for the program.

We deeply care for each other, and to demonstrate this, we need to be willing to push our friends and teammates to their highest level on the practice field and in the weight room. We create training situations using competitive cauldrons and mini games with times and conditions that make things very chaotic. It demands that the athletes think and act quickly to turn chaos into organization.

Being able to laugh at yourself can be critical for this age group. I'm not sure how to coach this; perhaps it develops over time. The past few years I have noticed that young athletes can be very serious and intense, which can inhibit the fun element of training. Students today are way more comfortable knowing what the plan is. As much as we ask the players to trust the leadership, and be OK with surprises and last-minute adjustments, unpredictability can really rattle them. Having clearly designated time blocks and describing the events within helps them collectively. They understand that training and match environments require open and flexible minds.

Enthusiasmos is one of my favorite words. I'd like to think I inspire players and coaches rather than motivate them to perform. I ask questions like *What does is feel like? taste like? smell like?* I create small-group feedback during training. In an era of player monitor systems that supply standardization and subsequent motivation, these human conversations and questions help athletes know themselves.

RECRUITING STRATEGIES

As the head coach, I am heavily involved in recruiting and work very closely with other coaches at Maryland. Coaches need to understand where they are and to listen to everyone in the athletics department in getting the behind-the-scenes stories. Every campus has a person who has researched the history of athletics and how it plays a role within the institution—past, present, and future. Sit down with them—maybe take them out for a meal—and your recruiting depth will soar. History tells the truth.

Once you know the background, the working environment, the programs, and the leadership style, then you can assess who is the right fit. If you are not recruiting at the level to win matches, start with the history of your product and work with like people. The talent is out there.

When meeting face-to-face with an athlete I am recruiting for the first time, I ask the athlete to share her hockey story. After listening to her experiences, I then share how hockey became my passion and such a huge part of my life. That connection concerning the love and commitment to excelling in the sport is a good starting foundation.

Be able to differentiate your university and program and set it apart from the other schools that your recruits are considering. I try to concentrate on what I perceive to be the needs of the athletes. In order to excel, they need to be satisfied with their choice once they are on campus. We had a meeting with a top recruit and her parents. Her parents are both doctors, and she wanted to be a doctor, so we pulled in quite a lineup of experts for them to meet from the medical school. That extra touch of delivering what the athletes are looking for will be important when it comes time for them to make the decision.

Athletics departments and university-wide campaigns can also help encourage and inform athletes and their families. Coaches should be aware of themes and campaigns taking place on their campuses and try to tie those ideas into the recruiting strategy of attracting talent to your program. We have a campaign going on to raise $1 billion. I did a lot of work on this five-year campaign with the university's central relations. The campaign theme, "One Maryland," was our recruiting theme during that campaign. I like to use images and visuals in recruiting. If you read all the information the university has to offer on its yearly theme and brand, it is perfect for us to use. Maybe it is a two- to four-year campaign pitch you can use in your recruiting strategies. I am always interested in what the incoming first-year students get in the mail each year from the University of Maryland. It was crab mallets and masks one year.

A lot of coaches study other programs to try to figure out how they can leverage their program against the competition to get recruits. I prefer letting the history, stats, and facts about our own program speak for themselves. It's easy for me to make the case for Maryland field hockey because that is what I know. Having never worked at another institution, I probably would not be that credible talking about another program.

We have a few new factors playing into recruiting conversations. One is changes in the rules regarding name, image, and likeness (NIL) and the extra money (or opportunity for the athlete to earn money) the NCAA now allows schools to offer. We have to be prepared to talk about how our university is working with athletes on that effort and what NIL company the university partners with on behalf of their student-athletes. Maryland is presently with Opendorse. The other new consideration is the transfer portal and the number of athletes turning to new fresh opportunities for various reasons. The extra year of eligibility with COVID-19 (entering classes of 2017-2020) has made it even more complicated and affected the numbers in the transfer portal for sure.

High school, junior college, and club coaches need to be aware of the vast differences between the various levels and available monies afforded to potential student-athletes. Schools in the Power 5 conferences (ACC, Big Ten, Big 12, Pac-12, SEC) can offer prospective student-athletes the biggest financial package. NCAA Division I, Division II, and Division III packages are different. There are also NAIA and NJCAA schools that have completely different rules and allocations for coaches and athletes. If you are a high school, junior college, or club coach, be current with your knowledge so you can be honest with your athletes early in the recruiting process. Guiding them to the appropriate level for their athletic skill and academic ability is key.

Identifying Athletes

Being familiar with the structures, systems, and evaluation processes of school clubs around the country and the world gets you ahead of the game. Clubs have their own cultures, just like leagues around the world do. I'm always interested in looking at the top clubs that have the cream-of-the-crop athletes. Historically, they have talented tier-one player squads that can tell you right away their potential. Right beneath those top teams are second, third, and fourth teams that include prospects that have the desire and vision to compete. If the club has quality fundamental coaching and history, players who are in the lower tiers can be very good in your program. Getting to know the top club directors and coaches can really help your presence as a top recruiter. Once you sign a player from a top club and a solid hockey-playing region, you'll have a presence there forever. This is why I like to be sure their character fits with what we're looking for and vice versa. We all need to be happy to *win*.

Everyone can identify the top athletes in your sport. To be successful in recruiting, you need to identify student-athletes you can actually get. There's no need to take up time and resources going after recruits you will not get. Be realistic and identify the prospects who will continue to move your program up in wins and the rankings without overshooting the mark. One step at a time. Signing a little better recruit each year will produce better results in the long run.

Many college coaches own and run local field hockey clubs in their communities. I have never done that. It would feel a bit awkward for me and my staff to have our own club and recruit some players and not others. We have lots of clubs in our area that provide playing opportunities for young athletes, and we get to watch them all. For hockey, playing on an artificial (carpet) turf is best for their skill development. Although our game keeps growing in popularity and number, there is a shortage of good synthetic surfaces.

It is imperative that you build a relationship with the coaches who run clubs in your community and around your state and region. Those coaches and club directors can provide you with the background on athletes in their program and others they may see at various events as they compete around the country. They will certainly be familiar with your program and what type of athletes you are looking for to improve your team. I am always excited when high school or club coaches call me to get an overview of my coaching philosophy and leadership style.

Adding Transfers

The transfer portal has become a new aspect of recruiting and been very effective for many programs to have immediate success. You have to decide if that fits into your recruiting plan and how. An athlete who shows up in the portal may be someone who you lost out on during the first go-round, and now they might be graduating early and are looking for an opportunity at another school. Keeping in close contact with club and high school coaches around the country will keep you alerted to students who may be interested in transferring. It is just another part of this complicated recruiting process.

Sometimes athletes make a decision early if their scholarship offer has a time line. I've seen several of these athletes commit and go to a university and then transfer later because they had not visited enough schools before making their decision. This happens a lot with international recruits because some do not have enough information and, in some cases, never took visits to the United States.

Dealing With Rejections

We realize we won't get every athlete we want, so we have a logical depth chart. It is important that we handle the rejection with a young prospect properly. I say, "Thank you for your interest. I wish you the best, and I'm sure I'll be seeing you in action." As disappointed as I am feeling, I rehearse it and say it so we can move on quickly. The athletes are now referring to this as the "break up call," apparently . . . too funny.

Unless you really think they might change their mind because of a clear miscommunication, I never go into the why or ask what we could have done differently. If a student-athlete wants a certain academic curriculum and a university is offering them a certain environment, or if they want warmer weather year-round, you just need to cut your losses and say, "Thank you for letting me know."

A recruit who told you no the first time around may want to transfer to your university later to be closer to home or for any number of reasons. Never burn bridges with a recruit and their club and high school coach if they rejected your first offer. They will remember how you responded to their rejection of your offer, and it may work to your benefit in the long run.

Filling the Depth Chart

Make sure your recruiting strategy is flexible, because situations can change on a monthly basis. Develop a depth chart of your current team by positions and classes, and do the same for the prospects you are recruiting. A recruiting strategy is much like putting together a giant jigsaw puzzle with pieces that are constantly changing. One of your current athletes may get injured and need another year of eligibility or perhaps medically be disqualified. Another may transfer out of your program. There are a variety of situations that cause the recruiting strategy to be adjusted. You have to be willing and able to adapt accordingly.

We typically start out identifying 12 to 18 athletes, with one-third being in state, one-third out of state, and one-third international. We look at players for multiple positions and those who are skilled enough in a variety of positions to move if needed. Identifying goalkeepers (GK), central defenders, and goal scorers is key, and every athlete should be training a specialty piece.

I certainly listen when a prospective student-athlete says she wants to play a certain position and the family asks, "Do you see her in that role?" Outside of a GK, I do not recall guaranteeing a prospect a particular position or role. That puts too much pressure on them and us to make it happen.

I'm a big believer in "serve the team" and "trust the leadership." For athletes and their families that might be a harder concept to understand today than when I first started coaching. I learned early in my coaching career that it is important to be able to speak to parents and be honest with them. I have found more and more parents today really want to be involved in the process. I will get on a call with parents and answer their questions up front.

TYPES OF SCHOLARSHIPS

There are two types of scholarships in the NCAA. There are "head count" sports, meaning a certain number of athletes receive aid up to a full scholarship. Sports like field hockey and other Olympic sports have scholarships known as "equivalencies." These sports are allowed a certain number of full scholarships (12 for field hockey), which are divided up among the whole squad. Some student-athletes may receive a full scholarship, and others on the team might just receive room and food or books or another combination, as long as the total for the team does not go over the allowed amount. Head count sports have a set number of scholarships that can be awarded to a certain number of students, and equivalency sports have a set number of scholarships that can be divided among any number of athletes.

I believe in equal opportunity and existence; consequently, every woman on the field hockey team at Maryland, for as long as I've been here, has signed a letter of intent to compete. I am hopeful that all sports eventually become head count sports or that most sports go to just tuition and fees to be more equitable.

For us to make a full scholarship offer, it must be very clear how dominant this athlete is in her arena. I have only offered a full scholarship two times in my career. If coaches want to compete for the premier athlete going up against the top schools, they have to accept that they may need to offer all six elements of a full scholarship: tuition, fees, room, board, books, and personal and miscellaneous expenses (PME). I recently offered all six elements for the first time. We have 12 full scholarships to offer. That comes to $300,000. Everybody on the squad is going to have a mix and match of that $300,000. If we pick up their tuition and fees and provide monies toward room and food to make it more affordable for their parents, they are pretty comfortable. The socioeconomic background of the field hockey player has risen. The families are typically able to personally cover what we do not.

Many athletes in field hockey are exceptional students. They can graduate early with their degree, which goes into our yearly calculations. We also have "gray shirt" athletes who graduate early from high school and start in January to get ahead academically, socially, and athletically.

In addition to having a depth chart to track your team and recruits, if you coach an equivalency sport, you will also need to have a detailed chart tracking the amount of aid everyone on the team is receiving and the projections for scholarship money available for recruits the next academic year.

RECRUITING CHALLENGES

Every coach has a list of things they find unpleasant about recruiting. For me, the biggest challenge in recruiting is the time lines put on athletes that pressure them to commit early.

Early Commitment Time Line

That early commitment expectation is a critical piece right now. Many coaches make the recruiting decision very black and white to their prospects: *This is the date we want you to commit by, and let's get this done. If it was the wrong decision, so be it; go someplace else.*

I prefer not to recruit in this manner. Pressing young athletes to make such an important decision before they have all the information only leads to more mistakes. I like to take the time to get to know them. The virtual calls on Zoom have actually been a super way to know whether you both want to arrange an official visit to campus.

Unfortunately, I don't always get an opportunity to have conversations with prospective student-athletes and their parents about the university, the area of the country, my coaching philosophy, the educational options, support systems, or many other considerations because of the recruiting time lines and pressure from other coaches to make an early decision. I may lose an athlete because I haven't been able to get to know them and their families well enough or provide them all the information they should know about our university prior to their choosing.

I wonder if we will backpedal a bit, to where prospective student-athletes engage in all their correspondence, research, and host-home visits and decide just prior to their senior year. Time will tell.

Change of Conferences

Over the past 25 years, many schools have changed conference affiliations, and that has significantly affected the recruiting by the coaches at those schools. In 2014, Maryland moved from the ACC to the Big Ten. That also required rethinking my approach to recruiting. We were in the ACC so long that I did not realize the leagues each have a culture of their own. I'm still learning, rewiring, and refiring in the powerful sports world of the Big Ten. I do enjoy competing with football in the fall season. It is very exciting, and the university towns are so vibrant and driven by *amazing* university sports.

The differences in the conferences are not so much in field hockey but in the energy, the region, and the history behind it. It's kinda cool. All of a sudden, Maryland is in the sunny South. Perfect! Bring your sunscreen.

What I didn't realize coming into the Big Ten was how special it would be to be a part of a big-time Power 5 conference that treats all sports and athletics personnel with the highest regard. I am very grateful.

Third-Party Influencers

It is important to determine early on who is around the prospective student-athlete who might have some influence on their selection of a university. While the parents will most likely serve in that role, you must also recruit the club coach and the high school coach. Because of the recruiting seasons, coaches may only be able to observe the athlete during the club season and see the club coach. Don't forget to get to know the high school coaches of the prospects. While you don't see them during club tournaments where you may be recruiting, that coach has known the athlete and their parents for a long time. The athletes may hang out in their high school coach's office during their free time at school. Taking time to get to know them may pay dividends if they are close to the athlete you are interested in recruiting.

You will want to get to know the parents of prospective student-athletes, but I am not sure that it is as important today as it once was. I've always been more comfortable working with athletes who make their own decision on what school to attend—the ones who are more independent and less risk-averse. The youngest children in families tend to have those characteristics and have done very well at Maryland.

As a coach recruiting today, you can see the anxiety in the eyes of these young athletes and their parents. With the expense of a college education hanging in the air, there is a lot on the line. They seem more fearful of making the wrong choice than enthusiastic about making the right one.

Recruiting internationally is becoming very similar to recruiting from within the nation. Parents and young athletes tend to be logical and thorough throughout the recruitment process, and coaches need to understand the commitment involved in parents sending their child to study and compete outside their country. Having an extensive international student-athlete guide is imperative for their success and comfort.

Negative Recruiting

Very early on in my coaching career, I had a challenging situation I am grateful for today. A young student-athlete made allegations that our administration and, in particular, the field hockey program, created a homophobic environment. I was accused of being homophobic and of treating lesbian athletes differently if they acted in an openly gay manner. The university retained a lawyer from the attorney general's office in Baltimore to work with me through the investigation. It seemed logical for me to personally and publicly "come out" in the legal setting in order to speak more openly about the case. After that, not every recruit or competitor let it rest. I had a competitor suggest to a very high-level recruit that my lifestyle may not be in their daughter's best interest. This was rough to hear. We were very far along in the recruitment process, and I felt confident this potential student-athlete and family would become Terps. I called the family and shared what I had heard. They simply stated their daughter was not comfortable attending Maryland. It was very clear that if you were openly gay and "out," recruiting could be affected. Encountering this attitude from a recruit's family was personally and professionally challenging. I had been brought up in an open European family that lived in Italy and the United States throughout the year, and I was encouraged from birth to be honest and comfortable in my skin. I got over this incident quickly, but having another coach use my sexual orientation to get an edge in recruiting was certainly disappointing.

AUTHENTICITY IS KEY

If I could give you one piece of advice as a coach and a recruiter, it is simply to be yourself. Be authentic. Student-athletes at Maryland do not focus on lifestyle as much as life living. They are very open, and they define the boundaries on how the team handles openly gay or lesbian teammates. I hope that in another 10 years, more coaches will feel uninhibited by their position and working environments and be OK with who they are and how they handle same-sex relationships inside their programs. Having been with my partner (now wife) for 30-plus years, it is comfortable, and past players and families are some of our best friends. Having the full support of your athletics department and community leaders makes life right. Protect your shell, but be you! Thank you, Maryland.

Be authentic in your coaching. There are a variety of coaching styles that work. Use the style that suits you and matches your personality. You can't imitate someone else and expect it to work for you. Recruits need to know who you are and understand your coaching philosophy before they can make an informed decision to attend your university and to play for you. I intend to be as authentic as possible when I meet with recruits in person.

How you present your program needs to match up with what is actually going on inside your program. Recruits having time alone with your players is key. Ask your current athletes to be honest about their experience at your university and with you as a coach. This all needs to line up if you expect long-term success in recruiting and coaching.

Zach Bland/Maryland Terrapins

TAKEAWAYS

- Identify the right level of talent to recruit to your program. Know the specifics you are looking for when you are evaluating, and know how you want to track that.

- Educate yourself on selling strategies. There are great business books available on selling yourself, your brand, and your business. Use what others have discovered works in business.

- Listen and learn the most important factors for each particular recruit, and design a strategy specific for each recruit based on what they are looking for. If you are so busy selling that you don't listen, you will miss out on any clues they are giving you. Let them know the benefits of attending your university and participating in your program, but also listen to what is important to them.

- Know the ever-changing recruiting rules and follow them. Once you or a staff member bend or break the rules for a recruit, they will own you forever.

- Take time to dig into some research on why the typical student decides on a school and understand the factors that are important in that decision, such as distance from home, academic major, and so on. Be ready to handle any objections or concerns a recruit might express. For example, if they say the school is too far from home, be ready to show them how quickly they can be home on a flight and how often they can go home. Remind them that they will be on campus for nine months of the year with holiday and semester breaks in between.

- Map out your recruiting strategy for the year, including expenses for travel to evaluate talent, official visits, home visits, and so on. Lay out a calendar for evaluation periods, official visit dates, camp mailings, and social media releases.

- Lay out the objectives for each telephone call to a prospect. Follow that plan each week.

- Determine the official visit itinerary and campus visit tours and meetings.

- Develop the strategy for offering a scholarship and a commitment time line that suits both you and the prospective student-athlete.

CHAPTER 15

DEFINING AND ADJUSTING ATHLETES' ROLES

Kelly Inouye-Perez

I was a catcher in softball, and so in that position I felt a responsibility to be a leader. As a catcher, a quarterback, or another similar role in other sports, you have a duty to be engaged with your teammates—to be aware of how they are doing and to tend to them if they need help or guidance. So, as catcher, I was attuned to all my teammates on the field and gave special attention to our high-maintenance pitchers.

Similarly, when I was an assistant coach, I was very close to all the student-athletes. It was such an easy job, really—a natural transition from what I did as a player and leader.

When I became a head coach, that's when things became very difficult for me. I had a certain perception of what a head coach should be and do, but until you are really in that role, you can't appreciate all the factors to consider and duties to fulfill. It was a real challenge. I was very lost.

When I first talked about the roles on the team, I got caught up in trying to make things fair for everyone. I overcommunicated. I went on and on about how I cared and this is what I have to do, and what you have to do. It was too much information. It was difficult, and the players were definitely struggling.

DETERMINING ROLES ON A TEAM

I've learned a lot after that rough initiation into head coaching. After that experience, I appreciated even more the significance of defining and adjusting athletes' roles to maximize the potential on a team. It is a critical part of our program, and a huge reason for the success we have experienced. It is a key ingredient for any coach to understand to be successful. Coaches must decide how they are going to get players on their teams to align.

A motivational speaker from the Army once gave me great insights on organizing and deploying personnel to make the most impactful, positive use of their collective talents. Through the conversation with this person, I learned about how the Army is structured, how systematic it operates, and the level of respect that is required to function effectively within that environment. He used one phrase that really stuck with me: "Mission first, team always." I really liked that concept. It made sense. He said, "It is the responsibility of each individual to figure out how they are going to help the mission of what you are trying to accomplish, knowing they are always going to be a part of this team."

I had it reversed in my mind. I always put team first, meaning I was focused on solving the people part of the difficult task of defining athletes' roles and trying to ensure that each player felt OK about their assignments and the expectations of them. But the "Mission first, team always" approach allowed me to determine and define more clearly what everyone's role should be, based on how they individually could contribute the most to achieving our shared goals. That vision and emphasis is essential in getting the most out of individuals to accomplish a mission.

"Mission first, team always" is also very easy for me to articulate to our team. We are on a mission to win NCAA Championships on the field, but our goal is also to win championships off the field and to be able to truly develop leaders in life.

That simple phrase allowed me to stop and think about the role of every player on the team. I was going to be able to have one-on-one conversations and be really clear about each individual role and how it would help the mission. I found myself really comfortable engaging in transparent conversations with every player on the team and for every position. It was much easier to define clear-cut roles.

I was able to make crystal clear to each player what their role would be. For example, "You may just be a base runner, but you will be fully engaged in all of the practices, and when it comes to game time, I am looking for you to be a runner for this player when it comes to these situations, late in the game or early in the game." I define the whole thing with the details so that they have a clear understanding of what I am thinking.

After that conversation comes the real test. I would say, "This is going to be your role, and I am not going to decide if you embrace this—you are." I explain their role and ask for their buy-in. It is very simple. "Either you buy in because that's how you help this mission, or you choose not to and this may not be the place for you." It is not emotional; it is straightforward and very clear. Ultimately, the athlete determines through her actions whether to accept the role for the team or hold on to her own ideas about what role she will fulfill.

When I first started clearly defining each person's role on the team, some of the athletes responded with comments like, "Well, I want . . . . What about . . . ? Why can't . . . ? Wait a minute . . . I'm not sure how that benefits me." Earlier in my coaching career, before I started making the roles very clear, I would go down that rabbit hole with them saying, "I do believe in you . . . I know you've done this. I've seen you do that. I know you haven't gotten as many reps . . . I'll get you more reps . . . . " When you are explaining, you are losing the discussion. Sure, I'd listen to them. They were asking questions and raising concerns typical of all athletes. As a former athlete, I get it. So I listened and understood where they were coming from. Then, in response I would say, "This is what I believe. This is the difficult part of my job, to really try to figure out how we are going to accomplish this team goal or mission. A big part of this is about me being clear and you understanding how important your role on this team is and how your role is valued. I respect what you can bring to the program. Your ability to own it, master it, and be prepared for it is how we are going to win a national championship." Then we flip it: "It is such an important role that without you in that role, we may not win a national championship. Your ability to buy in to this is important." I would say this to them in one-on-one meetings, and then I would announce it to the team so that everybody would understand where everybody else stood on each of the roles. But it's important to have those conversations with the individuals involved before I share the information with the team. No player should learn their role in a team meeting without them hearing it from the coach first. That shows respect for the athlete, and she will trust you more for doing that.

MAKING PLAYER ASSESSMENTS

Of course, determining and adjusting roles entails a great deal of evaluation. Much of this involves objective measures, but there is always a certain amount of subjectivity involved as well.

Metrics are big in softball right now. I ask my coaches to come up with baseline measures of what is expected so that everyone is on the same page. We can measure them, let them know what is expected and how far off they are, and create a path for everyone to be able to be "the one." There is a process, and we test them in every part of the game—offensively, defensively, pitching, fielding, hitting, throwing, and cardiovascular and sleep patterns.

Everyone's strength, power, speed, and cardio metrics are posted in the locker room. We expect to see improvement in those areas through the course of the year and the athletes' college careers. From the fall season to the spring season, there are certain expectations that everyone will improve in those areas so that when there is improvement by all the athletes, everyone gets credit for it because everyone is getting faster and stronger.

When it comes to pitching velocities, the pitchers are aware of their numbers, but it is not something that I am posting because that is irrelevant; everyone has to be the best version of themselves, but there are specific standards that we do share. When it comes to some of the basics, it is mainly things that are in their control.

The daily competition is to be a better version of yourself; it is not to be better than your teammate. We give them their metrics so that they can compete against themselves in things such as exit velocities, double plays, transition times, throwing velocities, and running speeds. Our whole philosophy is that you are a diamond in the rough, and that is why you are here. And with extreme heat and pressure, you will be a better version of yourself. The process we trust is to continue to beat yourself every day. The theme is, *Better version of yourself, better version of yourself, better version of yourself.* People don't really look at their teammates' metrics, they just want to know theirs and want to know, "Where am I? Did I improve today?"

Of course, relying on metrics alone to decide roles can get you in trouble. Other factors such as attitude and contributing to team culture are also important. Still, metrics can be applied beneficially if handled the right way.

Player Dashboards

I have developed a dashboard for every athlete. These are the basic foundations and expectations. The coaches let the athletes know where they are with the expectations. While that is part of it, there is also the dynamic that you may not be the best person for the job, but it is how this program is going to be successful.

In the fall season, we are collecting data and creating the personal dashboards. The athletes will be able to see metrics when they meet with the coaches during our player–coach meetings (PCMs) and get that information on where they stand. That includes academics. *Did I improve, did I improve, did I improve?* You are constantly working to beat your own metrics.

The dashboard is a term for a tool that I believe every coach should have for all their players. The dashboards are like something you would see in a car with a fuel gauge, speedometer, and odometer. We chart their offense, their defense, their strength and conditioning, and their mental skills. It can be as detailed as the coach needs it to be. It is a model that I've learned through some outside training. There is the physical aspect (screening). There is the mental aspect—knowing the player's EQ (emotional quotient). And there are the technical skills. A certification training session I attended also got me into what is the best equipment for that particular athlete to use.

While there is no universal dashboard, every coach at any level should know their athletes physically, technically, and personally. I have added to the dashboard mental, strategy, and conditioning skills—which are concepts from *Coach Wooden's Pyramid of Success* (2009). The biggest part of that is that I want my coaches to provide them with an expectation in every category. Every athlete wants to know what is expected and how are we going to help them get there. "This is what you expect? Where am I? How am I going to get to where I need to be?" When you bring clarity to that path, then you are going to get athletes to work hard. Any time you tell an athlete you just need to get better, or you need to be faster, you are leaving out the important details.

If an athlete wants to see where they are within the team, we can show them statistical graphs of where they rank within the team. The specific sport metrics that everyone sees and knows are easy to understand, such as batting percentage and on-base percentage. But rarely do I say she is beating you out because she is a 10th of a second faster than you—unless it is a pinch runner, because there is a speed factor. But it is also a matter of their technique in running bases and how they are reading a live situation. They can be extremely fast, but maybe they don't read well and their turns need to be tightened up. My ability to use that metric is good, but I also have to be able to discuss the other aspects of what is important. Maybe they have great instincts, but they are well below the speed needed to run the bases. "I need you to be better by this much, and when we get to the end of the season that extra step is why I'll be ready to go to you. Your instincts are great and your turns are good, but your speed needs to improve. You are going to take the rest of practice and do extra work at the speed station and skip the work on defense." If their role is speed-related, they are working out at the ladders and getting timed to be a better version of themselves in the area that I need them to be.

Those metrics come into play, and that dashboard is my expectation of them from their first year to their senior year, and there should be steady improvement. The clarity of what is expected to improve starts with my coaches. You have to let them know what you expect, where they are, and head them in the right direction with a detailed path. That is your job. You have to check in with them often to make sure they are on that right path. We all know how to do the eyeball test and say, "I know and I believe," but these players always need to know where they are at and what they can be better at. That is powerful coaching—when you provide that roadmap and you are with them.

We have athletes who enjoy coming to practice because it is not just going through reps with everybody doing the same thing. They will want to know, "What am I doing today?" We have sheets that will describe what each person is working on, and it may all be different. The system holds people accountable.

Analytics

I am using analytics for the individual growth and development of my athletes. It is information that is valuable in coaching my team, but it is not my lifeline. I think as a coach I should be responsible for being aware of and researching the various analytics to know what is out there in my sport. There are some players who have extreme tendencies that you better pay attention to and not put yourself in a position to not be prepared.

Coaches at all levels need to evaluate their players in their own way, and it doesn't have to be complicated or expensive. We just came back from a long break, and we are having our players hit off a tee. "I'm giving you 10 balls, and I want to see if you can hit the balls straight up the middle" to show me they are getting on plane and their swing path is where it needs to be. There is no need for coaching. It is a "captain obvious" drill, just seeing if you can hit a stationary ball. The goal was to hit the screen 40 feet away. If you hit the screen it counts; if you don't hit it, it doesn't count. Some of the girls got four out of 10 and six out of 10. The next time they just had to beat their previous score. Some beat it and some didn't, but instantly it was putting a little pressure on them to improve with an expectation of getting better.

Then we moved on to where you had to hit the screen three times in a row from a toss before you could go on to hitting a moving ball. A very basic drill to demonstrate whatever their metric is, and beat it. "If you can't do that, that's OK. That's just where you are right now. Let's get back to basics. Just so you know, getting your swing on plane is going to allow you to make adjustments to the fast ball, the off-speed ball, and the slow ball that are breaking in different planes. If you are not on plane and just come back with a swing, you are going to be vulnerable."

I'm starting them at ground level, and every coach should do that so they understand the basics. There is not really any coaching going on except for themselves. If they are running a speed drill, we use a stopwatch so everybody gets their number, then they try to beat their number the next time. If everybody beats their number, then maybe we drop any extra running segment we had planned. We try to use motivational things to get them to all make that extra effort. The players are setting their own basic metrics.

When it comes to all the measurements and metrics, they are really just standards for our program. I serve on a lot of committees to try to see if we can come up with standards for our sport. I have been in the room with everybody in the country, from USA staff to pros to college coaches, and we cannot align on some of the basic standards.

I just come up with my own tests. I'll put two cones 10 to 15 feet apart, based on their position in the field, and see how many times they can go back and forth in 30 seconds. I keep track of the measurements and set it up the same way every time for each player by position and remind them of their time before. I'll say, "Last time you did 12. Let's try to get 13 today." For the outfield, I have a 90-foot throw and a 120-foot throw, and it is from a rolling ball so that they have to pick it up and throw it. We do the same thing with timing the speed from glove to glove. There is always a determining factor. Somebody stretches or it is a bad toss. Whatever number they had before, they just try to beat it.

It is a matter of making up what is good for your team. You should never get hung up on what UCLA does, but focus on what your team does. What does that individual need to do, and how are you going to beat yourself? That makes it tangible and real, without worrying about what another person or team is getting for their scores. Always put yourself in a position to get better, and if you do that you are heading in the right direction.

Players' buy-in to their respective roles is necessary to prevent dissension and to optimize performance of the team as a whole. The most obvious confirming evidence that the role designations were properly made and that players are fulfilling them effectively is in the execution of your team in achieving its mission. However, we've found

UCLA Athletics

the personal dashboards and analytics to be helpful in supporting our decisions and the players' understanding of them.

Development and Improvement

If, as a player, I see that I am improving, that builds confidence. I'm feeling more productive and more prepared to be able to help my team. No, I might not be the best on the team in anything, but that isn't in my control. All I can control is the effort to improve and become a better version of myself.

That's why in sharing player assessments, we promote the positive. We don't do a lot of player comparisons or emphasize where individuals rank on the team in any given area. The measures I believe that should be focused on are the positive ones for individual team members.

Those are going to motivate each of them to be the best version of themselves, not the rankings that show them still lagging behind in several metrics as compared to their teammates.

So I will only post team figures in areas where the target is expected to be reached by each member of the team. Maybe it is something like getting a short sprint time at or under three seconds, which can mean the difference between being out or safe on the basepaths. That gets everybody fired up, and players root for each other to meet or beat the mark. So when it came down to one player who needed to lower her time and she did it, the whole team cheered for her and threw their gloves around and celebrated on the mound. It was like we had won a championship, but it was only fall ball and we were at practice.

This is exactly the kind of energy you want at practice every day. It came down to one person being a 10th of a second faster, and when the adrenaline came into play, she accomplished something she didn't know she could do. She became a better version of herself.

MAKING ROLE ADJUSTMENTS

We are fortunate to have really talented athletes with versatility. In the last six to eight years of coaching, I have asked some very talented athletes to play other positions. Those have been defining moments where I could have hurt the program and the girls could have quit, but they got to redirect their talent in a very unselfish manner. It is usually with one of my go-to players or superstars that I can redirect, and when they buy in, the team has nowhere to go but up.

For example, we had a top athlete I had recruited as a shortstop. When she started playing for UCLA she was the best hitter, but we needed her leadership behind the plate, even though she had never been a catcher before. She was having trouble buying in and adjusting to the position change. Her travel ball coach called and her mom called, both telling me that she was going to quit. Still, I stood firm and insisted, "I need you behind the plate." I said, "I actually understand your concern, but I want to get this team back to the College World Series." I absolutely needed her leadership, and that is how much I valued her leadership. I said, "This is how much I believe in you. You can be in a position to be a catcher and help our pitcher (a good friend and teammate who was an outstanding pitcher but struggling at the time), and possibly fail in a position you have never played before and still perform offensively. That's how much I believe in your confidence and ability to have an impact and get us back to the World Series." She almost quit and then she came back full circle and said, "Do you really truly believe this will work?" I said, "I absolutely believe this is the defining moment for our program." She made the switch reluctantly and we got ourselves back to the World Series.

That's a success story in adjusting a player's role, and it is her story. She's the one who made it successful. She had always just been asked to perform and be "the one," without really giving any thought to whether that role was maximizing her contribution to the team. She was helping the team more, which she found more satisfying than all her All-American trophies. And when her teammates realized this, it caused them to reflect and consider what, if any, changes they might make to be a greater contributor to the team mission. It is a big part of where we are now, because one of our star athletes bought in to a different role and embraced it.

I also have an amazing and brilliant assistant coach, Kurt Walker, who strategically can rotate players. We are not a program that locks into a starting nine and says it is what it is until someone messes up. We do just the opposite. We create a versatility in our team and get people into ball games more than any other program. The reason I do that is because I want to give people opportunities. The goal of the starting lineup is to get up by enough runs so that we can get the other players in and allow for the culture to be strong.

In game one of the College World Series in 2019, we were so far ahead of Oklahoma that I had players asking if they could pass the bat to another player. We were able to get everyone on the bench into the game. When I went to the press conference, they asked what was the biggest moment in that win. I said, "We made history, we gained confidence, and we were able to get every player in the game." That idea had not even been considered going into the World Series, but the team was thinking that. The success of the entire team allowed us to carry that on throughout the tournament and win an NCAA National Championship.

When the culture is that strong, you have a good thing going because players are so supportive of each other. That comes down to establishing and respecting what everyone's role is. Remember, we have clarity in letting players know what their role is. It may be rotating players in until I bring that conversation to you, to let you know you are going to be the one. Someone might ask, what do I need to do? I remind them you just need to know you are rotating and do the best you possibly can for this team.

COMMUNICATING ASSESSMENTS IN TEAM MEETINGS

One of the biggest learning situations I've had as a coach came after a very tough loss. Instead of composing myself and organizing my thoughts before talking to the team, I just went into the locker room and literally talked about everything we did wrong in the game. I noted the lapses, so by the final out I had a list of 28 things I had to criticize. And I read this list to the team right after the game with a very negative tone.

As I was going through the list, I looked up and saw the looks on my players' faces and thought, "OK, this is the worst meeting I could ever have." As a player, I would never want this. As an assistant, I would never want this. And I would have looked at the head coach thinking, "OK, you have lost it." But here I was, as a head coach, with this feeling of responsibility that I needed to share with them all that I knew we needed to work on.

Right after that I changed our process. I said, "No longer am I going to run the postgame meetings. I'm going to have the student-athletes

Keith Birmingham/MediaNews Group/Pasadena Star-News via Getty Images

run them." Here is what we do. I say very clearly that they have to step up and own whatever went wrong, so we always open it up, and even after practices, I'll call them together and say, "What can we be better at?" Then players own it. It is about having them communicate and own their responsibility, wherever they fell short.

I lead them through the discussion. The coaches potentially could add something, but I want it to come from the student-athletes, because as a coach, we all know you have a decision to make at the critical moment after a game about what you are going to highlight. There is that moment where there might be other things that you may cover, but you are not going to do the 28-point checklist. You are going to pick the things that you as a coach feel are relevant and need to be addressed. I have the athletes own it. There are times when I'll ask, "Is there anything else?" And I'll look right at one of the athletes, and they are all looking around, so I say again, "Is there anything else?" That's followed by nothing but quiet and awkward silence, so I say again, "Is there anything else we could be better at?" Then one of them might say, "Well I could have thrown more strikes." I'll say, "Awesome, I appreciate that." So, we teach them to own it, because that is much more beneficial than me simply calling them out.

Then we flip it, and I have them tell me some of the things we did well. That acknowledges and reinforces the things that we are doing well. And it shouldn't just be the obvious performance measure like getting key hits or making an excellent defensive play. Instead, try to help players appreciate the less tangible contributions that make a difference. For example, it might be noting that role players were prepared to come in during the sixth inning and produce a game-winning run or the bullpen catcher's good work with the pitchers. All of those little things that a team, and especially young women, notice, and they make sure everyone gets a positive shout-out. That is a feel-good moment, and we always leave every meeting on an upbeat note where all the roles are acknowledged.

Those feel-good takeaways by each player about the role they are playing is important to our culture, as is the appreciation of the effort everyone is putting in toward our success. While players who get less playing time might not seem as valuable as our star players, we make sure that they and their respective roles get called out and that they are assured the coaching staff and their teammates consider them significant in our mission.

It's best when most of the callouts come from the team members themselves. That means there is ownership by every individual and trust among all team members. If they fail to highlight contributions I considered significant, then I can add in as needed. I always have my checklist of things to make sure they are covering the key items, and if there is something they haven't mentioned, then I can address it.

COMMUNICATING ASSESSMENTS IN INDIVIDUAL PLAYER MEETINGS

When we schedule individual player meetings, I'll ask them to write down things they want to cover in a meeting. I've found it to be much better when they come prepared, so the points they want to make and the questions they want to ask will be covered and not get lost in whatever emotion is involved in the discussion. I listen completely to what it is they are addressing, and then I will ask them if I can respond. It's essential that the athlete be assured that she is being heard in the conversation. But listening did not always come easy for me as a coach. I have had to develop that skill.

In my early years as a head coach I was inclined to be a bit defensive and debate athletes when we would meet individually about an issue they had. Then I realized that just escalates everything, especially the emotions of the athlete. So now I say, "OK, go ahead and tell me what you want to talk about," and then I shut up until she is finished. I want the athlete to know she is running the meeting.

And, if it is a difficult matter she wants to discuss, I make sure to acknowledge the fortitude she is showing by meeting with me and addressing it. I might say, "Your ability to come in here and have this honest conversation with me is appreciated. I give you so much credit and respect. The fact that you are here speaks volumes, and that means that you care about this team." That sets the player at ease and gives her the green light to say what is on her mind.

I really want my athletes, as women, to be able to express themselves because it can be so hard for some of them. Young women want to be valued, they want to be heard, and they want to be appreciated. Confidence is a big part of that, so I really encourage them to communicate. I let them know that if you are not clear about something, then you are going to make up your own story. If you make up your own story, it may be wrong. It is better to be clear. We may agree to disagree, but let's be clear about everything before you make up your own story because that is a dangerous path to go down.

Sometimes I will ask the athlete to take notes during our meeting. That helps ensure that my statements and responses are accurately recorded and interpreted by the athlete and avoids a situation where the athlete has to try to recall what I said or guess what I meant. We'll review the notes together so that everything that was said is clear before she leaves the meeting.

I have a lot of individual conversations with our athletes. My assistants have asked if we might communicate too much with our players. But I would always rather communicate with the athletes one-on-one and make sure each of them has had a chance to express themselves, be heard, and be informed about matters pertaining to them that could in some way affect the team. Only after that do I feel comfortable sharing such items with the team.

That approach says to each athlete, "I care about you, I respect you, and you can trust me." And that goes a long way in developing a strong coach–athlete relationship with each player, regardless of her role.

DUTIES AND PERSONALITIES ON A TEAM

All the best teams in every sport have strong leadership among team members. But not every team member is going to be as suited as another for leadership responsibilities. Identifying and piecing together into a unit the various strengths and personalities on your roster is a big part of coaching effectively.

In the history of UCLA softball, we have never had captains. I don't determine who the captains are or put a C on your jersey. You earn that. It is your overall body of work, what you do on the field and off the field, and all those types of things that determine what people think of you. I'm not always with them, so I am not always able to know who those people are.

I do expect leadership from the player at the catcher position. Even if I have a first-year catcher, I'll tell her, "You better step up and open your mouth and not act like a first-year player."

Although we don't have captains, we do have a leadership group. Oftentimes it is comprised mostly of seniors who know and have met the expectations of our program. I don't like players getting to their senior year and not being great leaders. That means they are not great followers, and as a result the seniors turn into people you never thought they would be. Maybe they can't get the team to follow them even when they know it is their responsibility. That affects their play on the field, which affects the culture, which affects everything. Sometimes you have great seniors and sometimes you don't. And if you have a poor group of seniors who haven't bought in, feel entitled, and aren't the most talented, it will likely be a tough year.

I began looking for an approach that would ensure that we would, as a team, consistently have all our bases covered in terms of player leadership and role execution. When I read *The Tipping Point: How Little Things Can Make a Big Difference* by Malcolm Gladwell (2002), it seemed to relate to our teams and the roles we needed fulfilled. According to Gladwell, there are always the salespeople, the mavens, and the connectors that form the team's core group. I realized this during the season of our first national championship, when everybody was frustrated and stuck. So I decided to use things from that book that would create change—positive change, I hoped.

I set about identifying the salespeople, the powerful personalities on the team, the mavens, the connectors who were the glue on the team—the players who brought people together and who were always taking care of and supportive of everyone. Then the key was getting them all to fit together in the team's social dynamic, which is big. Salespeople, we need you to be up front and center. Connectors need to get buy-in from people. Reach out to your teammates and pull them together: "Come on everyone, we really need to do this if we want to win." Mavens, be clear, know what is going on, and ask questions. Just ask if you don't know.

When those three groups are functioning and working together effectively in a group dynamic, it can be very powerful. That's what happened in that championship year. We went from working against ourselves internally because of our differences to using our differences as our strength together as one unit. My adaptation of Gladwell's model designated a role for members of each class to fulfill:

- Seniors: influencers
- Juniors: leaders
- Sophomores: followers
- First-year players: learners

Instead of simply giving seniors leadership of the team, I have them lead through influence, and that is by supporting and really building up the younger Bruins. I tell them, "Seniors, it is your last lap. Enjoy it. Influence positively. Make sure everybody enjoys this ride. Take care of the younger Bruins. Bring them in and make sure that they know they matter."

The juniors are the leaders in our program. When I say leaders, I mean active leaders. When it comes to organizing events or picking uniforms or talking with the coaches or sending messages to the team—active leadership things that normally would have fallen on the seniors to do—the juniors have that responsibility in our program. Juniors are also an extension of the coaches to the rest of the squad, communicating and reinforcing what we say. I message through the junior leadership group, and they meet with me to ensure that they are meeting their responsibilities.

Sophomores have the responsibility of followership. A big part of being a leader is knowing how to be a follower. I tell them, "Next year, you will be the leaders, so if some of the things they are saying don't make sense, you better go get clarity and learn how to get buy-in because you are going to be next. I can tell you one thing. When you are a leader and you don't have people who are following, it is not a fun dynamic."

First-year players are learners. Come in and learn. Ask a lot of questions, use your resources, put yourself in a position where maybe you don't know it all but you are going to be taken care of by the senior class—which is another way in which seniors influence the team.

This model frees up seniors and allows them to benefit the program most. They still are leaders (from their experience as juniors) and have influence and can help make decisions, but it is not their responsibility. Their responsibility is to influence everyone positively.

At times, seniors will get so frustrated with their younger teammates for not understanding things or not buying in, so you need to remind them of the learning process they have had in their years in the program and to nudge their younger teammates in the right direction, but with some patience.

Recently we had two Olympians we weren't sure were going to come back to finish their eligibility. They were gone for a year, but now they have returned as seniors, so I told them to just enjoy the ride. I don't need you to come back in and be the voice right now. We are all happy they are back, but we don't need them to do the heavy lifting. Enjoy this ride, and if we need you, we will call on you. I involve them in the leadership meetings, but I don't have them be the voice. It frees them up to enjoy their last year. They can appreciate being with all their sisters instead of having to meet with the coaches all the time.

Another thing I learned from Gladwell's book is that sometimes your salespeople, the strong personalities, will get to thinking that they know all the answers, and that's when I as a coach need to step in for a course correction. And that isn't the only scenario in coaching when you have to deal with challenging individuals who have lost sight of their roles and responsibilities.

"DIFFICULT" PLAYERS

I once had a confrontation with a full scholarship athlete who wasn't just a starter—she was an All-American. Many team members had come to me saying they simply couldn't handle her anymore and didn't know what to do. She was causing problems, complaining, and not buying in, and nothing the junior leadership group did seemed to make a difference. So I told them, "OK, thanks. Now it is my turn and I will handle it."

This had come to a head when we were in the College World Series, so I arranged a meeting with the athlete and our leadership group and here's what I said. "We love you to death, but we're done with it. Either put yourself in a position to knock it off and do whatever you can to help this team, or I'm not going to put you on the bus." She looked around the room, and of course the rest of the group looked mortified. I said again, "I love you to death, but understand you are not bigger than this program, and you will not be the reason we do not win a championship this year. I will not let that happen." She looked surprised and said, "I didn't know everybody felt like this." I said, "Here is the bottom line. Buy in and create no distractions, or I will not put you on that bus. This is coming from me because we want to win. *We* want to win. We want you to be a part of this team, but understand this is how it is going to work." In that group dynamic, when she heard us say, "We want you; we need you," she was upset but heard the message and committed to changing her behavior.

In instances like those, where the leadership group feels helpless, a coach needs to step in. Some coaches have trouble confronting the team's superstar who has a strong personality and isn't responding to her teammates or those teammates are intimidated by her. But if the coach doesn't address it, the problem just festers. A coach can't ignore bad behavior that is detrimental to the team dynamic, culture, and performance. It is great when the leadership group can address such things, but it's the coach's responsibility to do so in being true to the motto: "Mission first, team always."

Since 2014, when the "Mission first, team always" motto first came about, I have let scholarship players go, suspended them with reason, disciplined them, and have even gotten to a point where I say, "This may not be the best fit for you and life is too short. You are important, and your college experience is important, but this may not be the best place for you." If they say I don't feel like I am able to be the best version of myself here, I'll remind them, "If that is what you believe, then this is not the best place for you." We are forthright and crystal clear that our program isn't about any one person. It's about all of us being the best version of ourselves in our respective roles.

COALESCING OF ROLES IN A TEAM CULTURE

A team is formed when each individual member feels a bond with, trust in, and responsibility to one another and to the group as a whole. Our team's culture results from everyone understanding and accepting that no one person is bigger than the program.

The foundation of Coach Wooden's pyramid of success is built on friendship, loyalty, and cooperation, and we believe that to be the bedrock of Bruin softball. It is about working hard and loving what we do with enthusiasm and industriousness, and doing so with a good attitude. All of those things become really important in our culture.

We talk about the value of each person on our team in our mission statement, which is "To develop powerful female leaders that are going to continue to thrive in the real world with the experiences they learn at UCLA." Nowhere does it say winning championships.

Our culture, while being team oriented, really focuses on taking care of the individual. Val (Kondos Field), our longtime gymnastics coach, introduced me to personal days. During this time and for this generation, you need personal days, not only for the athlete but to cover yourself. You better give them the time if they need it. Old-school coaching doesn't work anymore. You can't just tell them to suck it up and say if it is not bleeding or cut off, then get back out there. Personal days allow them to be the best version of themselves.

The softball complex should be our players' version of Disneyland. We want them to feel that this is the place to be—that it is not just one more thing on their daily list that they have to do. I want you to come onto the field and give your all and love what you do. It is hard, but you love it. If you do not, then you are not in the right place mentally, because this is fun. The challenge is fun when you do it together.

The main thing is that no one is bigger than the program. Everyone is held accountable to the same standards, and we represent something that is bigger than ourselves. Our alumnae are a big part of who we are, so they represent leaving the program in a better place. All of those things come with history and tradition, but our program is run through storytelling and how they are able to take care of each other and what people have done. The alumnae come back and share. It is a culture of what it takes to win, knowing we do have superstars and there are selfish moments, but if you really want to win, then you are going to do what is best for this program and trust that your coaches are going to take care of you along the way. If you do that, you will get what you want. But if you don't, you'll know exactly why you didn't win.

The key is the people and how you get to empower them to feel like they can make a difference, a contribution, for this team and this program, no matter their role. If you can build a culture that allows them to appreciate the little things, then you realize when you get to the end that there is no need to do more or be more—it is fun.

TAKEAWAYS

- Have a team mission or theme to guide your coaching decisions, such as "Mission first, team always."
- Use metrics to develop individual player dashboards for your sport to measure progress.
- Be clear in individual meetings on expectations and the player's role on the team.
- Value each athlete in your program, and make sure to listen to them when they want to talk to you. Have them come prepared with notes and leave with notes of what was discussed.
- Determine the best leadership method to be used within your team.
- Empower the athletes to be the best version of themselves every day.

CHAPTER 16

LEADING EFFECTIVELY AND COACHING PEOPLE UP

Jen Welter

The first time I was offered a coaching position with an NFL football team, I turned it down. Women don't coach football, so I thought "I can't do that." There had never been a woman coaching in the NFL, so I didn't consider it as an option.

Thankfully, Wendell Davis, a former Dallas Cowboy, would not let me turn down the opportunity. He literally said, "Not a lot of NFL coaches are going to give you this opportunity, and you are going to take this job." He said, "I can teach you how to coach football, but it is very different watching how those guys listen to you and see how they love you. That is truly special."

In pursuing my master's degree in sports psychology, one of my primary areas of focus was coach–athlete communication. I studied that area because in working with coaches on their communication skills—particularly football coaches—it was clearly an area that needed attention.

The leadership style of many football coaches tends to be autocratic, which doesn't allow for much two-way interaction between coach and athlete. Having worked with and learned from women coaches in other sports, it was clear that they looked at leadership a little differently, allowing, if not actively seeking, more exchanges with and input from athletes. That's closer to the leadership style and manner of communication that I will be advocating in this chapter.

LEADING WITH A VISION

The first thing that is so important for all coaches, but particularly head coaches, is to know where you are leading the group. Is there a common goal, a common vision, and buy-in from our athletes? Have we sought and listened to input from the coaching staff and the players? Have we all reached a consensus on what we want? When we are all on the same page, we can create a shared vision of who we want to be and how we want to approach it.

Not all teams that want to win a championship get there the same way. What is our team identity? As a team, we will determine the vision, what we want to achieve, and who we want to be on our journey. And the big key is, how do we get there collectively? Is the team identity outdated?

Oftentimes, there might be an old team trying to fit into a new model, and then there is friction. Creating a team identity and getting team buy-in are extremely important. Do we have the right personnel for the identity and image we want to project? If we start with those things and we have the buy-in from the players, then all the things that we do should reinforce that identity, whether it is the slogan that we use as a team or the practice focus. Our identity doesn't just start and stop with how we play on the field. It is who we want to be within our team and then to the world at large.

Strong leadership starts with the vision, and it has to belong to the team, not just be the coaches' idea. You have to create an "ours" mentality because then everybody is involved and has a little bit of ownership. We need to know each person fits into that equation. Whether as a position coach or as a player, everyone must see how important we all are to the mission.

One of the first things I think of when I see friction on a team or on a staff is what I lovingly call "misses in communication." Miscommunication implies that somebody said something wrong. But "misses in communication" means we are not on the same page. Is what I'm saying the same as what you are hearing, and are we all aligned? Start with a conversation about that alignment within your program.

In football, we have a head coach, an offensive coordinator, a defensive coordinator, and a special-teams coach. We want to get into our team identity and decide where we are going to hang our hat. What are we going to be known for, and what is the beat of the drum for this team? We have to make sure we all agree with what we have got to work with. We can't say we are going to live and die with our offense when we don't know what the quarterback is capable of doing. We have to get an honest assessment of our strengths and the things we need to work on because that is going to be our time allocation for practice. We are going to emphasize and highlight the things we want to be known for, but at the same time we are pushing to strengthen those areas that may be weaker. Once coaches know what they've got to work with, they need to decide how they are going to use what they have.

Every coaching staff has delegated duties. In football, we typically break up assignments into offense, defense, and special teams. So the head coach might have coaches with three different personalities over-seeing those areas, and needs to ensure each is coordinated in a balanced and respectful manner. The coaching staff, in turn, must decide how we get all the players involved, invested, and feeling appreciated, while also helping them to realize what, as a group, will be the team's true and most successful identity.

DEVELOPING A CULTURE

You must give players a voice in shaping the identity and setting the tone. With the most powerful teams I have ever been on, it was obvious the leadership was not from the top down. There was a way that the players set the expectations so that everyone wanted to be a part of our team. That came from the total team buy-in and not just one person. We all agreed that everybody has a role in leading this team. We all agreed that we all have our own special sauce within that process.

So we will give players more of a say on matters having to do with how we work together and present ourselves as a team. For example, we let players decide how they want to take the field and also to have input on warm-ups, which can set the tone and mood for a game. Do we want to have on our practice shirts? What is our team slogan? Players will be more into adopting the identity outlined by the staff if they get to make those types of decisions. We have agreed that this is what we are going to do to win games, and the players get more input on the style in which we do so.

Letting the players decide on things that may be a little less important to the staff can make a big difference in developing the team's culture. In simple terms, you might say that coaches determine the identity and strategies, but the players own the culture.

The players, as a unit, can say this is where the captains really should have a voice. We always want to be in touch with what is going on with team culture and the emotional and mental state of players. Because if you lose touch with that, then it is really hard to get them to buy in to an offensive play, defensive play, or other important ideas coming from the coaching staff.

The flair you use to present information is important. We were known for our defense, and we called it "team shutdown." If they don't score, they can't win. Whatever strategy you are using, the why is really important, especially to the younger athletes today. You have to bring them into the why and not just tell them to believe a theme that has been on the locker room walls for 87 years that they may or may not be able to relate to. Your game plan is part of it, and getting them to buy in by giving them a voice is a big part of it. The voice might be in the execution in the team culture and how that is translated. You want to make sure we are on the same page.

Sometimes, the game plan will adapt because of certain things you have seen in the team culture. Maybe you have some really "swaggy" receivers who thrive on big plays, and the rest of the team gravitates to it. There were some plays the old coach wouldn't have done, but a new trick play gives them life and the coach acknowledges that. We want there to be an exchange, and the buy-in has to be that communication is open both ways. We have roster changes and injuries and everything can change. If your team identity is centered around one player, you can be in trouble.

There has to be room to grow together, which means that communication is so important. Sometimes the players will say, "Hey coach, trust us. We've got this." I've seen great coaches have meetings with players asking for any suggestions they might have for the coaching staff. It may be one play in the playbook, but the fact that it came from the trenches means it has a good chance of being successful. That type of psychological input can be a big part of their success.

Good leadership entails listening to people. I've had the opportunity to work with great head coaches who appreciated that I had a doctorate in sports psychology, but they especially liked when they heard their players say, "Jen really talks to us." I didn't realize that was so rare or so hard for some coaches.

One time, a captain was not performing well. He had lost the locker room, so I asked the coach if he had ever talked with the player about how to be an effective captain. He said, "No, he just needs to be a captain." I said, "Do you know how much pressure he puts on himself to be a captain because he is not that type of leader naturally?" The player would ask me if he was making the right decisions with the team. It was as if it was paralysis by analysis, because you put a C on his chest. I said, "Try making him not a captain and see how he plays."

BUILDING A TEAM

Team building and team culture mean bringing in the individuals as a part of what this team looks like, so we know and appreciate them. Knowing more about each other builds relationships that, within a team, start to develop friendship and love and make me want to play for you more. What we are trying to do when we talk about team building is develop relationship tentacles by getting to know each other beyond the field, so we can appreciate, understand, and grow closer. When I care about my teammate, I will do a whole lot more than when I don't know someone or care about them.

Look at all-star teams. They have lots of talent but little cohesion. They're just a group of athletes assembled for a week at most with few shared experiences, objectives, or allegiances. Contrast that to a team that creates an identity over a period of time and speaks to each individual and is united in a desire to meet the standards to which they have all agreed. That is a real team with a culture that people take notice of and appreciate.

So, as a coach, you always need to be thinking how you can further cultivate that dedication—that commitment to a common purpose. How do you tap into the individuals within your team, give them a voice, help them share their identities, and create a team identity that honors the people who are a part of the team and that they are proud of? Something as simple as statements on practice shirts can remind and further strengthen the type of bond that embodies a successful team.

Life experiences build relationships and help us fortify ourselves and make us what we want to be and who we want to be and what we want our team to be. Team-building activities that really reveal the true part of players' selves, as opposed to something like bowling, are much more effective. You will get a lot more buy-in and authenticity if they know that you appreciate that being an athlete is more than just throwing a football. Have that conversation with your athletes. Ask them how they plan to use their athletic experiences in society, in their future careers,

Christian Petersen/Getty Images

in their own homes with their own families. This is harder to do with younger athletes, so you might have to guide them more.

The point is, when you convey to each of your players that you value them not only as athletes but as people, it shows that you sincerely care for and trust them as individuals. These types of conversations with your athletes will strengthen the team bond further and help you to relate to your athletes on a whole different level. Now the team is united not just on the field but off the field as well. It creates a deeper team culture and atmosphere that is much more likely to be sustained and be successful. And every time you make an effort to confide in them, letting them know you heard them and appreciate them, you are further strengthening the bonds between you and each of them. So, even though the athletes own the team culture, it is never truly established until and unless the coaching staff contributes and nurtures it in this way.

CHOOSING CAPTAINS

Some sports have a tradition of assigning players in certain positions to be captains. In football, it's often the quarterback. In basketball, it's typically the point guard. In baseball, it's usually the catcher. The rationale for this seems to be that because they are in a position to call plays and the ball is in their hands most every possession or pitch, they have the most control of things on the field or court.

The Belichick Way

I have had the opportunity to work under longtime New England Patriots Coach Bill Belichick, who as a leader is very clear about who he is and what he wants. There is the Patriots' way, and when you join that organization, you know you must buy in to the system, which puts the team first. The system does not abide prima donnas; no one is above the team. Yet, Coach Belichick will let the players add their own personal flair if it benefits the team.

It is a special environment where head coaches can ensure all players respect and adhere to the philosophy and strategy they are using, and everyone fits within the team identity. That is a situation all coaches want but seldom are able to achieve. Because he doesn't have to worry about the typical team dysfunctions that occur, Coach Belichick is able to get the most out of each player in the system, even players who had not enjoyed much success on other teams or who were not highly regarded as draft candidates. Also, because of the shared focus and diligence to detail among the coaching staff and team, Coach Belichick can optimize the use of the talent available to him in all situations. He has different game plans from the first half to the second half, and specific sets and plays or schemes for seemingly every time, down, and distance scenario. He is the ultimate chess master, but getting the excellent execution from his teams that he has for many years all starts with everyone on the team committing to the system and fulfilling the roles and tasks assigned to them each and every workout, practice, and game.

This orthodoxy in captain selection has shifted somewhat in recent years. I've seen teams respond well to rotating captains, but you don't want to throw someone into that role who is liable to make a mistake and harm the team.

It is a blessing to a coach when one of the better athletes on the team is also clearly viewed as a leader by other team members. What you don't want is for the choice of captains to become a political thing that divides the team. I recommend having those conversations early with the team and making a joint decision. Then, if somebody pushes back when the captain or captains are announced, you can say, "We talked about this. What has changed? We set that standard. Do we not agree with that, or what happened that shifted that focus?"

If you set a standard up front that is known by every member of the team and is applied consistently for everyone, then whatever situation arises can be dealt with according to whether the captain selected is meeting those standards or not. This also prevents any appearance of favoritism or special treatment by the coaching staff. The standards are set across the board and have been agreed to with team buy-in, so any decision consistent with them cannot be viewed as personal, preferential, or punitive.

USING A FEEDBACK LOOP SYSTEM

I came up with this system when I was consulting with various teams because I saw this gap in communication so often. I would sit down with a player and say, "Tell me what makes somebody great at your position." We would each list at least five things.

I would say, "I agree with your five, but I would also add communication." "Oh yeah, you're right, and maybe hustle." Then we agree on a list of seven things, or it may be a longer list. Then I would tell them, "I want you to rate yourself on a scale of 1 to 10 on those seven things. Take me through those, and let's see where you think you are." We would do this throughout the year, so we were always on the same page from a feedback perspective. You can increase the list, but it is important to always do the list together because it creates buy-in and gives the players a voice.

I've had athletes who just wanted me to operationalize it and give them the list, but then they didn't have a voice. It should not be just my list. It is our list and agreement on the things we need to do. It is also the verbiage of how you and the athlete are going to hear it. We come up with the list and then we both go through and rate the athlete on each item on the list on a scale of 1 to 10.

Everyone will have a bias on how they see themselves. When we go over the list, we see the differences. When I look at an athlete's self-rating, I know the lower the score the athlete has, the lower their confidence is in those areas. The things they feel best about are the ones where they rank themselves higher. Then we look at the differences and discuss what we should spend our time on improving. I get to see where the player is not feeling great, and then as a coach, I get to walk you from there to where I'm going to focus my attention on you. We can create an emphasis on the things the athlete needs to get better at and develop specifics on how we are going to help them get better.

Because you make it a feedback loop, we can always revisit it. Whatever was not great before, we should see it get better. This gives us a way to always check in with each other, and the athlete gets to see where I have them rated. If they want to be a starter, you can talk with them about the skills and performance of the player starting in front of them, and they need to match or exceed that player's contribution. Let them know that to earn the starting position, here are the things they need to improve. You make it concrete and tangible so that you're always on the same page.

The feedback loop is an important coaching concept because it clears up the feedback channel. It becomes something that makes us a team. Position coaches need to do this with each of their players, and then the head coach can also weigh in. Then you have an objective way to check in with your staff as well. This is a tangible way to always look at progress, and athletes need reminders. Athletes can say, "Remember when you used to rank me as five in this area and now my ranking is a nine." I'll remind them, "That is great progress. I am so proud of you." That could have been a confidence deficit for the athlete, yet as a coach you were able to build that up by catching them doing that skill well. They might be better than they think they are and just need to hear it from you. If they are rating themselves low on something, you know that it might be their confidence that is low and something you don't see as a weakness, but you can be sensitive to it in coaching that athlete. The feedback loop also takes care of that "miss in communication."

AVOIDING DISCONNECTIONS

This is a list of communication lapses that I have seen in coaching. See if you are doing any of these things:

- Trying to emulate other coaches. When a coach tries to be something she is not, players sense the inauthenticity in a heartbeat.

  A lot of female coaches try to model a male coach they have either played under or somehow came to admire. I didn't have any women coaches to observe in the NFL, but I certainly would not have succeeded if I attempted to be like any of the male coaches in the league. It is important to find your voice and your style and not try to model after someone else that you can't possibly be.

– Failing to fully engage and inform players. Too many times there is a disconnect between the coaching staff and athletes. One group is communicating among itself, and the other group is doing the same among itself, but the separation of the two is the problem. As you've read, I developed a feedback loop system for coaches to use with their athletes to avoid this situation.

When I was with the Arizona Cardinals, I used to listen to the staff and how they would evaluate players during film. I would share that information with the players, and they were totally surprised because no one had ever given them that feedback before. Clearly, the feedback loop was closed. And that is too often the case with most teams. So make sure you provide an environment that encourages reciprocal interaction, not a one-way conversation.

– Attacking the person rather than the problem. All athletes make stupid plays, but we can correct a bad play. However, in reacting to errors made by athletes, coaches too often let emotions get the best of them, and their actions or words are interpreted as personal by the athlete. She perceives that you are being mean to her and maybe even intentionally embarrassed her in front of her teammates and anyone else who observed the incident.

Once that trust is gone between a player and coach, it's hard to reestablish. That is why it so important from the outset for a coach to develop a personal relationship with each athlete. That means making it clear to every one of them that, yes, you are players, but first and foremost you are people I care about and from whom I want to gain your trust. That is essential.

If you see something off with a player, say, "You're not yourself today. Is everything OK?" Or say, "It's not like you to miss a play like that. Is there something on your mind?" And if she says, "Yes, can I talk to you after practice?" be sure to be available for that conversation. If you at least listen to them, they'll see that you care and will likely come back the next practice or game feeling better and playing sharper. They were reassured you value them as individuals, as humans, not just as an athlete. So they are going to be more understanding if you say or do something that it is not perfect, because they will know that it was perfectly intended.

– Calling out a player or coach in a group setting. This kind of action is a form of bullying and is not appealing or advisable in any circumstance. All it does is pit you against whomever you are singling out, who is certain to be offended and resentful that you did so before an audience, even if that individual had done something that warranted corrective action.

Instead, take that coach or player aside as soon as a private meeting is possible and have a strong one-on-one conversation. Allow the other to share her story on the matter as well. However things work out, it is necessary to clear the air, reach a mutual understanding on how to proceed, and then move on. Don't just let things continue to build or else the emotions involved are almost certain to erupt into a scene that is easily avoidable.

COACHING MEN VERSUS COACHING WOMEN

The difference in coaching each gender is the why. Women need to hear the why. A lot of times they want to understand how something connects while men have been more trained to just do it without questions. The why helps men, too, but women without the why will always push back.

I have found intentional communication is important with men as well. Male athletes are not used to that, but they respond positively to it. It made the national news that I was writing handwritten notes to players and leaving them in their lockers. It is not rocket science that you just care about somebody. Nancy Lieberman-Cline is a friend of

Christian Petersen/Getty Images

mine and said, "I just want you to know I write notes to the players, too." Some of the men said they had never had a coach show that they cared so much in their entire career.

Just being a good human being is important with both genders, but it is probably talked about more when coaching female athletes. Certain approaches might be expected when coaching men, but they liked a different caring approach when they got that from me. They still keep in touch with me and say, "You had more of an impact on me as a person than any other coach," and that is what it is all about in the long run. That is an advantage that female coaches have with female athletes. Female coaches are usually more intentional about that aspect, and it has been more accepted, but I don't think it is unique to female athletes. There have just not been as many women coaching men—yet.

We look to differences so much and assume that it is a competition, with one gender being a better coach than another. But the beauty of having a staff that is hopefully diverse in many ways is the athletes will relate to different coaches with respect to certain aspects. Guys talk to me about things they wouldn't have talked to a male coach about or feel like they could because the communication is more natural. There are also certain things they may not feel comfortable talking to me about, but the goal is to create a team environment where there is always a place for them to be heard. Athletes should have access to both genders because there is a distinct advantage to having a combination. We are better together.

TAKEAWAYS

- Having a clear vision of what success means in your program, and conveying it in a manner that makes others want to jump on board, is a prerequisite in leadership as a coach.

- Leading today's athletes means communicating that you value them and their input while seeking their buy-in and support of the direction you give them.

- Standards, agreed on by all your athletes and reinforced by team captains, are essential for effective leadership and the development of individual and self-responsibility within your program.

- Continually seeking your athletes' input through some type of feedback system will strengthen your connection to them and help you make more mindful decisions.

- Do a self-check of your interactions with the coaching staff and team to avoid common communication errors that can damage relationships and prevent you from excelling in your coaching role.

CHAPTER 17

TAKING AN ATHLETE-CENTERED APPROACH

Nancy Stevens

Ever since I entered coaching, I have sought to shatter the myth of the all-knowing, omnipotent head coach. When I was growing up and watching coaches, they were always presented as being invincible, and I was always very uncomfortable with that perception. Even today, when you turn on the television to a college basketball or football game, the cameras and commentary seem to be focused on the head coaches on the sidelines more than the action on the court or field.

So, the notion that the head coach is the main person and the focal point of a sports program and team is pretty much ingrained in our thinking. And though you see many organizations, including those in sports, adhere to that model, I was never comfortable with leading or managing my program in that way.

INVERTING THE PYRAMID

That led to my decision to invert the pyramid. Rather than putting myself at the top of our organizational chart, followed by my coaching staff, and then the seniors, juniors, sophomores, and lastly, the first-year student-athletes underneath, I place the athletes at the top with the coaching staff below the team. Imagine that—the head coach is at the bottom of the inverted pyramid!

It is a very different perspective and approach than the head coach making all the decisions, being the primary focus and the one always being interviewed. When I consider the role of the head coach, I think back to one of my favorite poets, Margaret Atwood, who wrote about being as unnoticed and necessary as the air.

That's how I have been leading and coaching my teams for 43 years.

After we inverted the pyramid structure within our field hockey program and empowered our players and staff, we changed the way we gather as a team into a circle formation. Those of you who have read the excellent book *Sacred Hoops* (1995), by former 11-time NBA champion coach Phil Jackson, might recall that he started and ended each practice with the players in a circle to symbolize forming a sacred hoop. So, all of our team meetings are conducted in a circle in our team room. Even when we are on the road, we'll set up the chairs in a circle in a hotel room. This may sound like a small thing, but what that change in the shape of the geometry and being in a circle demonstrates is that no one is dominant. Every person in the circle has an equal opportunity to make a contribution. That style of coaching dovetails well in working with this generation of student-athletes.

We try to make the experience athlete-centered rather than coach-centered. The recent research has shown that the athletes entering high school and college now have shorter attention spans. They are using almost a full 10 hours a day of screen and computer time. A professor at the University of Connecticut, Dr. Amy Gorin, has done a lot of research in this area and has made a few presentations to our coaches on this topic. It is important to know this valuable information because we need to adapt our coaching style to the people we are working with.

We used to have hour-long film sessions with our team. Because of the athletes' short attention spans, we can't do that anymore. We shortened our film review sessions to a half hour or less. That was a dramatic change. We reduced those film sessions by 50 percent and still had to fit in everything that is important to prepare the team for competition. You have to keep your explanations shorter. As a coach, you have to figure this out or you are not going to be successful with the athletes today.

Experienced coaches have found it is a challenge to coach athletes in today's world, and they are having to change the way they coach if they want to have a long career. Coaches need to examine how they should adapt to be a better coach for athletes at this time and realize what they have done in the past is not going to work with this newest generation.

Another method I use in coaching is to "catch them being good." Athletes have grown up being told how special they are by their parents, grandparents, and other significant people. You can continue to coach the way you have always coached thinking you need to criticize a player because they are not doing it your way or the best way, but it is just not going to work. You need to "catch them being good" and reinforce that behavior instead of criticizing them. We have found that repeated criticism crushes some players, so what is the gain from that type of coaching?

I recall Pia Sundhage, former coach of the U.S. National Soccer team for the Olympics and World Cup, said she works hard to make seven

UConn Athletics

positive comments for every criticism. That sounds like a good coaching tactic to me.

We often see men's basketball coaches screaming at their players, and I think to myself, do we see that type of behavior in any other profession? Would a CEO of an automobile dealership yell at the sales associate if the associate didn't reach a goal in sales for a quarter? Would a teacher yell at students in a classroom if the students didn't do well on a standardized test? Thankfully, there are more and more coaches that are changing and adjusting their coaching behavior, such as Pete Carroll, head football coach for the Seattle Seahawks. For example, he has his team doing yoga and is leading his team using a more player-centric style and approach.

SYMBOLS AND STORYTELLING OR NARRATIVES

I have used symbols and storytelling with my team for years. There was a terrific book published in 2016 by Nancy Duarte and Patti Sanchez titled *Illuminate: Ignite Change Through Speeches, Stories, Ceremonies and Symbols.* The book was a revelation for me, even though I had been doing this for years. It talks about the power of stories and symbols.

One of the stories we tell the team, mainly addressing it to the senior class, is about a housebuilder. The housebuilder was a longtime employee of a company building houses. Before he retired, the owner of the company came to him and said he wanted him to build one last home. The longtime employee was already thinking he was out the door, but he agreed to do one more job. He wasn't really mentally into it and haphazardly put the house together without using the best quality materials. At the end of the building process, the owner of the company came to look at the home and he handed his longtime employee the key to the house and said, "You've worked here for 30 years. I want you to have this house."

We convey that story to our team because we want them to understand it is their team. They are not running sprints for me, or lifting weights for me, but for their team and teammates. After telling them this story, we took a key and placed the key in the front of the team room so when they enter and leave, they were reminded daily that they are building this season for themselves. The effort we put into training every day is for us. Having the key displayed on the wall in our team room was a symbol to say that you are building your house and should take ownership.

Greg Schiano, head football coach at Rutgers University, uses an axe as a symbol in their training facility to remind the players to "keep chopping" every day and be focused on the daily process. P.J. Fleck, head football coach at the University of Minnesota, uses the theme "row the boat" as their team symbol or theme. The use of symbols is very powerful in motivating people in this young age group that we are coaching.

One of the things that has informed my coaching career is the writing of Joseph Campbell, who was a professor of literature at Sarah Lawrence College. His book *The Power of Myth* (1991) is about a hero's journey, which is what we have in athletics with overcoming adversity and the power of teamwork. As coaches, we are always combining symbols with narrative. Most teams will play a schedule of 25 games against schools in your conference, and some outside competition, before you get into the national or state championship. Is the narrative every week just, "Go out and beat the other team?"

Malcolm Gladwell's book *David and Goliath: Underdogs, Misfits, and the Art of Battling Giants* (2013) speaks eloquently about the power of narrative. Each year, the group of athletes on our team is different from the year before. At the beginning of each season, we find symbols that might speak to that particular team and also find a narrative that they will embrace. The narrative is overarching. Because you are not playing your top rival every game, maybe you don't need a narrative or symbol to get your team ready to play every game. I may need a narrative for maybe 10 or 12 games on our schedule, and for each team it is going to be a bit different. I have found the use of symbolism and narrative can be very impactful and works across all organizations.

Airbnb is a multibillion-dollar company now, but it started as two guys living in an apartment who needed money to attend a conference. They started renting three air mattresses and serving breakfast to people who stayed overnight. Now, whenever they have their annual meetings, they display their symbol, a mattress, which keeps them grounded on where they started.

At Nike, they have a company storyteller called an "EKIN," which is Nike spelled backward. The EKIN meets with all the new employees at the company and tells them the history of the company, which started with Bill Bowerman, an Oregon track coach, making the soles of a running shoe with rubber he put in a waffle iron. The new employees are asked if they would like the Nike swoosh as a tattoo somewhere on their body. That is a perfect example of symbolism and storytelling.

The way in which we develop our team culture each season is, in many ways, relatable to this passage from the book *Illuminate*, mentioned previously: "Illuminating a venture is leading travelers through a story. Many times it's a tale of intrigue, full of suspense, challenges, friendships, and sometimes a pinch of horror. When your venture is done, mine the speeches, stories, ceremonies, and symbols, for they are treasures for which you paid a great price, and they can hold great meaning" (Duarte and Sanchez 2016, p. 271).

Each year we get a different group of people. Maybe we have added nine first-year players and have lost six seniors. Now we have to create new symbols and narratives to take them through their journey and bring them closer and closer together. The book refers to stories and symbols as "collective effervescence," where "people's individual identities subside and they feel part of something larger than themselves" (Duarte and Sanchez 2016, p. 18). It really does speak to the team experience.

An example of this with our program happened one year during the preseason. When your team comes in for preseason, the anxiety level is through the roof because they are going to be tested. This is especially true for an aerobic sport such as field hockey, because we do fitness testing on the track, speed testing, and strength testing. I thought there has to be a way to relieve all of their anxiety because it is so counterproductive. In the team room, I placed a placard on the mirror—because as you already know, they are always in front of the mirror. The players take time to fix their hair before practice and before games. The sign on the mirror had three words: *You are enough.* I thought it would be a powerful message for them because in their minds, they are not enough. Especially coming in to the preseason they are thinking: Did I do enough work? Did I run enough? Did I lift enough? This anxiety seems to be toxic, so this was the message I wanted to give them as their coach. It was an unconditional embrace of *you are enough*. We talked about the message and let them know they didn't need to have anxiety about the preseason testing; this simply was a starting point for the season. We know we are going to get better incrementally every day. We used this narrative during the season, and the symbol was the sign with those three words. We left the sign up and moved on throughout our season.

Fortunately, we ended up in the NCAA National Championship game against the University of Maryland. All of the pressure was on us because we were 22-0 and ranked number one in the country. As a head coach, you know the locker room or team meeting room before a game can be filled with anxiety when you are playing for any kind of championship. I walked into the locker room and went up to the whiteboard and wrote three words: You Are Enough. When I turned around to look at the team, I could see the anxiety level on the team diminish and the belief in themselves rise up. I knew immediately the use of that symbol was going to work for our team that day. It was risky because it was an important moment in my coaching career and for the players' careers as well, so I wanted to get it right. I did tell them that everything that could have been said has already been said. I didn't need to tell them anything else except go out and be who you are.

As a coach, I have learned that less is more. When I first started coaching, during the pregame talk, I would have 20 different points that I wanted to make before we competed. I thought I had to cover everything. It is overwhelming for the athletes, and it doesn't engender a sense of trust because they already know those 20 things. I finally

understood that less is more and that I needed to show I trusted them. So, the night before the championship game, we had film sessions and simply reaffirmed with our players what we would need to do to win the national championship. They knew the set pieces we needed to run, and the individual position groups knew what they needed to do from our earlier meetings. When it came to the championship game, we wanted to have them play free.

I've subscribed to this approach for a long time as a field hockey coach, since taking Northwestern University to three Final Fours and then the University of Connecticut to 10 Final Fours. I have always been driven as a person, and like most coaches, I have a tendency to overdo it when it comes to preparation, details, and instruction. But the more I learned to let go, the better it was for me and our team.

By the way, in that national championship game versus Maryland, our players performed brilliantly. They had come full circle from the first preseason practice to the final game of the year. It was a powerful example of how trusting and letting go as a coach can benefit your players.

EMPOWERING PLAYERS

We have to learn to be more comfortable with giving up the reins and allowing players to take control of certain things. We let our players run some of our practices to engender trust. We have a leadership council with representatives from each class. Sometimes we have had the players design set pieces, which are our offensive plays, and they have come up with some great ideas. We have used those plays in our games, and when they score a goal, it is so powerful for the team.

This reminds me of a moment in the 2018 Super Bowl, which the Philadelphia Eagles won. The Eagles were driving down the field and near the end zone when the quarterback, Nick Foles, approached his head coach, Doug Pederson, and suggested they run a trick play on the fourth down inside the 10-yard line. It was a play called the "Philly-Philly" that they had practiced all season. The coach gave it quick approval, and they ran the play that had another player throwing a pass to the quarterback in the end zone. It worked perfectly, and they scored a touchdown. There is now a statue outside Lincoln Financial Field called the Philly Special, showing the quarterback and coach in that special moment, when a play at a crucial point in the biggest game of the season was decided by a player. They won the Super Bowl because the coach stepped aside and let a player call a play in the most important game of both of their careers.

Sometimes an image like a photo of water-skiers making a pyramid will stimulate a conversation with our team. We might ask, "What would you rather be during this season or during this game? Do you want to be remembered in the game by your three best players holding you up, or do you want to be the boat?" Think about whether you want to be the one who is driving the team and pulling some of your teammates with you, or just being comfortable having our best players pull us through the season. This is a very effective thought exercise that encourages interaction and accountability in a team.

I mentioned earlier Dr. Amy Gorin, professor at the University of Connecticut, who conducts research on various generations and has found that current students are very hesitant to make their own decisions. Everything is "crowdsourced," meaning they obtain input for a particular task or project by enlisting the services of a large number

Randy Faris/The Image Bank/Getty Images

of people via the Internet. An informing moment for me was a TED Talk (Zoref 2012). The speaker brought a live ox out on the stage and asked the crowd to tell him how much it weighed. The people in the audience laughed and thought that was impossible, but they did it and actually got the weight exactly right.

There are two ways to look at this type of leadership. It is as an abdication of responsibilities as the head coach or, if you are crowdsourcing decisions, you can say the collective knowledge of this group is going to be greater than what I necessarily know. This is what young people are used to doing. There is even a website called "decider.com" and everything is crowdsourced. People go there for decisions on what movies or television shows they should be watching.

We use this type of shared decision making with our team. It may be a small thing, but when we are taking a team trip, as the head coach I used to decide everything, even what we were wearing on our flight. I finally thought, why am I making all these decisions? Finally, I said to the captains, "You crowdsource and find out what the team wants to wear." They can use their cell phones and get in touch with each other quickly and ask, "What are we wearing on our team trip? What is our entertainment on the trip? Where are we eating?" It was a freeing experience for me, except that I had to trust my team that they wouldn't come back saying we want to wear our ripped jeans and our cutoff T-shirts. You are giving up control, and that is a small thing, but it does positively shape your team culture. We'll even crowdsource when to have team meetings, which may not always be when the coaching staff wants to have the team meeting.

We work hard to give our team a lot of decision-making power. We have to be ready to adapt as the generations change. We need to be reminded that research shows social media is the biggest factor in our athletes' lives, so you have to be aware of that and make it a positive for your team and the way you operate.

APPRECIATING THE ROLE OF PARENTS

Student-athletes are constantly attached to their parents with their cell phones. When most of us were in college, we called home maybe every two weeks or once a month. That might have been because when I lived in a residence hall, we only had one landline phone for 30 girls who lived on that floor. Now of course athletes can immediately let their parents know following practice that, "Nancy looked at me sideways today."

As coaches, we need to understand how much money parents have invested in their athletes' careers. When we were growing up, athletes played a sport in high school, which didn't have a cost; they went to one summer camp, and off they went to college. Now, parents are spending thousands and thousands of dollars for travel teams, club dues, and numerous summer camps. As coaches, we have to understand the students' constant attachment to parents through texting or any social media, and the investment parents have in their daughters, emotionally and financially. We have to honor that investment the best way we can.

In our program, we worked hard to keep in touch with the parents by having tailgates after our games, so the coaches would spend time with each parent. You are managing their expectations for their daughter's performance and role on the team, and you are managing their expectations for the team's performance. So, it was important to take time to visit with the parents at those tailgates and honor their investment in their child and their involvement in their child's life.

If we can get the parents pulling in the same direction and involved in a positive way, then it provides us with a tailwind for our program. If you alienate the parents or you are not open to listening to them if they have a concern, then you are going to have to manage a headwind. Obviously, we would all prefer a tailwind to get us where we want to go.

TAKEAWAYS

- Take time to examine the power in your program, where it resides and if the current system is working well. You may need to rethink the structure if you have been doing things the same way for many years. Think about your team meetings and where you are located when you are addressing the team.

- Empower your athletes with important decisions within the program. They should have more input in team travel itineraries so that they feel like their time is being well spent. Use some guided discovery methods to lead them to the right decisions for the team.

- Always be on the lookout for symbols and narratives that could be used with your team throughout the year. There are plenty of moving stories in advertising and on social media. Be ready to capture those for the right time and place with your team.

- Catch your athletes being good on the field, in the classroom, and in the community. It will pay big dividends. It is never wrong to catch them doing something right!

- Appreciate the role parents play. Enlisting the support of athletes' parents can make the experience better for players and coaches.

CHAPTER 18

STRENGTHENING COACH–ATHLETE RELATIONSHIPS

Teri McKeever

Like most of you, my own athletic experience informs how I communicate with the people I coach. Athletics for me was the first place that I felt confident. I am the oldest of 10 children, and my mom was my swimming coach. We trained in the backyard with my siblings and when it fit into her schedule, so there were a lot of things that I did on my own.

I began swimming competitively at 10. When I was 12 years old, I made it to the national finals. I wasn't exceptional, but I was swimming at a high level for my age group. I was never anyone who won big meets, but I was always hanging around the top.

When I got the opportunity to go to college and get a "real" coach, I really didn't get any better. Though I worked at it, no one pushed me to raise my performance to another level and be the best I could be. Perhaps because of that I was inspired to help other young women more fully realize their potential—to be the coach who connected with them, cared for them, but also challenged them.

I struggled early in my coaching career at the University of California. It is common for athlete–coach relationship difficulties to arise when athletes get a new coach they didn't sign up for and the coach inherits a team they didn't recruit. I also made the challenge more difficult by trying to coach like my successful counterpart, the coach of the men's team at Cal, instead of just being the best version of me. During that struggle, I met a friend I could talk with and started on a journey that helped me look at myself and my approach. I guess it wasn't until I was 35 years old that I learned that asking for help was a sign of strength.

In the course of those consults, and in the reflection period that followed, I began to focus on the experiences that allowed me to have good success, and on what I valued most in coaching. Then and even now, after more than 20 consecutive seasons of being ranked in the top 10, and after 11 straight years in the top three nationally, the thing I find special about what we do is finding a way to relate most effectively with each athlete we coach, to help every one of them reach their potential.

My coaching philosophy is based on developing the whole person. I really don't see myself so much as coaching as teaching, and having the good fortune to do so in a really amazing environment. That mentoring emphasis and my holistic aims have guided the development of athletes in our program and influenced how I interact with them. Through the years, this has allowed a variety of women to come into our program and be successful, not only as athletes and students but also women in their postcollegiate pursuits.

ESTABLISHING THE RELATIONSHIP

Because of my own experience, one of the first things I talk about with the team each year is how important it is to ask for help for yourself. I don't want them to feel like they have to pretend to have all the answers when that would be impossible. I encourage them to ask for help, and I share with them the experience I had that confirmed how important it is to do so, not only for an athlete but also for a coach.

I find it helpful to relate my experiences with them. Though it has been more than 40 years since I swam competitively, my swimmers still connect their own experience as young swimmers and women to those that I had growing up. They appreciate my stories of wondering what my strengths are, where I'm coming up short, and the process of trying to improve. We all walk through that journey, and that is something that I very much enjoy helping them navigate.

I talk a lot about that in the recruiting process because I think that a positive coach–athlete relationship starts from the very first interaction. I tell the recruits that if they come to Cal, then we will have a partnership. I tell them your job is to "coach me" to be the best coach for you. I say to them, "You have had a lot of success by the time you get here. Hopefully, you have some ideas of what works for you and you will communicate those to me, and then you also have to be open to some new ideas."

An "aha moment" for me came when talking with my coaching consultant, Kathie, about the differences in the relationships with the athletes with whom I have had the best connection and those with whom my communication has been difficult. The biggest difference is that the athletes who have thrived and with whom I developed a really great personal connection were willing to grow as people and to be invested in that journey of being challenged beyond the swimming pool to learn about their strengths.

I talk with the athletes about building a tool chest not only for the swimming pool but also with knowledge and skills in other aspects of life, for the years beyond their athletic careers. And when they do that, they aren't just helping themselves chart a better future, they are also helping me grow and develop my coaching tool chest as well.

Now it seems more athletes and their families are looking at the superficial things, such as cool Instagram accounts, and they are failing to see that it is the direct human connection that is going to allow them to have the college experience that most people dream of and talk about.

A strong relationship between coach and athlete is very important because the status of each of those individual relationships affects your entire team, whether you are coaching an individual sport or a team sport. If I don't have good relationships with the individuals, I probably don't have a good relationship with my team. If you have 25 athletes on your team, it is important to recognize you have 25 relationships that you need to intentionally work on developing.

Those of us who coach individual-oriented sports—like swimming, golf, track and field, and other activities in which athletes perform singularly, and their own success is mostly independent of other team members' performance—have a unique problem. Our athletes tend to believe that if they work hard enough, they can control their own athletic destiny. Though it can be a positive that they have the courage and sense of personal urgency to want to determine their own fate in competition, it also detaches them from the team. They do not need to rely on teammates

Courtesy of UC Berkeley and photographer John Polzer.

to help them be successful. And individual attention and "star" status is easier to claim. But, as coaches of our teams, our ultimate performance measure is how our group and program do as a whole.

So, when we meet with our team at the start of each season, I let them know the superstars among you are going to be superstars, and we want them to shine. But what is going to make the difference in our collective success is the improvement and contributions of those who are at other performance levels on the team. If each one of them raises their level a notch or two, really awesome stuff can happen.

This focus on collective success can be a new way of thinking for those athletes, so you need to almost teach them how to be part of the team. They are used to being the best athlete in their program, and the workouts revolved around what their needs were. The other team members kind of fit in around them. Therefore, when recruiting athletes I have to explain what my ideas are for the team and that the program is bigger than one person. It's about caring about the welfare and performance of each member, respecting them, and being honest with each other.

My ideal team culture is personal excellence, accountability, adaptability, and authenticity.

There is definitely a blue-collar mentality at Cal because it is a large public institution. We aren't coddling our athletes or holding their hands to make things easy for them. You are going to have to learn how to navigate, advocate for yourself, take initiative, and have an opinion in a respectful way.

A lot of coaches talk a lot about diversity, but they don't really encourage it in terms of different points of view. I don't want or expect our athletes to just go along with the flow. I want them to have an opinion and be able to articulate that and stand up for it. When I have been most successful in recruiting, I have had people all along that spectrum, and they appreciate each other. People who are open-minded and willing to be challenged are a joy to coach.

I will, at times, bring in experts on certain topics and have them talk to the team, even when the person has a point of view that I don't fully endorse and my athletes might not be very receptive to them. During the course of the presentation, I might say, "I personally agree with that," or "That one was a little harder for me to go along with." The point is, I believe it's healthy to expose athletes to new ideas and different ways of thinking about things. One concern I have had more recently is that young people have adopted a position on most matters without even really thinking through the issues or implications related to their stance. So I want to encourage them, both as athletes and citizens, to think for themselves and be informed before just deciding something is best for them because that's what their parents, teammates, or friends told them. If you're going to be a great athlete or a great coach, you need to take in all the information available and then use what you find helpful and consistent with bettering yourself and those around you. That is a skill that will serve anyone well as they move through life.

Managing Conflict

If you aren't having conflicts on a team, then the athletes and those coaching them are not being authentic. If there is no butting of heads or questioning in a respectful way among athletes and coaches, then I don't think you're challenging each other enough. That might be uncomfortable for some and create some tension at times, but that's OK when the individuals involved are striving to improve themselves and the team and not motivated by a personal agenda.

We talk a lot about what the differences are between being a good teammate and being a good friend. You can have a poor teammate who can be a good friend, or you can have a really good teammate, but she's not really a friend. Athletes need to be able to distinguish and deal with those different scenarios and, when there are conflicts, learn how to resolve them.

We use role-playing as a way to address such interpersonal issues before they come up. For example, about a week before we go to our first big invitational meet in the fall, I'll talk with the athletes about what their responsibilities are in the team area of the facility. We'll talk about if you have a bad swim, what is appropriate behavior and what is not appropriate behavior. Then, if I see one of my athletes pouting about her performance, I can remind them of that talk and how such behavior is not allowed here. Or I'll have the captain talk to her about getting over it and supporting her teammates, or have her pity party elsewhere, in private.

So we try to anticipate a wide variety of challenging situations and discuss what our expectations are in responding to them. The athletes need to know and agree to what behavior is and is not acceptable. We will also do somewhat the same thing during recruiting, where we might come up with situations similar to the ones we have seen the recruit struggle with while evaluating her. It is telling whether the recruit realized her responses could have been better or believes she acted perfectly fine in those scenarios.

In the last couple of years, I have arranged more role-playing in small groups, and then observed the interaction among the groups afterward, and perhaps talked with them about the important takeaways from the situation. We also have small groups that discuss social issues and try to determine ways to have a positive impact.

Challenging Athletes

When you reflect on the best coach or teacher who brought the most out of you as an athlete or student, it is almost certain to be someone who challenged you beyond your comfort zone. When I recruit my athletes, I let them know I am not going to be their best friend. Nor am I going to be their mom. I am going to be a coach who expects a lot out of them and will constantly push them to continue to grow. That won't happen if I have to tell them everything they have to do. When athletes ask me a question, I like to turn it around and ask them a question to help them figure out the answer instead of telling them what my thoughts are. I like to "teach them to fish, not fish for them." After listening to them think the situation through, I'll certainly share my thoughts.

I tell our athletes that their job is to find their role on the team. We're not all the fastest swimmer or a straight A student, but we expect you to challenge yourself to be your best in both the pool and the classroom. Your job is to find a role that is unique to you. So, what is that? I can't tell you what that is, but you have to find it and be vested in finding it with your teammates.

At times during my career, I have felt like I needed to apologize for demanding excellence and having a very high bar. Now, as a more experienced and confident coach, I don't feel that way anymore. In fact, seeking a level of excellence and accountability is who we are, so athletes must accept that and embrace it to be a part of this team. There is going to be a level of expectation. I don't care if you are the fastest swimmer or the slowest swimmer; there are high expectations.

As a young coach, I coached to the middle, because I wanted people to like me and I didn't want to disappoint anyone. I didn't like it when they went home angry with me. What I have come to understand is that I'm not really coaching if I am worried about an athlete liking me and

Al Sermeno

me being uncomfortable sometimes. I am asking you to be uncomfortable, and I need to be willing to be uncomfortable sometimes. I need to coach toward the highest level of what our goals are as a program, and then everyone's job is to rise to that level. I'm not bringing my standards down so that you are more comfortable.

You need to have a really clear idea of your nonnegotiables and communicate that to your athletes. I don't believe life, let alone sports, is black-and-white. I think there is a lot of gray area in both. And the better you manage the gray in your individual life as coach or athlete, as well as your collective life as a team, the better we are going to do. As the head coach, I am going to make decisions sometimes when our athletes don't know all the information, and they must trust that I am making that decision in the best interest of the team and respect it, with the understanding that no one is always right.

If we are going to say that we want to contend for a national title, then everybody needs to do things that are aligned with that, and that's where you find what your role is because the roles will not be all the same. But it doesn't mean because an athlete didn't make the travel team that we are expecting any less commitment from that athlete in helping our team achieve that national championship goal.

Learning From Failing

A former student-athlete of ours who is now working on her PhD said, "One of the best things I learned swimming at Cal is how to fail and quickly move on." I thought that was an awesome compliment because when I was her age, even the prospect of failure petrified me. In fact, even when I started coaching at Cal, the thought of possibly failing almost paralyzed me. I was so afraid to make a mistake.

Now I realize how much I benefited from taking some hard knocks when I was competing as an athlete and later learning how to be a better coach. Sure, there were some hard times that I would not want to go through again, but what I learned about myself and handling difficult situations was life-changing. It has also helped me assist athletes in dealing with failure, and also in gaining a more mature perspective about what failure is and is not.

So when an athlete is despondent about placing third at the Olympic trials and not making the Olympic team, I let her know that if that is the worst thing that ever happens to her, she will have lived a very blessed life. I know such things seem catastrophic in the moment, but I try to help such athletes look at the big picture and how they can learn and grow from the experience. It's important to talk with them and help them move on.

I might also enlist the help of others to assist athletes in dealing with what they perceive to be failure or major difficulties. Now that I have been here long enough, if there's a young lady who is struggling with something academically or personally, or her health, there might have been an athlete before her with similar concerns, and I'll try to connect them. That is a huge asset that we have. The longer you coach the more experts—former athletes in your program—to call upon.

As their coach, I will consider their individual goals within the context of the collective goals of our team. When I see or feel that we're not moving toward them, I will address the team. But if an individual has a goal saying they want to be an All-American, and they're not living up to that standard, privately I will have a conversation with them. "These are the things I don't think are in line with you saying you want to be an All-American. Have you changed your goal?" They will usually say, "No, Teri, my goals are the same." I'll respond by saying, "OK, then these few things need to be improved upon or I'm not going to allow you to say that is what your goal is anymore. You don't get to say you want that and then not live that every day."

NURTURING LEADERS

We try to develop leadership skills in all of our athletes, even those who aren't inclined to want to take a leadership position. The value of learning how to make good decisions and to accept responsibility for your actions applies to all of them and is apparent in how they perform as athletes and students. Yet, we don't expect each athlete to have the qualities a team needs in its captain or captains.

One exercise I've done in determining captains is to have the team select them, but not in the traditional manner. Instead, I surveyed the team about the experiences, accomplishments, and qualities they thought were essential for an athlete to have to be considered for the captain role. Must they be a senior? An NCAA qualifier? Have a certain grade point average? What qualities are most important? And so on. Then I tabulated the responses and shared the results with them.

After that, we had athletes who were interested in serving as a team captain submit a job description to my assistant for what they thought a team captain on the team should do and what their own strengths and weaknesses were. We had 10 athletes submit the required material to be a candidate for captain one year. Those applications were then distributed to the team with the names removed.

Then I had each team member send me their top-three votes, and I got together with my assistants and an executive coach who works with us and we counted the votes. We did not count them in front of the team, but we honored their votes and tried to make sure at least everyone got one of their top-two choices to serve as one of the captains that year. We ended up with four captains, and then we had those people meet with the coaches at least once or twice a month, and they also met with the executive coach I work with to go over leadership skills without the coaches there. That has been very valuable.

We spend time coaching our leaders to have a lot of ownership in the team. I feel like this is my program, but last year we did a whole

Captains Take the Lead

I had problems with an athlete one year and suspended her for a variety of reasons, but she spun the story to make it look like I was the problem. The captains and the rest of the team realized I wasn't the one out of line, so I asked the captains how they thought we should deal with the situation. All four of them agreed that it would be best if they went and talked to the disgruntled athlete. So, they did just that, and the outcome was much better than if I had been involved in that discussion.

thing on expectations and I had nonnegotiables that I gave them. And then I gave them all these different categories and they needed to write down the expectations for themselves within the program. They boxed themselves in way more than I would have done. But now they have this document with standards they have created and must live up to.

Because swimming has such a large roster, we separated the athletes on our team into "family pods." To determine the pods, the coaches and captains from the previous year divided the team members up by the various classes of students. So the first-year students are split up and roommates are split up so that we can stretch connections. I would then meet with each family pod. When I brought up the family pod system for managing our team during one of my presentations at a national coaching convention, many of the male coaches in attendance looked at me like I had come up with a cure for a major disease.

USING COMMUNICATION TO HELP ATHLETES KNOW THEMSELVES AND GROW

With athletes being bombarded by messages in all forms of communication available now, it is important to help them discern whose opinion really matters. It is frightening how young people are so concerned with how many likes they have on an Instagram picture. Why worry about what someone who doesn't even know them is saying about them? And even if the person messaging about them is someone they know, they need to be able to gauge how much that person's opinion really matters.

I like to share with my athletes the following quote to help them consider whose opinions and regard are really important in their lives.

Life is a theater, so invite your audiences carefully.

Author unknown

Not everyone is worthy of having a front row seat in our lives. I tell our student-athletes that you are going to have many people come in and out of your lives and unfortunately some of them will not be the type of people that will add positive things to your life. You might find the time spent with them is too draining and the friendship or relationship does not seem to be going anywhere positive. Keep them at a distance. You will have lots of different opportunities for relationships in all areas of your life and you need to choose to spend time with the ones that are encouraging to you. One way to evaluate a relationship with a person is after you spend time with them, do you feel better or worse?

The more you surround yourself with people who show respect, peace, love, and honesty, the easier it will become for you to decide to keep that person as a good friend and have them sit in your "front row" of life. Everyone we associate with closely will have a major impact on our lives and everything in it, so always be aware of who you have chosen to sit in your front row.

This gets them to think about what matters, like defining success, whether that is team success or individual success. What does success look like for you? It needs to be your definition, not the definition you read in a magazine or what someone else thinks success looks like. Each athlete needs to be able to determine and articulate that for herself.

Recruiting the right people is not just about how fast they can go in the pool. I also want to know things about them personally. I'll ask them questions as simple as, "If I were to talk to your high school or club coach, what would they say they will miss the most about you when you have gone off to college?" Some of the recruits can tell you right away, and others say I don't know. I want to coach people who have some level of self-awareness or have at least been triggered, so there is a curiosity there.

I like athletes who are willing to try new things that might be better than the old way. If something we're doing during practice doesn't work, I'll stop them in the middle of the workout and say, "That's not working like I thought it would," and apologize and start over with something else. That type of coaching is definitely outside of the norm, so I need athletes who respond well to trying something different, not getting upset that they are being asked to do something new or criticizing the coach and thinking she doesn't know what she is doing. That's why, for me, finding athletes who have the confidence to explore and to extend themselves is important.

The traditional swimming model is train to train. I think training should be about performing, and performing is very different from training every day; it has different aspects and different qualities of things and a different mindset. When you go on a job interview, that is a performance. When you get behind the swimming block, that is a performance. So how do you bring those tools to those situations when you want to perform and get your message across, or get that job, or do well on an exam? That's the performance mindset we are striving to have.

In trying to determine which athletes have the mental capacity to approach things in that way, we have often used the DiSC behavior assessment tool over the past 15 years. The DiSC (Dominance, Influence, Steadiness, Conscientiousness) model of behavior was originally proposed in 1928 by William Moulton Marston, a physiological psychologist with a PhD from Harvard. We believe the time invested in this evaluation is worth it, not only because it helps the coaching staff better understand our athletes but also because it helps the athletes better understand themselves.

We, the coaches, also benefit from knowing the personality differences between athletes in terms of what motivates them, their behavior style differences, and so on. The DiSC behavior assessment tool is really beneficial in that it helps my athletes understand that if they have a bump with me, or when I am being more direct, it is more my behavior style—and it is not that I am mad at them, and it is not personal. That is a hard lesson I have had to learn. When someone gives me feedback, it is not directed at Teri personally, but Teri as a coach. It helps them understand that when I might jump on an athlete, I'm not saying they are bad, only that that specific behavior they are showing is not good. They are learning that feedback is information and doesn't have to be something negative.

I had three individuals, including our executive coach and two other people, make a presentation. One topic was looking at my style as the coach and asking how can you be more effective when you want to communicate with Teri, or with the assistant, Dani? That has been a really important piece in the last couple of years. I told the athletes this summer that if you can walk away from here and see your style, and understand how it really helps you show up in the world, and know where you have to adapt and what environments cause you stress, then that is a better gift we can give you than helping you go faster in a 50-meter freestyle.

I can't put enough value on what coaching has brought me. I have such great joy in seeing people develop, in having athletes simply ask how your dog is and just having that personal connection with those student-athletes. It looks different than it did 30 years ago when I coached at Fresno State, but those relationships are still what gets me up in the morning. I finally made that connection in my head that I can coach the way I think is needed; I just need to find people who want that in their sport.

TAKEAWAYS

- Know yourself as a coach as well as the type of athletes you will work best with in your program.
- See the big picture of coaching. It is really all about developing our athletes into the best version of themselves for life.
- Take the time to really get to know every student-athlete in your program. That strong relationship will improve performances because you took the time to show them you cared about them as people.
- Coach to the highest-level athlete in your program. Make sure all the athletes understand those expectations before they get into your program, so there are no surprises.
- Have athletes work with you to plan their progress and workouts. You will get more buy-in and teach them how to be responsible for their own success.

CHAPTER 19

GROWING ATHLETES HOLISTICALLY

Becky Burleigh

We had a player who was a very high achiever. She was invited into the full national team program as a college player, which is pretty unusual in soccer. Everything should have been going great for her, right? The many hours and great effort and sacrifice she had put into becoming one of the top players at her level had seemingly paid off. Instead, those accomplishments were somehow making her miserable. Seeing her in that state of despair really opened my eyes and affected how I've coached since then.

The identity of that player was "what you do" and not "who you are." The question every coach must answer is, "How are we contributing to that belief?" How can we model appreciating the young individuals under our guidance as people, not just athletes?

When we talk about growing athletes holistically, we could start with an "a person is more than a player" philosophy. That was born out of seeing players who had their total identity tied to their sport. Although that probably serves athletes well in many respects as they're progressing rapidly in their careers, it also can cause a lot of problems. What usually happens is when they're playing well, they feel good about themselves and when they're playing poorly, they feel bad about themselves.

So, we take a different approach in coaching and try to separate the two—the person from the player. We work to help our athletes understand that separating those two things doesn't affect performance in a negative way. It just allows them to have an identity as a person and an identity as a player.

PLAYER TESTIMONIALS

Thank you for pushing me and helping to mold me into the person I am today. I think I could have gone somewhere else and ended up a completely different person. The culture you set up here has really driven everything I have done and everything I will do.

Susi

You helped change the patriarchal athletic landscape and forged a path for female athletes and coaches. Your influence is vast as you have empowered each member of your teams to recognize their strengths, work to be their best, and find the power within each one of them to build meaningful lives.

Katie and Connie

ONE-ON-ONE MEETINGS WITH PLAYERS

We started by creating more programming to demonstrate our appreciation for the players as people, and to give them space and time to talk about themselves. As a staff, we schedule a meeting with each player every week. I usually start those meetings with the simple question: "What's the most important thing we need to be talking about?" From there, the subject can get much deeper and more meaningful to the athletes.

I remember one player meeting started out with her talking about a chemistry class that she was struggling with, and it ended up being a discussion about how she was the first in her family to go to college. There was a lot of pressure on her to go to medical school. She didn't really want to do that, but she was afraid she would let her family down if she didn't. I tried to navigate that school discussion with her, discovering what she really wanted to chase and not what her family wanted her to chase.

Meeting individually with athletes is essential to discover and gain access to what they are thinking and experiencing. This is another reason why effective communication skills are so important in coaching. If you don't communicate successfully and fail to connect with your athletes, it will significantly limit your potential impact and opportunities to establish key relationships.

Our individual meetings with the players don't have a set agenda, so the meetings last various amounts of time. I make these meetings a priority in my schedule, even though it is a large time commitment. I think it is probably one of the most important things I do as a coach. I always feel like I could spend another two hours a week preparing for my next opponent or rewatching our own game film, or I could spend that time talking to our players and getting to the heart of the matter as far as things that are going on. I personally feel like my return on investment (ROI) is better spent in the player meetings. I feel I can coach the players better if I get to know them better. I think they can take my coaching better if they get to know me better.

With my open-door policy, I end up seeing more people than are in my group every week anyway, because people are just going to come in to talk about things. We had a couple of athletes who transferred in, and some of them will say, "The only time I met with my coach was during the recruiting process and if I was in trouble." In our soccer program, coaches having meetings with players is such a common, all-the-time thing there's no nervousness about it. The players will say, "Yeah, I met with coach today," and it is not a big deal. It helps them learn skills to talk to people who are technically in more power and control than they are. It gives them an opportunity to bring up their own concerns.

I know some coaches have difficulty meeting with each individual on their team every week because they don't have enough staff to fit everyone in on their schedule. Not every coach is fortunate to have the size of staff that I do. We can divide the team into three groups, and each of us has a different group each week, so it is not me personally meeting with every player on my team every week. I am meeting with one-third of our athletes every week. If I were coaching at a high school, club, or smaller college and I didn't have that size staff, then maybe I could only meet one-third of the team one week, one-third of the team the next week, and so on.

Our players can never say they didn't have the access to be able to speak with a coach, which is key to staying on top of team or player issues that might be brewing. I understand why some coaches don't do it, but it is important to me because of my style of coaching. It would be hard to coach the way I coach without athletes having that kind of access. Bill Beswick, an English sports psychologist who works with elite soccer players, made this point very well: "It is a significant moment when a coach realises that success is about 'human beings' as well as 'human doings'" (2016, p. 63).

PLAYER TESTIMONIAL

Thank you for being a coach who valued me as a person and supported me emotionally, physically, and mentally. I can recall many moments of you providing me support, such as finding me a nutritionist to provide me the food I needed for my special diet, setting me up with a therapist when I needed extra emotional support, listening to me speak at church and asking me questions about my faith. You supported me in my decision to get married while still in school. You taught me to endure mentally, and I felt appreciated, loved, and valued as a member of the Gator soccer team and now family. I will treasure those moments and memories.

Ananda

TEAM MEETINGS

In the off-season, team meetings include what we call "Real World Weekly," where we address subjects with the team that *they* wanted to learn about. We ask our players at the beginning of the semester to identify three things that they want to dive into a little bit deeper that have nothing to do with soccer. Then we try to create a curriculum around those topics, which have ranged from finances to motor scooter maintenance to social etiquette and really all sorts of things. While most NCAA schools have a life skills program that offers basic educational sessions on standard subjects, our approach is specifically tied to what the players want to learn and get excited about.

Through all of these sessions, what really comes through is that the more investment we made in the person, the more willing they are to be invested as players. It's not a zero-sum game. There is a component to these sessions that even when you're not talking about something to do with your sport, that investment pays off in your sport, even though that is not why you do it.

Some coaches still don't believe there's a time or place to be doing those types of activities with their team because they want to focus primarily on the performance. But I believe players who feel invested in and who feel more at peace with things that are going on outside their sporting life are generally more productive.

When we first started this type of activity, it took a little time to get the players to buy in to this part of our program, but there is a really simple way to talk about it. We talk about character skills, and that we have a performance side, which are things you do by yourself, and a relational side for things you do with other people. We asked our players, "Do you think that you can get better at those character skills?" They all said yes. "Do you think that when we are working on those performance skills, it can make you a better player?" They all said yes. "If you think about the relational skills, will that make you a better teammate?" They all said yes. "So, if you're a better player and a better teammate, do you see how that is going to improve your results?" Once you get them to that point, they've now bought in to why these discussions are important.

We have done this for at least the past six seasons. We have now progressed to asking them questions like, "What are the top-three things that can get in the way of us maximizing our abilities as a team?" I would say 95 to 100 percent of those things are human-related and not sport-related. It's not that we are not going to score enough goals or we can't defend at a high enough level. It's always things like communication, trust, selfishness, and distractions. When the team tells you the things they think can bring us down, you can see that they are now bought in to the need to have those discussions. They're giving you the answer to the test.

These off-the-field discussions take time, and we count them as part of our 20 hours a week. It is easy for us to fit these activities into our allowable practice and game times because they are short 10- to 15-minute discussions. The frequency of doing this would vary because some of them are integrated into your training. For example, we have a drill in soccer called "Shots and Crosses." It is working on taking shots at the goal and hitting crosses for another person to score. You can set the number of goals they are trying to score within a certain amount of time and at a high level where it's really difficult to achieve. Then, while I'm coaching that drill, I am seeing how they react to the pressure mounting on them while trying to accomplish that goal as the clock ticks down. So, yes, there is a part of us coaching and knowing that was a poor cross and that's why you can't score. But there's also the part of watching them start yelling at each other and getting frustrated because the time is running out, and that is not going to help you score, either. It is in drills like that when we are able to address the human-related issues that come up under stressful situations.

When we get the topics from the student-athletes, I find the people to share their expertise with them. For one of the sessions, I asked one of the men who works on campus in maintenance to teach them how to change the oil in their car and made sure they knew how to change a tire. He also did motor scooter maintenance for us one year. We also had a former player who worked in a scooter shop in town, so she did a session with us one time and it was great. It was probably the most popular session because nobody wants to spend the money on their scooter maintenance.

In short, seek opportunities to empower your athletes to grow using their sport and to create better people. The beauty of sports is that it can provide experiences that teach young people how to deal with stress and wins and losses in their lives. There is not a better environment to experience growth because of the physical, mental, and emotional challenges that sports put on an individual.

TESTIMONIAL

The "Real World Weekly" program has been incredibly valuable to our student-athletes due to the fact they miss out on many regular student college experiences that teach critical life skills. In a subtopic of finance, our video coordinator was very knowledgeable, so Becky allowed him to take the lead. Within this moment, he was our leader.

An assistant coach

UNDERSTANDING YOUR ATHLETES

I gauge the leadership I provide my team and program based on the answer to one basic question: Do I make people around me better? If I don't, then I'm not a good leader, regardless of all the stuff I try to do.

In order to make people around me better, I have to understand myself, and I have to understand them. We use the Dominance, Influence, Steadiness, Conscientiousness (DiSC) behavior assessment tool in our program to address both of those areas (see figure 19.1). There are other tools that do the same thing, but the DiSC profile is one of the easiest behavior profiles to understand, discuss, and apply.

While our players know there are different DiSC profiles, I'm not saying they can all necessarily execute the flexibility in behavior that DiSC tries to teach you, but they can all talk in that language with the self-awareness of who they are, as well as the awareness of others. I wish they all could say, "That person is a high C, and this is how I should communicate with that person." But it certainly seems to have improved their self-awareness. We are seeing a positive change with athletes having more social awareness.

In recruiting, I explore beyond whether an athlete has the physical talent to be successful. It is also about the fit. So, when I recruit young women for my program, once we determine that she has the base level

Dominance (D)	Influence (I)	Steadiness (S)	Conscientiousness (C)
Big-picture thinker	Collaborative	Accommodating	Accurate
Competitive	Communicative	Calm	Ambitious
Confident	Disorganized	Cautious	Careful
Decisive	Energetic	Cooperative	Competent
Demanding	Enthusiastic	Deliberate	Detail-oriented
Direct	Influential	Dependable	Expert
Enjoys power	Lively	Helpful	Independent
Fast-paced	Networker	Indecisive	Overanalytical
Firm	Open	Kind	Precise
Impatient	Optimistic	Listener	Private
Outspoken	Outgoing	Loyal	Quality-driven
Results-driven	Relationship-driven	Patient	Quiet
Skeptical	Sociable	Sincere	Reflective
	Trusting	Stable	Systematic
		Supportive	
		Tactful	

FIGURE 19.1   DiSC behaviors.

of talent needed on the field, I begin to really try to get to know her and her personality and determine if she will fit into our team culture.

I know for sure I have lost recruits because of my directness. I want to have honest conversations with them about a variety of topics that I think are important. There was one player who had a lot of interesting things posted on her social media. I asked her to talk to me about her strategy with social media and why these things were really important to her. I am not saying that every student-athlete who posts all about their sport on their social media is focused and every student-athlete who posts things dealing with their social life isn't focused, but just having those conversations might shed some light on their priorities.

I'm guessing they are not having this conversation with other coaches recruiting them. I know there was one player in particular who I'm sure we lost because I asked her some pretty hard questions about her social media, but I had to because I'm not sure she would've been a great fit for us, so I'm OK losing a recruit like that.

More importantly, I want to know what their DiSC style is, and that is easy to figure out once you start to see the patterns of behavior. I don't want to have an oversupply or an undersupply of a particular DiSC style on my team. For example, if our entire team was "high D," we would have lots of players with a high pace and high standards, but there is only one ball and they would all want it, so we need to be aware of that. Or if we had an oversupply of "I" personalities, we might make a great sorority and have a lot of fun, but maybe we are not going to get a whole lot done. I want to understand each recruit's drivers and why they play the sport, so I will try to dig into that a little deeper.

Unfortunately, the recruiting model and time restrictions sometimes don't really allow you a lot of time to get as deep as you might like with the individual. I also take time to talk to other people around them to find out how consistent people's views of that person are, especially from people who don't have a vested interest like their club or high school coach. For example, in recruiting, our number one source of information is the club coach they play for, but they want their athlete to come to a school like Florida because it gives prestige to their club. Of course, they are not going to be a neutral party, but if I talk to a coach who plays against that team regularly, they can tell me what that recruit was like when their team was winning big, losing big, or doing anything else that they noticed. That person has no skin in the game, and so that is going to be a much more neutral source.

When you talk to a whole bunch of these more neutral sources, and they are all saying the same things about the player, then you have a better picture of what the recruit is going to be like when she gets to your campus. We have a player coming in to play for us next year. The number one word that came up when people talked about her is *appreciation*—how appreciative she is of everything. Six different people have used that word to describe her, so you know the consistency that you're getting across the board is because the student-athlete clearly displayed that character skill often.

I am not a bait-and-switch or dog-and-pony-show person when it comes to recruiting. I am a really big believer in finding the right fit for the people we recruit to our program and trying to ensure our program meets their needs—and that they will be successful in our culture and system. I will tell them how much I want them, but at the same time, I'm not going to act one way in recruiting and then act another when they get to campus.

It is not just trying to convince them to come here because of this amazing experience they had in the 48 hours during their visit. I am going to give recruits a true picture of who we are and what we do. Then it is up to them to decide if they fit that model.

For example, I had very direct conversations recently with two committed recruits about the challenges our team has had in discussing political and social justice matters. I asked them, "How do you handle it when you have different political views than some of your teammates? Maybe your teammates will unfollow you because they say they don't want those messages on their feed?" It is interesting because it can be a risk to have those conversations, since it is showing the warts of your program. But it is important for them to know this is what they're coming into, and if they're still on board with that, we are going to be fine.

GIVING ATHLETES A VOICE

Effective communication with athletes is more important in coaching than it has ever been. That entails being more transparent in our relationships with them and more respectful of their views and right to speak out. And when we allow our players to have more of a voice, we need to be prepared to deal with their transparency as well.

This more open line of communication between coaches and athletes is now an expectation of younger athletes who were never subjected to the "my way or the highway" approach some coaches have taken in working with players in the past.

But we coaches need to realize that providing the "why" we are doing something involving our athletes is not a threat to our authority but rather an opportunity to educate and to gain trust. Rather than looking at this as a loss of any power, we need to see it as a chance to increase athletes' respect for what we are doing and a way to increase their buy-in to it. Yes, it is a paradigm shift for many coaches, but in reality, it is a win-win situation for our athletes and ourselves.

We need to look to empower our athletes, not control them. We need to help young women find their voices. Many young girls want to please everyone. I'd like to help break that mold of them being pleasers and help them learn to respectfully speak up and not always be willing to go with the flow because someone else says that is how it should be. Some coaches might be afraid of that, but in the end, you are going to create a stronger bond with your athletes because you are empowering them. You are also helping them develop a life skill that they will take with them. How do you create a world where they care about your opinion

but their actions are not dictated by your opinion? The aim should be to positively influence and not seek to control in your interactions with them.

I took a course called "Fierce Conversations" where we discussed tools to have confrontational conversations and team conversations. Don't ever have a team conversation about something that you already have your mind set on how you want it. A team conversation should be held when you are open to subscribing to the consensus your players reach, after providing the information that will be useful in coming to a decision. Teaching the skills to have confrontational conversations by reducing the emotion involved is a very necessary part of learning how to deal with conflict.

TESTIMONIAL

By observing you over the years, I learned ways to deal with conflicts, how to communicate effectively, the importance of making your voice heard, and the importance of listening and being a shoulder to lean on when needed.

Meggie

Name, Image, and Likeness

Social and legal changes outside your program can affect how you work with your athletes to develop them as players and people. A recent example of one of those changes involves the name, image, and likeness (NIL) concept, which could alter college athletics in a significant way. NIL would allow student-athletes to profit from their name, image, and likeness through avenues such as endorsement deals and marketing and promotions without regulation.

This may serve to augment our holistic coaching approach to athlete development because our student-athletes will be able to learn so many small business skills and real-world skills from dealing with their name, image, and likeness if they choose to get involved. I have athletes on our soccer team who are not necessarily the star players, but they have followers on Instagram who ask them about different products. So, I truly think there's a huge upside to NIL.

Athletes outside the major revenue-generating sports of football and men's basketball are less likely to get the big money from sponsoring local businesses, but they are savvy enough that they will find ways to get monetary reward through other means. One of our former players has built her business on creating social media platforms for people. She is going to speak to our team about it because I feel like she is a great resource for that. She was not a superstar like Alex Morgan, but she is somebody who has built something from the ground up and monetized it. If that had been legal for her to do when she was in college, she would've been so ahead of the game as a young entrepreneur.

SOCIAL MEDIA

One forum in which the voice of the athlete is more prevalent than ever can be a challenge, however. Most athletes have outward-facing social media as well as inward-facing social media. You can post things on your private Instagram page or Snapchat that is not going out to everyone, and it can be really negative or not as nice as it maybe should be. But their public-facing social media could be totally different.

Social media is a really amazing tool that can help us connect with our athletes, but when they slip and put something that negatively or improperly presents their views, it has a real downside for them—and for the program they represent. Furthermore, our athletes are not likely to easily shrug off a negative or demeaning post by someone outside the program, even if the person responsible for the post doesn't even know them.

I am now coaching athletes who have never *not* had social media, and I am concerned about the effect it has on their long-term mental health. While I am a fan of the careful and proper use of social media, in general I don't like the effect it has on our players. President Theodore Roosevelt reputedly said, "Comparison is the thief of joy," and social media has magnified that 10,000 times, especially for young women. I believe it has a worse effect on women than it does on men because we often care so much about what other people think about us.

On the other hand, social media can be a great platform for education if focused on individuals and organizations that are somehow enhancing our knowledge and appreciation of the things that are important in our lives. I'll find interesting or educational things from others and repost them. It is educational and enjoyable for me. I can follow any coaches at any level and have access to the best coaches in the world. I would never have access to them without social media.

For example, Kara Lawson, women's basketball coach at Duke University, puts a lot of good content out on Twitter, and while I'm not actually in her basketball practices, I do get to see little glimpses of her in the gym and see what she is thinking and doing, and I think that's pretty insightful.

I also search for and save things from social media to use with my team. If our team is struggling with being resilient, I'm going to search for things I think can provide a bite-size, media-driven clip of resilience that my team will relate to. It is much more effective than me standing up and talking to them about resilience. I can show them a 45-second video as opposed to me just talking at them.

So, while social media certainly has its ugly side, if used constructively and responsibly by you and your athletes, it can be an excellent tool for learning and sharing. In that way, you are promoting the kind of open exchanges with your athletes—giving them a voice—that benefits them, you, and your program.

SUPPORT FROM OTHERS OF INFLUENCE

While coaches can significantly enhance both the athlete side and the person side of the players under their guidance, we can't do it alone. The backing of the athletes' parents and the program's administrators is also crucial.

The parents, or other adult figures who serve a similar role in the athletes' lives, are likely to have the most influential voice. Ideally, you want that parental voice to be one that is supportive of your efforts to build on your developmental work with their children. The odds of getting such support are much better if you share with the athlete's parents your plan for further nurturing their daughter's life and athletic skills when she enters the program.

Similarly, take time to explain your holistic approach to coaching to the administrator(s) overseeing your program. When tough actions are necessary in an effort to grow your athletes, knowing the administration has your back is very important. So, make sure your administrator is on board with how you intend to handle things.

As a head coach, you don't want to be surprised about something going on in your program, and your athletics administrator doesn't like surprises, either. For example, I am never going to think about removing an athlete from my team without having multiple conversations with an administrator before that happens. If I am even thinking about it, I am going to involve my administrator in that discussion.

Some coaches may not want to see their administrator when the team is performing poorly. They can become very self-isolated, which is understandable because the athletic environment tends to reward on-field success and shun failure, but holing up in the office only compounds the problem. So, when my team is going through a rough stretch and has had a few bad games in a row, I will reach out to our administrators, let them know what is going on, and explain what we're doing to turn things around. I want to have that face-to-face interaction to control the narrative on the situation rather than have them draw negative conclusions from the results and having that impression linger. It is remarkable how much this simple, proactive communication can do to retain your administration's support of your efforts.

TAKEAWAYS

- The payoff of developing athletes holistically is that we are empowering them to think independently and reducing their reliance on the coaching staff to solve problems. Since many of the issues that come up on teams exist in spaces outside actual training and playing time, these skills can help the athlete feel more prepared to lead at these times.

- Sharing our philosophy on holistic coaching during the recruiting process shows the athletes and parents that we have a genuine concern for their daughter as a person; she will not be defined by her playing time or her playing role on the team. This reassures the athletes and their parents that everyone in our environment will be valued.

- When players talk about their experience in our program, they almost always reference how we developed them as people, not just players, and how that has provided important skills for them in their nonsporting life. That should be a major objective of every coach.

CHAPTER 20

KEEPING IT FUN WHILE INSTILLING THE VALUES

Lonni Alameda

I was coaching softball at Florida State University (FSU), and we were playing in the NCAA regionals against the University of South Alabama in 2013. We were down by five runs in the top of the sixth inning. We were playing against one of the best ERA pitchers in the country, and our team had several of our usual starters injured and out of the game. It seemed South Alabama had the game well in hand.

I was talking with my coaches in the corner of the field about what we should say postgame and what to talk about in the end-of-year meetings because we thought the season was about to end. We overheard the veteran players on the team who were injured and out of the game coaching up and cheering on the younger ones. Everything they were talking about were our core values. They were "all in" as to what we had been instilling for years. We loaded the bases in the bottom of the seventh, hit a game-tying grand slam and then a solo shot in the eighth inning. Winning that game advanced us to the NCAA Softball Super Regional, the first one since I had started coaching softball at FSU.

That game and those precious moments of the players coaching and supporting each other was the intersection of being a transformational coach and seeing the results on the field. I realized that day that being myself, having fun, and sticking to core values I believed in as a coach was going to work.

ESTABLISHING CORE VALUES

Core values are much more than slogans on wall posters or coaching clichés. They are those things that are so important and essential to you that they direct your ethical compass and steer your behavior.

A coaching staff and team need to come to an agreement on the core values that will guide their actions, on and off the field, and then live them. Our staff and players talk about core values all the time. We post our core values in the locker room, and when we needed them the most and in the biggest moment of our season, our core values showed up. Our players were talking it and living it. And then the transformational side of coaching met the transactional side of coaching. Our staff had given the team all the information they would need to be successful, which was transactional communication. At that point in time, we witnessed our team taking the situation into their own hands and transforming themselves into a winning team. Winning that super regional confirmed that the ingredients we had been putting into our team practices and meetings had nurtured our players in the core values and team culture that made that comeback possible.

Establishing values in a program is so important. Values create a common language and allow everyone on the team to be accountable. Knowing your values allows relationships to be built through an appreciation for everyone's past story while binding the team to the culture of the program itself. I have always had values on my previous teams, but I never clearly defined them or captured them on paper. The values are never going to change for me.

On the other hand, how players on each year's team translate those values to actual expectations and behaviors does often differ from one season to the next. So it is essential that you talk through with your athletes how they define the application of the values on a practical level. These interpretations establish the foundation for our team standards and guidelines. For example, a team one year may interpret "family" as being checked in at meals—therefore, no cell phones allowed. The next year, a team may not think that is important and have another way to represent what family is to them. To an extent, there is freedom to interpret things differently depending on what resonates with a specific group of individuals.

To help ensure that each athlete's interpretation of the values is consistent across the team, we have a little storytelling exercise in which each player describes what a core value means to them. We start this very early in the season and typically address one core value per week. We invest time in this process to make sure we are all on the same page, even if it cuts into our on-field practice schedule. It is that important to our softball program.

And that does mean everyone in the program. In addition to the players, you must ensure that the staff and all the support personnel know what you are talking about when you are talking about your core values and buy in to it. So, every year we always go back to the beginning and revisit the most basic concepts to confirm that everybody is speaking the same language. Take time to articulate what your core values are and how they can help you uphold the standard with your players.

In 2012, we had two new coaches on staff and we did an exercise with the sports psychologists. As a staff one night, everyone was given five index cards to write down what we thought about various things such as, "When we hold up a jersey, what are the five words that come to mind about the jersey?" Then we all put our cards on the table together and started going through them, seeing if there were any similar ideas. Everyone had family, so that was good, and we repeated that activity for a variety of items. We then did that same exercise with the team. After that we gathered in a classroom for three hours and came up with what our core values were for the program, knowing that the values of the coaching staff and the players had to mesh. Here is what we came up with:

A WINNING CULTURE

Florida State Softball has a foundation of core values that drive team motivation and success, both as softball players and individuals.

Family
Smart
Aggressive
Competitive
Committed

FAMILY

- At Florida State Softball, you become more than a softball player. You become family.
- FSU Softball is more than a team. We are a sisterhood of athletes who accept, protect, and honor each of our members.
- We respect, love, and accept one another and embrace the diversity and differences of each of our players, coaches, and support staff.

SMART

- Here at Florida State Softball, we recognize that you are a student before athlete.
- You will leave here with a degree along with a championship mindset and a forever-family.
- We have a tradition of excellence in the classroom and on the softball field.

AGGRESSIVE

- Here at Florida State Softball, we believe that the best things in life aren't handed to you. You work hard and you take them.

- On the field, we play aggressively. We take extra bases, we swing hard, and we never give up the fight.
- We take what we want, and we don't apologize for our success.

COMPETITIVE

- At Florida State Softball, we have the "next pitch" mentality, meaning the game isn't over until the last out is made. This mindset is the competitive force that drives Florida State Softball to continue fighting even when all odds are against us.
- The "next pitch" mentality is our reaction to failure. You swing and miss, so what? Next pitch. You give up a three-run bomb, so what? Next pitch. When you are truly competitive, what happened in the past does not matter, because the next pitch presents an opportunity to change the whole game.

COMMITTED

- Here at FSU Softball, commitment is everything. When you show up to practice, workouts, and games, you commit yourself to your team, its values, and the legacy of Florida State Softball.
- What we do every day determines how successful we are the next day, so we strive to be the best version of ourselves to ensure the team is the best it can be.
- We "GATE" before every practice and game. GATE stands for "Give Your All to the Team Every Day." We never do anything halfway. A hundred percent of our effort is given to our team always.

If the players had identified winning as a core value, we would have had a problem. I'm more about the process than the outcome. I couldn't live with just winning every day. Don't get me wrong. We talk about winning, but it is more about winning the moment, winning the day, and eventually, competitive winning. Winning the College World Series Championship is a result of meeting those individual challenges of the moment and making the necessary attitude adjustments along the way.

The balance between transformational coaching and transactional coaching is a challenge for every coach. I understand that my team wants to win and, in fact, needs to win for me to keep my job. But I also believe I'm cheating my athletes if the sole or primary determinant of whether they find their sport experience satisfying is whether they win or not. So, it's essential that I keep the best interest of my players foremost in mind while I also prepare and coach them, to the best of my ability, to give them a good chance of competitive success.

DRAWING THE LINE

Our goal as a softball program is to live by the core values we've specified and the standards we've set to reflect them every day. We want to make sure everyone has a deep understanding of what an "above the line" and "below the line" action is. While it is not an expectation that no one will ever do something below the line, as a group we can clearly say, "That is below the line," and the person who did such an action will understand why that is the case. The above and below the line concept came from the book titled, *Above the Line: Lessons in Leadership and Life from a Championship Program*, written by Urban Meyer, the former college football coach and head coach of the Jacksonville Jaguars. We used some of his ideas and concepts as we met with our team.

At the beginning of each year, players will be presented with the FSU softball core values and the absolutes that go along with them and how to be accountable. Over the years, we have added to these core values and how you live them every day. These are the nonnegotiable parts of our core values. You have this Florida State spear, and you always want to live above the spear and above the line. While the idea came from the Meyer book, our practice of the idea was figuring out how do we live it, and how do you get to a common language, such as someone holding me to the standard of tucking in our shirts by saying, "Hey, you are below the line right now with your shirt untucked." It is not someone calling you out but rather holding you to the standards and being accountable.

But you also need to keep in mind that living values involves learned behaviors. First-years and seniors may be at two different ends of the spectrum in their ability to interpret and apply the values into everyday life. Just as you have flexibility on the field and court with how players learn, have flexibility off the field as well. It is about teaching and growing each individual, and some will take a lot more time and energy than others.

What happens when they don't live up to those standards? You talk about the clear-cut expected behavior, you talk about the behaviors above and below the line—and we always have conversations about those—but you also need to know that we can handle the "middle area." There is a gray area sometimes, and you just hope it is not too big. But I tell them, "If you have trust in the process and you have trust in me as the head coach, then you as a teammate will fully understand how I handle an individual player who may be a little bit in the gray area, but it will get them above the line."

The value of trust is important in a program, and it is huge for us. How we build that is with communication and listening, and the skills and character side of it is important. I am probably going to be a little more lenient with a first-year player coming into the program than I am with a senior. I am holding that first-year to a standard and will get them above the line. All the recruits are familiar with this concept before they join our softball program. The minute I can start writing recruits, I am writing to them about our core values. Before a new player steps on campus, we form a summer sister group, and the values have already been defined to them and they clearly understand what it means. That early educational piece is big for building our team culture.

Finding individuals who will flourish in your program as a student-athlete with the core values that guide it will significantly reduce the number of incidents falling below the line or below the spear. Players will only flourish if they can be themselves, and in being themselves they are living the values. That core values–authentic athlete match is very important. Our core values have made being authentic appealing to them.

The DiSC (Dominance, Influence, Steadiness, Conscientiousness) profile assessment can be a useful tool in helping athletes know themselves better and the coaching staff know them better as well. While many Major League Baseball teams use it to assist their evaluation of draft prospects, we use it once players are in the program. We've found that our athletes are strong on their mental skills and that they are oriented in such a way that the program's core values are a comfortable fit.

LIVING THE VALUES

Anytime there is a chance to show how a core value is being demonstrated, we highlight it. We do that in the following ways:

- *Speak it*—when someone is living your values on the field. That is what we mean by "aggressive" base running. That play was "smart."
- *Show it*—in videos, with pictures, on social media.
- *Quiz it*—player A pop quiz: Talk to me about one of the core values. What does it mean, and how can it be applied in this situation?
- *Identify it*—any chance you have as a coach to reinforce the behaviors (both positive and negative), do it. *Tip:* We can all find the negative, so key in to showing the positive as much as possible.

We have a saying in our program: "Do you post the values or do you live them? If you live them, you shouldn't have to post them."

When an individual not directly associated with our team walks into our program, it is my expectation that they could identify our core values by watching our team in action. In my experience, there is no osmosis when it comes to values. Just because they are on the wall

FSU Athletics

doesn't mean they are a part of who you are. It is about action and how you live each value on a day-to-day basis.

What would someone observe when they look at our program? What you would see in our program is us having fun and the players' passion for the game. They are relaxed in big moments and are competitive. We get a lot of comments from people saying, "It looks like a family." We hug them, love them, and if they fail at something, our coaching staff is more in their hip pocket than when they are succeeding. As a family, if someone falls down you pick them right back up. There is no berating, no yelling.

Creating a Positive Team Culture

These values that your players live serve to create a positive team culture. A strong base of values is reflected in these four attributes:

1. *Authenticity:* People for so long had told me that I can't be who I am and win at a high level. I was challenged with that for a long time. To win the NCAA National Championship and win the way we won was affirmation that the values we believe in and strive to live every day are a path to success. You can win a variety of ways, but you have to be true to who you are.

2. *Transparency:* Everyone in the program—team and staff—knows what the mission is and how they are expected to act. There are no games. The standards and the values are what they are, and we have all agreed on them.

3. *Accountability:* A first-year player, a senior, a coach, or a support staff member has the same responsibility to hold anyone accountable. It is never personal, but it is about the values and standards of the program.

4. *Inclusion:* Everyone has a past, and it is valued within the program. Where you came from is important. Players and coaches are all different and may react to situations differently, and that is encouraged. How can we make that fit into our greater values and mission as a team, understanding that the mission of the team comes first?

Roster decisions and recruiting targets are significantly influenced by how the coaching staff believes players will fit in and contribute to the culture we are seeking to establish and maintain. The number one question I ask myself when bringing someone into our program is, "Can they flourish in the environment we have created?" Some might take a while to acclimate and adjust—after all, every day in a competitive sport setting isn't sunshine and roses. But once they are in the program, remember you made the decision to have them on the team. So it is important that you provide them every opportunity to succeed and invest in helping them do so.

On the other hand, no matter how strong your culture is, it can be shaken or seriously damaged by having the wrong people in your program. When that happens, you have to intervene, sooner rather than later.

Having Fun

Every individual has a unique definition of fun. Some of our players actually thrive on challenging physical workouts, while others cannot wait to finish them. One thing we are pretty certain of is that our athletes started playing softball because they found it fun, and we want to continue to honor that joy during practice and competition.

We always incorporate fun in practice. Sometimes, to lighten up the mood, we will have players throw with their nondominant hand (left-handed if they are right-handed) or play in different positions during practice. This usually sparks some humorous moments and laughs, which can provide a much-needed break from the focused and more serious approach we take in our drills and performances on the field.

Maybe at the end of warming up our arms, we'll all shoot threes into the softball bucket. Everyone is trying a different style, like a hook shot or some creative way of doing it, so it is really fun. Sometimes it might go on a little long and I'll have to rein them in, and we'll move on to the next softball activity. They enjoyed each other and were acting like kids for a second, and then we moved on. There is a fine line between fun and silliness. We ride that line sometimes but try not to cross it. Fun serves several worthwhile purposes, whereas silliness serves none.

Fun needs to be incorporated in practice and competition when appropriate, then you need to be able to transition back to a more serious mode quickly and regain focus on the task at hand. That is exactly what happens in a softball game. You go out in the field and are pitching and fielding, then when you come back in the dugout, there are six minutes before someone actually puts the ball in play, so you have to relax a little bit and have fun, cheer, and then get back out there. You have to develop that sense of when it is time to turn the fun switch on and off.

During that extremely competitive national championship tournament, there were things that happened that shouldn't have, such as when our third base player, Jessie Warren, threw a ball down the right field for an error or our center fielder and second base player missed a ball that was an easy pop fly to catch. I walked out to the circle and they were laughing, saying we are the cardiac kids, so we are supposed to play like this. We break from the circle and they get the next out, and they are back in the dugout relaxing again.

It is extremely difficult for anyone to maintain their focus for three hours. In softball, if you focus at practice for three hours, focus two hours

FSU Athletics

for every game for 56 games, and then you try to be the best you can at game 70 of the season, you are going to be mentally and emotionally done. We need to be focused and intense when necessary, but we also need to be able to relax and enjoy the experiences through the season, too. Keeping that fun component, that aspect that first drew you and your athletes to your sport, is essential to retain through a coaching and playing career, regardless of the level of competition.

TAKEAWAYS

- As a coach, you need to know your core values and nonnegotiables, then work with the team to see how they can bring each one of those into the program and live them every day.

- Be your authentic self as a coach. If you are just starting out, it may take a few years to figure out your style, but your philosophy probably won't change.

- Establish the line with your team early on with expected behaviors by identifying the "above the line" and "below the line" actions.

- Playing a sport should be fun. Work hard to keep that aspect alive in practice and in games. Athletes perform better when they are relaxed and having fun. Teach them when to focus and when to laugh.

BIBLIOGRAPHY

Beswick, B. 2016. *One Goal: The Mindset of Winning Soccer Teams.* Champaign, IL: Human Kinetics.

Brown, B. 2018. *Dare to Lead: Brave Work. Tough Conversations. Whole Hearts.* New York: Random House.

Campbell, J. 1991. *The Power of Myth.* New York: Anchor Books.

Conscious Leadership Group. 2014. "Locating Yourself—A Key to Conscious Leadership." November 15, 2014. Video, 3:35. www.youtube.com/watch?v=fLqzYDZAqCI.

Coyle, D. 2018. *The Culture Code: The Secrets of Highly Successful Groups.* New York: Bantam Books.

Duarte, N., and P. Sanchez. 2016. *Illuminate: Ignite Change Through Speeches, Stories, Ceremonies and Symbols.* New York: Portfolio/Penguin.

Gladwell, M. 2002. *The Tipping Point: How Little Things Can Make a Big Difference.* Boston: Little, Brown and Company.

Gladwell, M. 2013. *David and Goliath: Underdogs, Misfits, and the Art of Battling Giants.* Boston: Little, Brown and Company.

Jackson, P., and H. Delehanty. 1995. *Sacred Hoops: Spiritual Lessons of a Hardwood Warrior.* New York: Hyperion.

Kerr, J. 2013. *Legacy.* London, UK: Constable & Robinson.

Meyer, U. 2017. *Above the Line: Lessons in Leadership and Life from a Championship Program.* New York: Penguin Books.

Morin, A. 2015. "7 Scientifically Proven Benefits of Gratitude." *Psychology Today,* April 3, 2015. www.psychologytoday.com/us/blog/what-mentally-strong-people-dont-do/201504/7-scientifically-proven-benefits-gratitude.

Reynaud, C., ed. 2005. *She Can Coach!* Champaign, IL: Human Kinetics.

Robbins, M. 2020. *We're All in This Together: Creating a Team Culture of High Performance, Trust, and Belonging.* Carlsbad, CA: Hay House.

Sandberg, S. 2013. *Lean In: Women, Work, and the Will to Lead.* New York: Alfred A. Knopf.

Tuckman, B. 1965. "Developmental Sequence in Small Groups." *Psychological Bulletin* 63 (6): 384-99. https://doi.org/10.1037/h0022100.

Wooden, J., and J. Carty. 2009. *Coach Wooden's Pyramid of Success: Building Blocks for a Better Life.* Grand Rapids, MI: Baker Publishing Group.

Zoref, L. 2012. "Lior Zoref: Mindsharing, the Art of Crowdsourcing Everything." Filmed March 2012 at TED2012, Long Beach, CA. Video, 11:20. www.youtube.com/watch?v=din2UVvRnGU.

INDEX

Note: The italicized *f* following page numbers refers to figures.

ABOUT THE EDITOR

Courtesy of USA Volleyball.

Cecile Reynaud, PhD, was the head coach of the Florida State University (FSU) volleyball team from 1976 until her retirement in 2001, compiling an impressive 635 wins and seven conference championships in her 26 years at the helm. She was twice named Atlantic Coast Conference Coach of the Year (1992, 2000) and has been inducted into the halls of fame of numerous sport organizations, including the FSU Athletics Hall of Fame (2009), the American Volleyball Coaches Association (AVCA) Hall of Fame (2017), and the USA Volleyball (USAV) Hall of Fame (2020). In 2016, she received the Harold T. Friermood "Frier" Award, the highest award given by USAV.

Her career spanned international competition as well. She served as an assistant coach for the World University Games (1983) and went on to coach the U.S. Junior National Team (1985). Reynaud held the positions of deputy competition manager for the 1996 Centennial Olympic Games in Atlanta and competition secretary for the Goodwill Games. In 2012, she served as the team leader for the U.S. Women's Sitting Volleyball National Team at the Paralympic Games. In 2013, she was the team leader and assistant coach for the U.S. Women's National Team for the FIVB World Grand Prix, and in 2014 she served as the team leader for the Men's U.S. Volleyball Team at the U21 World Championship in Mexico.

In a leadership capacity, Reynaud has served on the boards of directors of USAV and AVCA and is a past AVCA president and USAV chair. She has also served on the Performance Enhancement Team for the USA Volleyball Sitting Volleyball National Team and the Commission on Youth Athlete Safety for USA Volleyball. She has served on the boards of directors for the Side-Out Foundation, the FSU Varsity Club, and her local sexual and domestic violence organization. In addition, Reynaud served as board president of WeCOACH, the premier membership organization dedicated to the recruitment, advancement, and retention of women coaches of all sports and levels.

After her coaching career, Reynaud was a research associate professor at FSU, where she taught graduate and undergraduate classes in the sport management department until her retirement in 2015. She serves as color analyst for collegiate volleyball matches on various television networks and has authored or edited several books, including *The Volleyball Coaching Bible* (Volumes I and II), *101 Winning Volleyball Drills*, *Coaching Volleyball Technical and Tactical Skills*, and *She Can Coach!*, as well as numerous volleyball DVDs.

ABOUT THE CHAPTER AUTHORS

FSU Athletics

Lonni Alameda

Florida State University has competed in the NCAA Division I softball playoffs every year since Lonni Alameda took the reins as head coach in 2009. During that span, she has led the Seminoles to seven Atlantic Coast Conference (ACC) Championships, four College World Series (CWS) appearances, and one NCAA Division I National Championship. Lonni has been selected ACC Coach of the Year five times, and she and her assistant coaches were honored as the 2018 National Coaching Staff of the Year by the National Fastpitch Coaches Association (NFCA). Before becoming the head softball coach at Florida State, she was the head coach at the University of Nevada, Las Vegas. After the 2021 season in which Florida State finished runner-up in the CWS, her overall coaching record stood at 761-338-3.

Rachel Balkovec

Rachel Balkovec

Rachel Balkovec is the first female manager in minor league baseball history, tapped by the New York Yankees to manage the Low-A Tampa Tarpons in 2022. She first joined the Yankees in 2019 as a hitting coach and started her pro baseball career as a strength and conditioning coach in the St. Louis Cardinals' minor league system in 2012. As a NCAA Division I softball player, she played catcher, first for Creighton University and then for the University of New Mexico. Rachel began her professional career as a part-time strength and conditioning coach for the St. Louis Cardinals' minor league club in Johnson City, Tennessee, and she was named the Appalachian League's strength coach of the year. In 2014, she became the full-time strength and conditioning coordinator, the first time a woman had held that position in baseball. In 2016, she was hired by the Houston Astros to be their Latin American coordinator for strength and conditioning, and two years later she was promoted to be the strength and conditioning coach for the Class AA Corpus Christi Hooks.

Becky Burleigh

Having started the University of Florida women's soccer program in 1995, Becky Burleigh served as head women's soccer coach of the Gators until her retirement at the end of the 2020-2021 season. Under Becky's leadership, Florida won the Southeastern Conference (SEC) regular season championship 14 times and captured 12 SEC tournament titles. The Gators made the NCAA Division I Women's Soccer Tournament 22 times while Becky was at the helm. She was named national coach of the year in 1998 when the Florida Gators defeated the perennial powerhouse North Carolina Tar Heels, 1-0, in the final match to capture the NCAA Division I National Championship.

Denise Corlett

Only one person can say she served on the Stanford University women's volleyball coaching staff over the 31 years in which the program won nine NCAA Division I Women's Volleyball national titles and 18 Pac-12 Conference Championships and amassed an 875-146 (.857) overall record. Denise Corlett was a key factor in the Cardinal's sustained success, and along the way was twice recognized as the American Volleyball Coaches Association's (AVCA) Assistant Coach of the Year and was inducted into the AVCA Hall of Fame in 2020. She was also a coaching staff member of national teams competing in World University Games as well as the 2003 Pan American Games. As a student-athlete at UCLA, Denise was a three-time All-American in volleyball, played basketball, and was a member of a national championship badminton team.

Melody Davidson

Hockey Canada Images

After leading the Canadian National Women's Ice Hockey team to gold medals in the 2006 and 2010 Winter Olympics, Melody Davidson served in a managerial role overseeing the Canadian national team in winning another Olympic gold medal in 2014 and a silver in 2018. Prior to that, she was the head coach of the Cornell University Big Red women's ice hockey team and head coach of the Connecticut College Camels women's ice hockey team. Her role in the Olympics earned her various honors, including induction into the Alberta Sports Hall of Fame and the Canadian Olympic Hall of Fame. She was also recipient of the 2010 Jack Donohue Coach of the Year Award. In June 2020, Melody joined Own the Podium as a high-performance advisor.

Kelly Inouye-Perez

Courtesy of ASUCLA Photography.

In her first 15 seasons as UCLA's head softball coach, Kelly Inouye-Perez has amassed an overall record of 672-180-1 (.788) and the Bruins have won two (2010 and 2019) NCAA Division I Softball Championships. They have reached the Women's College World Series for six straight seasons. During that span, her players have earned 32 NFCA All-American Awards, 67 All-Region honors, and 89 All-Pac-12 accolades. Kelly's ties to UCLA run deep. As a standout player, she led the Bruins to the NCAA Division I National Softball Championships in 1989, 1990, and again in 1992. Kelly also served as an assistant softball coach at UCLA for 13 seasons and appeared in the NCAA Championship game seven times, winning NCAA Championships in 1999, 2003, and 2004.

Roselee Jencke

Rowville Secondary College

After a celebrated netball playing career with the Australian Diamonds National Team that captured the gold medal at the 1991 World Netball Championship, the silver medal at the World Games in 1985, and the World Netball Championship in 1987, Roselee Jencke was awarded the Medal of the Order of Australia in 1992. As Diamonds number 89, Roselee played in 43 test matches for the Australian Diamonds. She then moved into coaching, serving as an assistant coach for the under-21 Australian netball team and specialist coach for the Australian Diamonds before taking the head coaching position for the Queensland Firebirds from October 2009 to 2020. She guided the Firebirds to five ANZ Championship Grand Finals, three ANZ Premierships, and an undefeated season in 2011. She was awarded coach of the year in 2011, 2015, and 2016; the inaugural Joyce Brown Coach of the Year in 2014; and Queensland Coach of the Year in 2015. She remains active in coaching developing coaches and talent identification.

Valorie Kondos Field

Commonly referred to as Miss Val, Valorie Kondos Field served as the head women's gymnastics coach of the UCLA Bruins from 1991 to 2019, where she led her team to seven NCAA National Championships. Under her tutelage, the UCLA women's gymnastics team won 19 Pac-12 Championships and 16 NCAA regional titles. She is a four-time Pac-12 Conference Coach of the Year, a three-time West Region Head Coach of the Year, and the Pac-12 Gymnastics Coach of the Century. She was also voted NCAA Coach of the Year four times. Miss Val has coached 20 individual gymnasts to 36 individual NCAA Championships, five Honda Awards, and two Pac-12 Scholar Athletes of the Year. During her coaching career, she coached numerous Olympic gymnasts. Miss Val retired from coaching in April 2019 and is a popular public speaker, including a TED Talk that has garnered over 4 million views.

Melissa Luellen

Currently the head women's golf coach at Auburn University, where she led the Tigers to the 2021 Southern Conference (SEC) Championship, Melissa Luellen has long been recognized as one of the top golf coaches at the college level. Before Auburn, Melissa was the head women's golf coach at Arizona State for 13 years; before that, she was the head golf coach at the University of Tulsa for two seasons. During her very successful tenure at Arizona State, Melissa led her program to an NCAA team title, two Pac-12 Conference Team Championships, and was named Pac-12 Conference Coach of the Year three times. Prior to coaching, Melissa was a four-time All-American at the University of Tulsa and capped off a stellar collegiate career by capturing an individual NCAA title while leading the Golden Hurricane to the NCAA National Golf Team Championship in 1988.

Cal Athletics

Teri McKeever

One of the most accomplished swimming coaches in the United States, if not the world, Teri McKeever has led the University of California women's swimming and diving program to four NCAA and five Pac-12 Team Championships. In 2020, the Golden Bears placed fourth at the NCAA Championship to extend their streak of top-five finishes to 15 years in a row, the longest run in the country. A nine-time Pac-12 Conference Coach of the Year, Teri was inducted into the Cal Athletics Hall of Fame in 2018 and the College Swimming and Diving Coaches Association of America (CSCAA) named her National Coach of the Year five times. Teri served as head coach of the 2012 U.S. Women's Olympic swimming team and as assistant swimming coach in the 2004, 2008, and 2020 Olympics.

Greg Fiume/Maryland Terrapins

Missy Meharg

The University of Maryland field hockey team captured seven NCAA National Championships and 26 conference titles during Missy Meharg's 33 seasons as head coach. Missy has been voted national coach of the year nine times and conference coach of the year nine times. Six of Missy's field hockey players have competed on U.S. Olympic teams, and many of the Maryland Terrapins student-athletes have played on their respective national teams. Missy served on the U.S. National Team coaching staff from 1993 to 1997 while assisting in the World Cup, Pan American Games, and the 1996 Olympics. She has coached 50 All-Americans, including six national players of the year. Missy was NBC's field hockey commentator for the 2012 London Olympic Games. She has served on the University of Maryland's senate and senate executive committee as well as being very active with the board of trustees for USA Field Hockey.

Baylor Athletics

Felecia Mulkey

While leading her teams to 10 National Collegiate Acrobatics and Tumbling Association (NCATA) Championships, Felecia Mulkey has an amazing 108-5 record over 11 seasons as a head coach of acrobatics and tumbling. She is in her eighth year as the head coach at Baylor University after winning four consecutive NCATA titles at the University of Oregon. During her coaching tenure at Baylor, she has led the Bears to five straight NCATA Championships with a 65-2 record and rides a 38-meet winning streak as she has coached 19 NCATA All-Americans. Prior to her coaching stint at Oregon, Felecia built the competitive cheer program at Kennesaw State University into a national powerhouse. She was inducted into the Kennesaw State Athletics Hall of Fame in 2019.

Courtesy of Arthur Images.

Carla Nicholls

Currently the Para Performance Lead and head coach for Athletics Canada, Carla Nicholls was part of the national team staff at the 2008, 2012, and 2016 Olympic Games. She has held various coaching positions, including head coach, at numerous events, including the World U18 Championships, World U20 Championships, Pan American Games, World University Games, and Commonwealth Games. Carla is an International Association of Athletics Federations (IAAF) Level 5 Elite Coach in horizontal jumps and National Coaching Certification Program (NCCP) Level 4 in athletics. She is an advocate of women in coaching and a graduate of the Coaching Association of Canada's Women in Coaching Apprenticeship Program.

Carol Owens

Carol Owens

In her 22 seasons as a member of the women's basketball coaching staff at the University of Notre Dame, 13 as an associate head coach, Carol Owens has helped lead the Fighting Irish to two NCAA Division I Women's Basketball National Championships (2001 and 2018). During that span, Notre Dame competed in seven NCAA Women's Basketball Championship games and reached the Final Four nine times. Carol was named the 2019 Women's

Basketball Coaches Association (WBCA) Division I Assistant Coach of the Year. In 2001, she was named one of the top-five assistant coaches in the country by *Women's Basketball Journal*. In 2011, *CollegeInsider.com* named her as one of the top assistant coaches in the nation. She was inducted into the A STEP UP Assistant Coaches Hall of Fame in 2019.

Courtesy of Kelly Backus/ESPN Images.

Carolyn Peck

Before becoming a basketball analyst for ESPN and the Southeastern Conference Network, Carolyn Peck was the head coach for the women's basketball teams at Purdue University and the University of Florida and also the first head coach and general manager in the history of the WNBA's Orlando Miracle. Carolyn was a standout basketball player at Vanderbilt University and played professionally before entering the coaching profession as an assistant coach at the University of Tennessee. She was also an assistant coach at the University of Kentucky and Purdue before becoming the head basketball coach at Purdue in 1997. Under her leadership at Purdue, the Boilermakers captured the 1999 NCAA Division I Women's Basketball Championship.

Rowing Australia/Delly Carr

Ellen Randell

Currently residing in Sydney, Australia, Ellen Randell is considered one of Rowing Australia's outstanding coaches in the sport. Based out of the Hancock Prospecting Women's National Training Centre, Ellen began coaching rowing teams in the late 1980s. A highly experienced rowing coach over the last 30 years, she specializes in coaching women and is expert in open and lightweight rowing (sweep and sculling). Ellen has coached four Australian women's crews to World Rowing Championship gold medals as well as multiple other medals. She rowed for Australia in 1983 and 1984 and has coached for Australia since 1987, including for 21 World Championship regattas and three Olympic Games. Ellen won World Championship titles in 1989, 1995, 2007, and 2008.

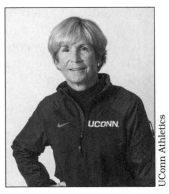

UConn Athletics

Nancy Stevens

The former head field hockey coach of the University of Connecticut, Nancy Stevens was named the recipient of the 2021 NCAA President's Pat Summitt Award. UConn won three NCAA Division I National Field Hockey Championships, appeared in 24 NCAA National Field Hockey Tournaments, reached 18 NCAA Quarterfinals, 10 NCAA Semifinals, and 19 Big East Conference titles during her 30 years as head coach. Before coaching at UConn, Nancy was the head field hockey coach at Northwestern, where she led the Wildcats to eight consecutive NCAA Division I Quarterfinal appearances, three NCAA Division I Semifinals, and four Big Ten Championships in her nine seasons at the school. Nancy finished her career in 2020 with a record of 700-189-24 and is the only coach in the history of the sport to reach 700 wins. She has also been an integral part of the national coaching staff for USA Field Hockey.

Courtesy of Stanford University.

Tara VanDerveer

The Setsuko Ishiyama Director of Women's Basketball at Stanford University for 35 seasons, Tara VanDerveer is widely recognized as one of the top coaches in the history of collegiate and international women's basketball. She has been inducted into both the Naismith Memorial Basketball Hall of Fame and the Women's Basketball Hall of Fame and is a five-time national coach of the year and 15-time Pac-12 Conference Coach of the Year. Tara has led Stanford to three NCAA Division I Women's Basketball National Championships, 13 Final Four wins, 23 Pac-12 regular season titles, 14 Pac-12 Conference Tournament Crowns, and 32 trips to the NCAA Tournament. She has also served as head coach of the USA Basketball National Team and led the national team to the gold medal at the 1996 Olympic Games.

Calvin University Sports Information

Amber Warners

Over 21 seasons as head coach of the Calvin University volleyball program, Dr. Amber Warners has compiled an impressive win-loss record of 604-94 (.865) and three NCAA Division III National Championships (2010, 2013, and 2016). She was selected as the American Volleyball Coaches Association (AVCA) Division III National Coach of the Year four times (2010, 2012, 2013, and 2014). Warners has led her team to 17 consecutive berths in the NCAA Division III Volleyball Tournament, advancing to the Great Lakes region NCAA Finals 12 times, advancing to the Elite 8 eight times, Final 4 seven times, and National Runner-up twice. Amber was also a very successful softball coach at Calvin as she led the Knights to two NCAA Division III Tournament berths and a NCAA Division III Softball College World Series appearance in 1997.

Jen Welter

Jen Welter

The first woman to coach in the National Football League, Dr. Jen Welter was hired as a linebackers coach for the Arizona Cardinals in 2015. In 2018, she was hired by the Atlanta Legends of the newly formed Alliance of American Football (AAF) as a defensive specialist. She was the head coach of the first Australian women's national team in 2017. She played running back in a men's professional football league with the Texas Revolution and was hired as the first woman coach in men's professional football, helping coach the most successful Texas Revolution season in franchise history. Before joining the world of professional football, Jen played women's professional football for 14 seasons, which included four World Championships, two gold medals, and eight All-Star selections.

Strengthening the voice and presence of women coaches

WeCOACH, a 501(c)3 non-profit, is the premier membership organization committed to recruiting, advancing, and retaining women coaches across all sports and levels.

With the purpose of strengthening the voice and presence of women coaches, WeCOACH provides educational programs that center around personal and professional development. Focusing on the challenges women face to stay in, feel supported in, and advance in the coaching profession, our premier development programs include:

- NCAA Women Coaches Academy and Academy 2.0
- High School Women Coaches Leadership Academy
- BreakThrough Summit
- WeAMPLIFY
- Mentor Program

Whether you're a current coach, a retired coach, an administrator, or a fan, consider becoming a WeCOACH member or making a personal donation. Visit **wecoachsports.org** to learn more!

All Sports. One Voice. WeCOACH!

12/21